TABE®:
POWER PRACTICE

Second Edition

LEARNINGEXPRESS®

NEW YORK

Copyright © 2017 LearningExpress.

All rights reserved under International and Pan American Copyright Conventions.
Published in the United States by LearningExpress, New York.

Cataloging-in-Publication Data is on file with the Library of Congress.

ISBN 978-1-61103-100-3

Printed in the United States of America

9 8 7 6 5 4 3 2

Second Edition

For more information on LearningExpress, other LearningExpress products, or bulk sales, please write to us at:
    224 W. 29th Street
    3rd Floor
    New York, NY 10001

CONTENTS

CONTRIBUTORS

Stephanie Moran
GED® Program Manager, Durango Adult Education Center
Durango, Colorado

An adult educator at the center since 2000 and an adjunct instructor of literature, reading, and composition at Southwest Colorado Community College since 2001, Stephanie Moran earned her M.A. in English from Bowling Green State University and graduated *summa cum laude* from the University of Northern Colorado in English and in elementary education. Since 2002, Moran has used the TABE® as the primary assessment for non-ESOL adult learners at her center. She has both administered the TABE® and taught students the skills needed to improve their scores on a post-test for state outcomes. She also designed the bridge curriculum that successfully transitions GED® test and high school graduates into college and onto career paths.

Moran regularly presents at national and regional adult education conferences, including COABE, has taught English at six colleges and universities, and is the recipient of the 2011 Award of Excellence for "significant contributions to the field of adult education in the state of Colorado" from the Mountain Plains Adult Education Association.

Jane Thornton Silveria
State Supervisor and Assessment Specialist
Office of Workforce Education
Florida Department of Education
Tallahassee, Florida

A *magna cum laude* graduate from Barry University with a B.S. in accounting and certified at the University of West Florida in the Individualized Manpower Training System, as well as the System for Applied Individualized

Learning, Jane Silveria has served as an assessment specialist at the Florida Department of Education since 1990. In addition to rewriting state board rules, providing training on new assessment instruments, and overseeing the career education programs at juvenile justice facilities, a major part of Silveria's responsibilities is reviewing and recommending the state's assessment instruments for adult and career education students. She has been the assessment expert for CTE for the past 23 years. She oversees the certified TABE® trainers and provides training for test administrators throughout the state.

Additionally, she has taught college classes in accounting and business mathematics, overseen the state's vocational basic skills remediation program, provided consulting services to education agencies and community colleges, and served as an active force in implementing career and technical programming in Florida's juvenile justice facilities.

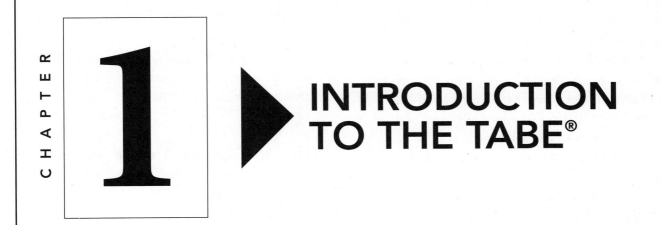

1 ▶ INTRODUCTION TO THE TABE®

The TABE®, or Tests of Adult Basic Education, is an accurate assessment tool to help place adults into the most beneficial educational settings, which is crucial in all adult learning environments. Because the TABE® assessment series has an extremely well-established and deserved reputation in the field of testing adults, you can be confident that this test will be useful whether you are an entering college student, an adult education student working toward your GED® test credential, or a person entering a new job or seeking to advance your career.

Who Takes the Exam and Why

The TABE® is a placement assessment that is one of the most established in the field. The first TABE® rolled out in 1966 and has been expanded and updated several times over nearly 50 years. The most prevalent edition is TABE® 9&10, and hundreds of thousands of adults take this most recent version of the TABE® annually. In fact, the TABE®, published by McGraw-Hill, is the most commonly used test by adult education centers in America.

Test-takers include anyone entering an adult education center who wants to improve his or her literacy or English language skills and eventually earn a GED® test credential, which is the high school equivalency exam. Because it measures basic skills, the TABE® can be a good predictor of how a student may perform on the GED® test. The TABE® is also frequently administered by workforce centers, community colleges, unions, non-profits, and technical and trade schools to assess students' abilities and progress. It is used across many occupational fields for training and employment purposes, particularly to evaluate candidates' eligibility to enter certain certificate programs.

Numerous state agencies also use the TABE® because it reflects the recent changes in standards for adult education. TABE® accurately estimates literacy and numeracy skills as well as functional workplace skills for military professionals looking to advance, people in correctional settings, welfare-to-work clients, and public school districts that want to evaluate their secondary students' readiness for credit-bearing college courses. A great benefit of the TABE® is that it offers both diagnostic and prescriptive information that helps the student, client, and teacher or adviser develop a solid study plan for skills improvement and an increase in scores on post-tests. Another benefit is that you can take the TABE® on a computer, on the Internet, or in a paper-and-pencil format.

Frequently, the agencies and educational entities mentioned above expect their students or clients to take timed pre- and post-TABE® exams, usually to evaluate progress and growth and to reassess whether a tester's program is the most useful and appropriate one for its students. Post-tests also serve to meet the state and national reporting demands from OVAE (Office of Vocational and Adult Education), NRS (National Reporting System), and WIA (the Workforce Investment Act). Because adult education programs receive government funds, they are required to report their progress to the NRS.

What to Expect on the Tests

TABE® 9&10 assesses a person's basic skills abilities in three major areas: Reading, Mathematics, and Language. It covers a series of major skills and subskills across those three domains and offers optional tests in Language Mechanics, Vocabulary, and Spelling.

The Reading Test

For the Reading test, Level A, you will be assessed on how well you understand, explain, and analyze material using three types of literacy: prose literacy, document literacy, and quantitative literacy. The reading passages you will find on the test are based on practical kinds of reading from life and business, such as instructional texts, typical workplace documents, and readings using contemporary visual formats. Questions will address how well you can construct meaning from context and apply that meaning in new situations. Graphic information such as a travel itinerary will test your document literacy, while quantitative literacy questions will examine how well you can combine what you read with basic mathematical or analytical concepts and operations required for problem solving and decision-making.

The Mathematics Computation Test

The Math Computation test, Level A, assesses how well you can solve basic mathematical problems using addition, subtraction, multiplication, and division of whole numbers, fractions, and decimals. You also will find questions that deal with basic algebra and percents. No calculator may be used on this section. The skills assessed in this section are the building blocks of all mathematical problems and are necessary for college math courses and the GED® test. The practice exams that follow do not require advanced knowledge of math; instead, they will help you recognize the formulas and methods you will need to solve basic problems and succeed on this section of the TABE®.

The Applied Mathematics Test

The Applied Math test, Level A, assesses how well you can perform more complicated mathematical problems. These are the types of problems that you find in everyday life and work and test the skills that will be needed for college coursework; for career programs such as nursing, electronics, and information technology; and for success on the GED® test. These skills are also very important in most job settings. You will need to be able to analyze data from graphs, charts, and diagrams, and questions also will address measurement, geometry, algebra, and problem solving. For example, for problem solving, the practice exams will help you recognize the processes necessary to formulate problems, determine and apply strategies to solve problems, and evaluate and justify solutions to problems.

The Language Test

The Language test, Level A, assesses your understanding of the writing skills necessary for college-credit-bearing courses or for remedial or developmental education coursework that will improve your skills. The goal is to indicate how ready you are to tackle the intensive writing required in most college courses or in coordinator and managerial types of jobs. Typical questions address the standard skills of sentence formation— for example, distinguishing a complete sentence from a sentence fragment, identifying proper punctuation for sentence sense, and recognizing subject-verb and pronoun agreement. Such skills are essential for writing that is concise and clear enough for readers to comprehend the flow and logic of a document or other text, such as a college paper or an accident report at work. For those entering a career path or seeking to climb a career ladder, the Language test examines your experience and understanding of business letters and related documents, such as memo or report writing, among other skills.

The Language Mechanics, Spelling, and Vocabulary Tests

The Language Mechanics test, Level A, hones in on the more highly developed skills needed for those courses or fields (at a management level, for example) that require more specialized or formal writing skills, such as composing, editing, revising, and extended writing. The Spelling and Vocabulary tests, Level A, support all of these assessment purposes and serve to examine your ability to spell correctly in both an academic setting and the workplace.

How to Apply to Take the Tests

To apply to take the TABE®, you will need to meet with an adviser at your high school or college/technical school, an intake person at your adult education center, your case manager at a workforce center or the department of human services, or the personnel/ human resources director at your workplace. At some sites, administrators will offer both the shorter Survey form of the TABE® and the longer Complete Battery.

The Number of Test Items

The Survey of the TABE® contains 25 items each in Reading, Mathematics Computation, Applied Mathematics, and Language, with each test timed at 25 minutes, for a total of 100 items timed at 1 hour 40 minutes.

The Complete Battery includes 50 items in Reading (timed at 50 minutes); 40 items in Math

Computation (24 minutes); 50 items in Applied Math (50 minutes); and 55 items in Language (55 minutes), for a total of 195 items timed at 2 hours, 59 minutes. The optional tests include Vocabulary (20 items, 14 minutes), Language Mechanics (20 items, 14 minutes), and Spelling (20 items, 20 minutes), all of which are included here in *TABE® Power Practice*.

Both the Survey and the Complete Battery forms include a Locator test timed at 37 minutes. This pre-test places you in a "Level" category that will decide your content range for the reading, math, and language portions: L, E, M, D, or A. The Locator test is typically used in the adult education setting but not in the career, college, or workforce setting. The "A" level is typically given in these settings. You may score such that you will take one test at an M level and another test at a D or an A level. Some test-takers may take the Locator test and all of the assessment tests in one long session, but many test centers will divide the tests into two sessions. If you have a preference, inquire if your testing center can provide your preferred seat time.

When you take the post-test you will retest at those same original levels, with few exceptions. As whatever agency or educational entity you are working with will have its own requirements for a post-test, make sure you know what is expected of you. Usually you will study for a specific number of hours before being allowed to take the post-test, often at least 60 hours; that number will vary based on a state's or workplace's expectations.

How the TABE® Is Scored

You can count on TABE®'s accuracy because it is "normed," or made valid, based on a field study that includes more than 30,000 adult learners! It is both a norm-referenced and a criterion-referenced test that is relevant to everyday adult lives and aligned with national adult education standards. A norm-referenced test means that your performance is compared to a nationally representative sample; that is, some learners will be at the higher end of correct answers, and some will always be at the lower end. With a norm-referenced test, the number of correct answers that you score is compared to the scores of all other test-takers. The two groups that the TABE® uses for norm-referencing purposes are an adult student group from basic education, corrections, career, technical, and college settings, and a second group composed of juvenile basic education students, up to age 14.

A criterion-based test will score your performance relative to the objective structure (the skill being tested). In other words, all learners can potentially perform at the same level. Therefore, a criterion-based test shows how well or how poorly you did on a particular task. Both kinds of norming can be useful to you and the school or agency with which you are working to assess your skills and customize a plan for your future.

CTB of McGraw-Hill, which publishes the TABE®, earned a seven-year approval from the U.S. Department of Education and NRS as an official assessment, meaning that it "pass[ed] stringent federal accountability standards for learner outcomes." Furthermore, the TABE® is correlated to GED® test scores and the NALS, the National Adult Literacy Survey, which measures the three categories of applied literacy (prose, document, and quantitative). Scores are also correlated with SCANS, the Secretary of Labor's Commission on Achieving Necessary Skills, which are workplace competencies that reflect a worker's job performance. Thus, your TABE® results can be utilized in a variety of ways to improve your performance at school or on the job. All of these approvals and correlations mean that you can depend on TABE®'s validity as an accurate assessment.

Your role is to give the test your best effort, answer questions to the best of your knowledge, and guess intelligently when necessary. However, make sure you don't guess wildly, because that may give you a higher or a lower score than your actual ability level reflects. Because one of the main purposes of the

TABE® is to place you in the best learning environment based on your actual skills, pure guessing defeats that purpose. The test administrator will review these guidelines with you before you take the test; this will allow you to approach the test confidently and with a sense of the goals you want to achieve. Your guide also will let you know when the test will be scored, how to obtain the results, and what they mean based on your individual situation.

If You Are an Adult with Special Needs

The concept of "universal design" has been embedded in the TABE®, meaning that the people who designed this test created it with the goal of making it available and accessible to as many people as possible, including people with a disability. If you are an adult student and require or need formal accommodations, speak to the test administrator. Because administrators are not allowed by federal law to ask you whether you have a learning disability, you must disclose that information. You will be required to provide documentation of your disability and then work in a confidential environment with a staff person familiar with the Americans with Disabilities Act (ADA) and its accommodations policy. Once your documentation has been provided, the TABE® and your administrator can offer procedures to help you. These might consist of a private room; extended testing times; large print, audio, or Braille editions of the test; assistive technologies; and more.

TABE® Power Practice Exams

TABE® Power Practice, 9&10 for Level A, provides you with two paper-and-pencil practice exams and one computer-based practice exam. All three practice tests mirror the actual TABE® exams in testing level, content, and topics covered.

Here are some features of the practice exams that will help you do your best when you take the actual TABE®:

- Each question has an indisputable correct answer.
- Incorrect answer choices are plausible but clearly wrong.
- For both correct and incorrect answers, there is an explanation telling you why it is right or wrong.
- Each practice test contains the complete battery of 255 questions and answers for the four main and three optional areas: **Reading**, **Mathematics Computation**, **Applied Mathematics**, **Language**, **Language Mechanics**, **Vocabulary**, and **Spelling**.

Whatever your circumstances, relax, take a deep breath, listen to or read the directions, have confidence in yourself, and know that you are moving in a positive direction—your future!

2 ▶ THE LEARNINGEXPRESS TEST PREPARATION SYSTEM

I t takes significant preparation to score well on any exam, and the TABE® is no exception. The LearningExpress Test Preparation System, developed by experts, exclusively for LearningExpress, offers a number of strategies designed to facilitate the development of the skills, disciplines, and attitudes necessary for success.

Preparing for and attaining a passing score on the TABE® requires surmounting an assortment of obstacles. While some may prove more troublesome than others, all of them carry the potential to hinder your performance and negatively affect your scores. Here are some examples:

- Lack of familiarity with the exam format
- Paralyzing test anxiety
- Leaving preparation to the last minute
- Not preparing

- Failure to develop vital test-taking skills such as knowing:
  - How to effectively pace through an exam
  - How to use the process of elimination to answer questions accurately
  - When and how to guess
- Mental and/or physical fatigue
- Test day blunders like:
  - Arriving late at the testing facility
  - Taking the exam on an empty stomach
  - Not accounting for fluctuations in temperature at the testing facility

The common thread among these obstacles is control. While a host of pressing, unanticipated, and sometimes unavoidable difficulties may frustrate your preparation, there remain some proven, effective strategies for placing yourself in the best possible position on exam day. These strategies can significantly improve your level of comfort with the exam, offering you not only the confidence you'll need but also, and perhaps most importantly, a higher test score.

The LearningExpress Test Preparation System helps to put you in greater control. Here's how it works. Separated into eight steps, the system heightens your confidence level by helping you understand both the exam and your own particular set of test-taking strengths and weaknesses. It will help you structure a study plan, practice a number of effective test-taking skills, and avoid mental and physical fatigue on exam day. Each step is accompanied by an activity.

While the following list suggests a time for the completion of each step, these are only guidelines. The regular practice of certain steps may require a more substantial time commitment. It may also be necessary and helpful to return to one or more of them throughout the course of your preparation.

Step		Time
Step 1.	Get Information	1 hour
Step 2.	Conquer Test Anxiety	20 minutes
Step 3.	Make a Plan	20 minutes
Step 4.	Learn to Manage Your Time	10 minutes
Step 5.	Learn to Use the Process of Elimination	20 minutes
Step 6.	Reach Your Peak Performance Zone	10 minutes
Step 7.	Make Final Preparations	10 minutes
Step 8.	Make Your Preparations Count	10 minutes
Total		**2.5 hours**

We estimate that working through the entire system will take you approximately three hours. It's perfectly O.K. if you work at a faster or slower pace. It's up to you to decide whether you should set aside a whole afternoon or evening to work through the LearningExpress Test Preparation System in one sitting, or break it up and do just one or two steps a day over several days.

Step 1: Get Information

Time to complete: 1 hour
Activities: Read the Introduction to this Book

Knowing more about an exam can often make it appear less daunting. The first step in the LearningExpress Test Preparation System is to determine everything you can about the type of information you will be expected to know for the TABE®, as well as how your knowledge will be assessed.

What You Should Find Out

Knowing the details will help you study efficiently and help you feel in control. Here's a list of things you might want to find out:

- What skills are tested?
- How many sections are on the exam?
- How many questions are in each section?
- How much time is allotted for each section?
- How is the exam scored and is there a penalty for guessing/wrong answers?

- Is the test a computerized test or will you have an exam booklet?
- Will you be given scratch paper to write on?

You will find answers to these questions in Chapter 1 of this book and on the CTB TABE® website.

Step 2: Conquer Test Anxiety

Time to complete: 20 minutes
Activity: Take the Test Stress Quiz

Now that you know what's on the test, the next step is to address one of the biggest obstacles to success: *test anxiety*. Test anxiety may not only impair your performance on the exam itself but also keep you from preparing properly. In Step 2, you will learn stress management techniques that will help you succeed on your exam. Practicing these techniques as you work through the activities in this book will help them become second nature to you by exam day.

Combating Test Anxiety

A little test anxiety is a good thing. Everyone gets nervous before a big exam—and if that nervousness motivates you to prepare thoroughly, so much the better. Many athletes report pre-game jitters, which they are able to harness to help them perform at their peak. Stop here and answer the questions on the Test Stress Quiz on the following page to determine your level of test anxiety.

Stress Management before the Exam

If you feel your level of anxiety is getting the best of you in the weeks before the exam, here are things you can do to bring the level down:

- **Prepare.** There's nothing like knowing what to expect to put you in control of test anxiety. That's why you're reading this book. Use it faithfully, and you will be ready on test day.

- **Practice self-confidence.** A positive attitude is a great way to combat test anxiety. Stand in front of the mirror and say to your reflection, "I'm prepared. I'm confident. I'm going to ace this exam. I know I can do it." As soon as negative thoughts creep in, drown them out with these positive affirmations. If you hear them often enough, and you use the LearningExpress method to study for the TABE®, they will be true.

- **Fight negative messages.** Every time someone talks to you about how hard the exam is or how it's difficult to pass, think about your self-confidence messages. If the "someone" with the negative messages is you—telling yourself you don't do well on exams, that you just can't do this—don't listen. Listen to your self-confidence messages.

- **Visualize.** Visualizing success can help make it happen—and it reminds you of why you're doing all this work in preparing for the exam. Imagine yourself in your first day of classes or beginning the first day of your dream job.

- **Exercise.** Physical activity helps calm your body and focus your mind. Besides, being in good physical shape can actually help you do well on the exam. Go for a run, lift weights, go swimming—and exercise regularly.

Stress Management on Test Day

There are several ways you can bring down your level of test stress and anxiety on test day. They'll work best if you practice them in the weeks before the exam, so you know which ones work best for you.

- Breathe deeply. Take a deep breath in while you count to five. Hold it for a count of one, and then let it out on a count of five. Repeat several times.
- Move your body. Try rolling your head in a circle. Rotate your shoulders. Shake your hands from the wrist.

TEST STRESS QUIZ

You need to worry about test anxiety only if it is extreme enough to impair your performance. The following questionnaire will provide a diagnosis of your level of test anxiety. In the blank before each statement, write the number that most accurately describes your experience.

0 = Never
1 = Once or twice
2 = Sometimes
3 = Often

_____ I have gotten so nervous before an exam that I put down the books and did not study for it.

_____ I have experienced disabling physical symptoms such as vomiting and severe headaches because I was nervous about an exam.

_____ I have simply not shown up for an exam because I was afraid to take it.

_____ I have experienced dizziness and disorientation while taking an exam.

_____ I have had trouble filling in the little circles because my hands were shaking too hard.

_____ I have failed an exam because I was too nervous to complete it.

_____ **Total: Add up the numbers in the blanks above.**

Your Test Stress Score

Here are the steps you should take, depending on your score. If you scored:

- **Below 3:** Your level of test anxiety is nothing to worry about; it is probably just enough to give you that little extra edge.
- **Between 3 and 6:** Your test anxiety may be enough to impair your performance, and you should practice the stress management techniques in this section to try to bring your test anxiety down to manageable levels.
- **Above 6:** Your level of test anxiety is a serious concern. In addition to practicing the stress management techniques listed in this section, you may want to seek additional, personal help. Call your local high school or community college and ask for the academic counselor. Tell the counselor that you have a level of test anxiety that sometimes keeps you from being able to take an exam. The counselor may be willing to help you or may suggest someone else you should talk to.

- **Visualize again.** Think of the place where you are most relaxed: lying on the beach in the sun, walking through the park, or wherever relaxes you. Now, close your eyes and imagine you're actually there. If you practice in advance, you will find that you need only a few seconds of this exercise to experience a significant increase in your sense of relaxation and well-being.

When anxiety threatens to overwhelm you *during* the test, there are still things you can do to manage your stress level:

- **Repeat your self-confidence messages.** You should have them memorized by now. Say them quietly to yourself, and believe them!
- **Visualize one more time.** This time, visualize yourself moving smoothly and quickly through the exam, answering every question correctly, and finishing just before time is up. Like most visualization techniques, this one works best if you've practiced it ahead of time.
- **Find an easy question.** Skim over the questions until you find an easy question, and then answer it. Getting even one question answered correctly gets you into the test-taking groove.
- **Take a mental break.** Everyone loses concentration once in a while during a long exam. It's normal, so you shouldn't worry about it. Instead, accept what has happened. Say to yourself, "Hey, I lost it there for a minute. My brain is taking a break." Close your eyes, and do some deep breathing for a few seconds. Then go back to work.

Try these techniques ahead of time and see if they work for you!

Step 3: Make a Plan

Time to complete: 20 minutes
Activity: Construct a study plan

There is no substitute for careful preparation and practice over time. So the most important thing you can do to better prepare yourself for your exam is to create a study plan or schedule and then follow it. This will help you avoid cramming at the last minute, which is an ineffective study technique that will only add to your anxiety.

Once you make your plan, make a commitment to follow it. Set aside at least 30 minutes every day for studying and practice. This will do more good than two hours crammed into a Saturday. If you have months before the test, you're lucky. Don't put off your studying until the week before. Start now. Even 10 minutes a weekday, with half an hour or more on weekends, can make a big difference in your score.

Step 4: Learn to Manage Your Time

Time to complete: 10 minutes to read, many hours of practice
Activities : Practice these strategies as you take the sample exams

Steps 4, 5, and 6 of the LearningExpress Test Preparation System put you in charge of your TABE® experience by showing you test-taking strategies that work. Practice these strategies as you take the practice exams in this book and online. Then, you will be ready to use them on test day.

First, you will take control of your time on the TABE®. Start by understanding the format of the test. Refer to Chapter 1 to review this information.

You will want to practice using your time wisely on the practice tests, while trying to avoid making mistakes at the same time as working quickly.

- **Listen carefully to directions.** By the time you get to the test, you should know how it works. But listen carefully in case something has changed.
- **Pace yourself.** Glance at your watch every few minutes to ensure that you are not taking much more than one to two minutes per question.
- **Keep moving.** Don't spend too much time on one question. If you don't know the answer, skip the question and move on. Mark the question for review and come back to it later.
- **Don't rush.** You should keep moving; but rushing won't help. Try to keep calm and work methodically and quickly.

Step 5: Learn to Use the Process of Elimination

Time to complete: 20 minutes
Activity: Complete the worksheet on Using the Process of Elimination

After time management, the next most important tool for taking control of your test is using the process of elimination wisely. It's standard test-taking wisdom that you should always read all the answer choices before choosing your answer. This helps you find the right answer by eliminating wrong answer choices. Consider the following question. Although it is not the type of question you will see on the TABE®, the mental process that you use will be the same.

9. **Sentence 6:** I would like to be considered for the assistant manager position in your company my previous work experience is a good match for the job requirements posted. Which correction should be made to sentence 6?
   a. Insert *Although* before *I.*
   b. Insert a question mark after *company.*
   c. Insert a semicolon and *However* before *my.*
   d. Insert a period after *company* and capitalize *my.*
   e. No corrections are necessary.

If you happen to know that sentence 6 is a run on sentence, and you know how to correct it, you don't need to use the process of elimination. But let's assume that, like some people, you don't. So, you look at the answer choices. *Although* sure doesn't sound like a good choice, because it would change the meaning of the sentence. So, you eliminate choice **a**—and now you only have four answer choices to deal with. Write **a** on your note paper with an **X** through or beside it. Move on to the other answer choices.

If you know that the first part of the sentence does not ask a question, you can eliminate choice **b** as a possible answer. Write **b** on your note paper with an **X** through or beside it. Choice **c**, inserting a semicolon, could create a pause in an otherwise long sentence, but inserting the word *However* might not be correct. If you're not sure whether or not this answer is correct, write **c** on your note paper with a question mark beside it, meaning "well, maybe."

Answer choice **d** would separate a very long sentence into two shorter sentences, and it would not change the meaning. It could work, so write **d** on your note paper with a check mark beside it, meaning "good answer." Answer choice **e** means that the sentence is fine like it is and doesn't need any changes. The sentence could make sense as it is, but it is definitely long. Is this the best way to write the sentence? If you're not sure, write **e** on your note paper with a question mark beside it.

Now, your note paper looks like this:

a. X
b. X
c. ?
d. ✔
e. ?

You've got just one check mark, for a good answer, **d**. If you're pressed for time, you should simply select choice **d**. If you've got the time to be extra careful, you could compare your check mark answer to your question mark answers to make sure that it's better. (It is: Sentence 6 is a run on and should be separated into two shorter, complete sentences.)

It's good to have a system for marking good, bad, and maybe answers. We recommend using this one:

X = bad
✔ = good
? = maybe

If you don't like these marks, devise your own system. Just make sure you do it long before exam day—while you're working through the practice tests in this book and online—so you won't have to worry about it during the exam.

Even when you think you're absolutely clueless about a question, you can use the process of elimination to get rid of one or more answer choices. By doing so, you're better prepared to make an educated guess, as you will see in Step 5. More often, the process of elimination allows you to get down to only two possible right answers. Nevertheless, as explained in Chapter one, rapid guessing is a strategy that should be avoided in the TABE®. It will result in the computer program giving candidates easier items, which you may also get wrong if you are guessing and running short on time.

Try using your powers of elimination on the following questions. The answer explanations show one possible way you might use the process to arrive at the right answer.

Use the process of elimination to answer the following questions.

1. Ilsa is as old as Meghan will be in five years. The difference between Ed's age and Meghan's age is twice the difference between Ilsa's age and Meghan's age. Ed is 29. How old is Ilsa?
   a. 4
   b. 10
   c. 19
   d. 24

2. "All drivers of commercial vehicles must carry a valid commercial driver's license whenever operating a commercial vehicle." According to this sentence, which of the following people need NOT carry a commercial driver's license?
   a. a truck driver idling his engine while waiting to be directed to a loading dock
   b. a bus operator backing her bus out of the way of another bus in the bus lot
   c. a taxi driver driving his personal car to the grocery store
   d. a limousine driver taking the limousine to her home after dropping off her last passenger of the evening

3. Smoking tobacco has been linked to
   a. increased risk of stroke and heart attack.
   b. all forms of respiratory disease.
   c. increasing mortality rates over the past ten years.
   d. juvenile delinquency.

4. Which of the following words is spelled correctly?
   a. incorrigible
   b. outragous
   c. domestickated
   d. understandible

Answers

Here are the answers, as well as some suggestions as to how you might have used the process of elimination to find them.

1. d. You should have eliminated choice **a** right off the bat. Ilsa cannot be four years old if Meghan is going to be Ilsa's age in five years. The best way to eliminate other answer choices is to try plugging them in to the information given in the problem. For instance, for choice **b**, if Ilsa is 10, then Meghan must be 5. The difference between their ages is 5. The difference between Ed's age, 29, and Meghan's age, 5, is 24. Is 24 two times 5? No. Then choice **b** is wrong. You could eliminate choice **c** in the same way and be left with choice **d**.

2. c. Note the word *NOT* in the question, and go through the answers one by one. Is the truck driver in choice **a** operating a commercial vehicle? Yes, idling counts as operating, so he needs to have a commercial driver's license. Likewise, the bus operator in choice **b** is operating a commercial vehicle; the question doesn't say the operator has to be on the street. The limo driver in choice **d** is operating a commercial vehicle, even if it doesn't have a passenger in it. However, the driver in choice **c** is not operating a commercial vehicle, but his own private car.

3. a. You could eliminate choice **b** simply because of the presence of the word *all*. Such absolutes hardly ever appear in correct answer choices. Choice **c** looks attractive until you think a little about what you know—aren't fewer people smoking these days, rather than more? So how could smoking be responsible for a higher mortality rate? (If you didn't know that mortality rate means the rate at which people die, you might keep this choice as a possibility, but you would still be able to eliminate two answers and have only two to choose from.) And choice **d** is plain silly, so you could eliminate that one, too. You are left with the correct choice, **a**.

4. a. How you used the process of elimination here depends on which words you recognized as being spelled incorrectly. If you knew that the correct spellings were outrageous, domesticated, and understandable, then you were home free. If you knew the correct spelling of one or two of these words, you could improve your chances of guessing correctly by using elimination. Surely you knew that at least one of those words was wrong!

Step 6: Reach Your Peak Performance Zone

Time to complete: 10 minutes to read; weeks to complete!
Activity: Complete the Physical Preparation Checklist

Physical and mental fatigue can significantly hinder your ability to perform as you prepare and also on the day of the exam. Poor diet choices can, as well. While drastic changes to your existing daily routine may cause a disruption too great to be helpful, modest, calculated alterations in your level of physical activity, the quality of your diet, and the amount and regularity of your rest can enhance your studies and your performance on the exam.

Exercise
If you are already engaged in a regular program of physical activity, resist allowing the pressure of the approaching exam to alter this routine. If you are not, and have not been engaged in regular physical activity, it may be helpful to begin during your preparations. Speak with someone knowledgeable about such matters to design a regimen suited to your particular circumstances and needs. Whatever its form, try to keep it a regular part of your preparation as the exam approaches.

Diet

A balanced diet will help you achieve peak performance. Limit your caffeine and junk food intake as you continue on your preparation journey. Eat plenty of fruits and vegetables, along with lean proteins and complex carbohydrates. Foods that are high in lecithin (an amino acid), such as fish and beans, are especially good brain foods.

Your diet is also a matter that is particular to you, so any major alterations to it should be discussed with a person with expert knowledge of nutrition.

Rest

For your brain and body to function at optimal levels, they must have an adequate amount of rest. It will be important to determine what an adequate amount of rest is for you. Determine how much rest you need to feel at your sharpest and most alert, and make an effort to get that amount regularly as the exam approaches and particularly on the night before the exam.

It may help to record your efforts. What follows is a "Physical Preparation Record" for the week prior to the exam; you may find its use helpful for staying on track.

Physical Preparation Checklist

In the week leading up to the test, you may be so involved with studying (and, unfortunately, stress) that you neglect to treat your body kindly. The following worksheet will help you stay on track.

For each day of the week before the test, write down what physical exercise you engaged in and for how long and what you ate for each meal. Remember, you're trying for at least half an hour of exercise every other day (preferably every day) and a balanced diet that is light on junk food. These practices are key to your body and brain working at their peak.

For the week before the test, write down what physical exercise you engaged in and for how long, and what you ate for each meal. Remember, you are trying for at least half an hour of exercise every other day (preferably every day) and a balanced diet that is light on junk food.

Exam minus 7 days

Exercise: _____ for _____ minutes

Breakfast: _____

Lunch: _____

Dinner: _____

Snacks: _____

Exam minus 6 days

Exercise: _____ for _____ minutes

Breakfast: _____

Lunch: _____

Dinner: _____

Snacks: _____

Exam minus 5 days

Exercise: _____ for _____ minutes

Breakfast: _____

Lunch: _____

Dinner: _____

Snacks: _____

Exam minus 4 days

Exercise: _____ for _____ minutes

Breakfast: _____

Lunch: _____

Dinner: _____

Snacks: _____

Exam minus 3 days

Exercise: _____ for _____ minutes

Breakfast: _____

Lunch: _____

Dinner: _____

Snacks: _____

Exam minus 2 days

Exercise: _____ for _____ minutes

Breakfast: _____

Lunch: _____

Dinner: _____

Snacks: _____

Exam minus 1 day

Exercise: _____ for _____ minutes

Breakfast: _____

Lunch: _____

Dinner: _____

Snacks: _____

Step 7: Make Final Preparations

Time to complete: 10 minutes to read; time to complete will vary
Activity: Complete the Final Preparations worksheet

You're in control of your mind and body; you're in charge of test anxiety, your preparation, and your test-taking strategies. Now, it's time to take charge of external factors, like the testing site and the materials you need to take the test.

Find Out Where the Exam Is and Make a Trial Run

Make sure you know exactly when and where your test is being held. Do you know how to get to the exam site? Do you know how long it will take to get there? If not, make a trial run if possible, preferably on the same day of the week at the same time of day. On the Final Preparations worksheet, make note of the amount of time it will take you to get to the test site. Plan on arriving at least 30 to 45 minutes early so you can get the lay of the land, use the bathroom, and calm down. Then figure out how early you will have to get up that morning, and make sure you get up that early every day for a week before the test.

Gather Your Materials

Make sure you have all the materials that will be required at the testing facility. Whether it's an admission ticket, an I.D., a second form of I.D., pencils, pens, calculators, a watch, or any other item that may be necessary, make sure you have put them aside. It's preferable to put them all aside together.

Arrange your clothes the evening before the exam. Dress in layers so that you can adjust readily to the temperature of the exam room.

Fuel Appropriately

Decide on a meal to eat in the time before your exam. Taking the exam on an empty stomach is something to avoid, particularly if it is an exam that spans several hours. Eating poorly and feeling lethargic are also to be avoided. Decide on a meal that will sate your hunger without adverse effect.

Final Preparations

To help organize your final preparations, a "Final Preparations" worksheet follows.

FINAL PREPARATIONS

Getting to the Exam Site

Location of exam site:_____

Date:_____

Departure time:_____

Do I know how to get to the exam site?   Yes _____   No _____   (If no, make a trial run.)

Time it will take to get to exam site: _____

Things to Lay Out the Night Before

Clothes I will wear   _____

Sweater/jacket   _____

Watch   _____

Photo ID   _____

Four #2 pencils   _____

Other Things to Bring/Remember

_____   _____

_____   _____

_____   _____

_____   _____

Step 8:
Make Your Preparations Count

Time to complete: 10 minutes, plus test-taking time
Activity: Ace the TABE®!

Fast forward to test day. You're ready. You made a study plan and followed through. You practiced your test-taking strategies while working through this book. You're in control of your physical, mental, and emotional state. You know when and where to show up and what to bring with you. In other words, you're well prepared!

When you're done with the test, you will have earned a reward. Plan a celebration. Call up your friends and plan a party, have a nice dinner with your family, or pick out a movie to see—whatever your heart desires.

And then do it. Go into the test, full of confidence, armed with test-taking strategies you've practiced until they're second nature. You're in control of yourself, your environment, and your performance on the exam. You're ready to succeed. So do it. And look forward to your future as someone who has done well on the TABE®!

3 ▶ PRACTICE EXAM 1

T his practice exam for TABE® 9&10, Level A, is a paper-and-pencil version of the computer-based exam you will see on test day. It mirrors the actual TABE® in testing level, content, and topics covered.

    This practice test contains a complete battery of 255 questions and answers for the four main and three optional areas on the TABE®: **Reading**, **Mathematics Computation**, **Applied Mathematics**, **Language**, **Language Mechanics**, **Vocabulary**, and **Spelling**.

    The tests in this book will show you how much you know and what kinds of problems you still need to study. Mastering these practice tests will allow you to reach your highest potential on the real TABE®.

Reading

1.	a	b	c	d	18.	a	b	c	d	35.	a	b	c	d
2.	a	b	c	d	19.	a	b	c	d	36.	a	b	c	d
3.	a	b	c	d	20.	a	b	c	d	37.	a	b	c	d
4.	a	b	c	d	21.	a	b	c	d	38.	a	b	c	d
5.	a	b	c	d	22.	a	b	c	d	39.	a	b	c	d
6.	a	b	c	d	23.	a	b	c	d	40.	a	b	c	d
7.	a	b	c	d	24.	a	b	c	d	41.	a	b	c	d
8.	a	b	c	d	25.	a	b	c	d	42.	a	b	c	d
9.	a	b	c	d	26.	a	b	c	d	43.	a	b	c	d
10.	a	b	c	d	27.	a	b	c	d	44.	a	b	c	d
11.	a	b	c	d	28.	a	b	c	d	45.	a	b	c	d
12.	a	b	c	d	29.	a	b	c	d	46.	a	b	c	d
13.	a	b	c	d	30.	a	b	c	d	47.	a	b	c	d
14.	a	b	c	d	31.	a	b	c	d	48.	a	b	c	d
15.	a	b	c	d	32.	a	b	c	d	49.	a	b	c	d
16.	a	b	c	d	33.	a	b	c	d	50.	a	b	c	d
17.	a	b	c	d	34.	a	b	c	d					

Language

1.	a	b	c	d	20.	a	b	c	d	38.	a	b	c	d
2.	a	b	c	d	21.	a	b	c	d	39.	a	b	c	d
3.	a	b	c	d	22.	a	b	c	d	40.	a	b	c	d
4.	a	b	c	d	23.	a	b	c	d	41.	a	b	c	d
5.	a	b	c	d	24.	a	b	c	d	42.	a	b	c	d
6.	a	b	c	d	25.	a	b	c	d	43.	a	b	c	d
7.	a	b	c	d	26.	a	b	c	d	44.	a	b	c	d
8.	a	b	c	d	27.	a	b	c	d	45.	a	b	c	d
9.	a	b	c	d	28.	a	b	c	d	46.	a	b	c	d
10.	a	b	c	d	29.	a	b	c	d	47.	a	b	c	d
11.	a	b	c	d	30.	a	b	c	d	48.	a	b	c	d
12.	a	b	c	d	31.	a	b	c	d	49.	a	b	c	d
13.	a	b	c	d	32.	a	b	c	d	50.	a	b	c	d
14.	a	b	c	d	33.	a	b	c	d	51.	a	b	c	d
15.	a	b	c	d	34.	a	b	c	d	52.	a	b	c	d
16.	a	b	c	d	35.	a	b	c	d	53.	a	b	c	d
17.	a	b	c	d	36.	a	b	c	d	54.	a	b	c	d
18.	a	b	c	d	37.	a	b	c	d	55.	a	b	c	d
19.	a	b	c	d										

Language Mechanics

1.	ⓐ	ⓑ	ⓒ	ⓓ
2.	ⓐ	ⓑ	ⓒ	ⓓ
3.	ⓐ	ⓑ	ⓒ	ⓓ
4.	ⓐ	ⓑ	ⓒ	ⓓ
5.	ⓐ	ⓑ	ⓒ	ⓓ
6.	ⓐ	ⓑ	ⓒ	ⓓ
7.	ⓐ	ⓑ	ⓒ	ⓓ

8.	ⓐ	ⓑ	ⓒ	ⓓ
9.	ⓐ	ⓑ	ⓒ	ⓓ
10.	ⓐ	ⓑ	ⓒ	ⓓ
11.	ⓐ	ⓑ	ⓒ	ⓓ
12.	ⓐ	ⓑ	ⓒ	ⓓ
13.	ⓐ	ⓑ	ⓒ	ⓓ
14.	ⓐ	ⓑ	ⓒ	ⓓ

15.	ⓐ	ⓑ	ⓒ	ⓓ
16.	ⓐ	ⓑ	ⓒ	ⓓ
17.	ⓐ	ⓑ	ⓒ	ⓓ
19.	ⓐ	ⓑ	ⓒ	ⓓ
20.	ⓐ	ⓑ	ⓒ	ⓓ

Vocabulary

1.	ⓐ	ⓑ	ⓒ	ⓓ
2.	ⓐ	ⓑ	ⓒ	ⓓ
3.	ⓐ	ⓑ	ⓒ	ⓓ
4.	ⓐ	ⓑ	ⓒ	ⓓ
5.	ⓐ	ⓑ	ⓒ	ⓓ
6.	ⓐ	ⓑ	ⓒ	ⓓ
7.	ⓐ	ⓑ	ⓒ	ⓓ

8.	ⓐ	ⓑ	ⓒ	ⓓ
9.	ⓐ	ⓑ	ⓒ	ⓓ
10.	ⓐ	ⓑ	ⓒ	ⓓ
11.	ⓐ	ⓑ	ⓒ	ⓓ
12.	ⓐ	ⓑ	ⓒ	ⓓ
13.	ⓐ	ⓑ	ⓒ	ⓓ
14.	ⓐ	ⓑ	ⓒ	ⓓ

15.	ⓐ	ⓑ	ⓒ	ⓓ
16.	ⓐ	ⓑ	ⓒ	ⓓ
17.	ⓐ	ⓑ	ⓒ	ⓓ
19.	ⓐ	ⓑ	ⓒ	ⓓ
20.	ⓐ	ⓑ	ⓒ	ⓓ

Spelling

1.	ⓐ	ⓑ	ⓒ	ⓓ
2.	ⓐ	ⓑ	ⓒ	ⓓ
3.	ⓐ	ⓑ	ⓒ	ⓓ
4.	ⓐ	ⓑ	ⓒ	ⓓ
5.	ⓐ	ⓑ	ⓒ	ⓓ
6.	ⓐ	ⓑ	ⓒ	ⓓ
7.	ⓐ	ⓑ	ⓒ	ⓓ

8.	ⓐ	ⓑ	ⓒ	ⓓ
9.	ⓐ	ⓑ	ⓒ	ⓓ
10.	ⓐ	ⓑ	ⓒ	ⓓ
11.	ⓐ	ⓑ	ⓒ	ⓓ
12.	ⓐ	ⓑ	ⓒ	ⓓ
13.	ⓐ	ⓑ	ⓒ	ⓓ
14.	ⓐ	ⓑ	ⓒ	ⓓ

15.	ⓐ	ⓑ	ⓒ	ⓓ
16.	ⓐ	ⓑ	ⓒ	ⓓ
17.	ⓐ	ⓑ	ⓒ	ⓓ
19.	ⓐ	ⓑ	ⓒ	ⓓ
20.	ⓐ	ⓑ	ⓒ	ⓓ

Mathematics Computation

	a	b	c	d
1.	a	b	c	d
2.	a	b	c	d
3.	a	b	c	d
4.	a	b	c	d
5.	a	b	c	d
6.	a	b	c	d
7.	a	b	c	d
8.	a	b	c	d
9.	a	b	c	d
10.	a	b	c	d
11.	a	b	c	d
12.	a	b	c	d
13.	a	b	c	d
14.	a	b	c	d
15.	a	b	c	d
16.	a	b	c	d
17.	a	b	c	d
18.	a	b	c	d
19.	a	b	c	d
20.	a	b	c	d
21.	a	b	c	d
22.	a	b	c	d
23.	a	b	c	d
24.	a	b	c	d
25.	a	b	c	d
26.	a	b	c	d
27.	a	b	c	d
28.	a	b	c	d
29.	a	b	c	d
30.	a	b	c	d
31.	a	b	c	d
32.	a	b	c	d
33.	a	b	c	d
34.	a	b	c	d
35.	a	b	c	d
36.	a	b	c	d
37.	a	b	c	d
38.	a	b	c	d
39.	a	b	c	d
40.	a	b	c	d

Applied Mathematics

	a	b	c	d
1.	a	b	c	d
2.	a	b	c	d
3.	a	b	c	d
4.	a	b	c	d
5.	a	b	c	d
6.	a	b	c	d
7.	a	b	c	d
8.	a	b	c	d
9.	a	b	c	d
10.	a	b	c	d
11.	a	b	c	d
12.	a	b	c	d
13.	a	b	c	d
14.	a	b	c	d
15.	a	b	c	d
16.	a	b	c	d
17.	a	b	c	d
18.	a	b	c	d
19.	a	b	c	d
20.	a	b	c	d
21.	a	b	c	d
22.	a	b	c	d
23.	a	b	c	d
24.	a	b	c	d
25.	a	b	c	d
26.	a	b	c	d
27.	a	b	c	d
28.	a	b	c	d
29.	a	b	c	d
30.	a	b	c	d
31.	a	b	c	d
32.	a	b	c	d
33.	a	b	c	d
34.	a	b	c	d
35.	a	b	c	d
36.	a	b	c	d
37.	a	b	c	d
38.	a	b	c	d
39.	a	b	c	d
40.	a	b	c	d
41.	a	b	c	d
42.	a	b	c	d
43.	a	b	c	d
44.	a	b	c	d
45.	a	b	c	d
46.	a	b	c	d
47.	a	b	c	d
48.	a	b	c	d
49.	a	b	c	d
50.	a	b	c	d

Reading

Read the following passage and answer the questions that follow.

Dining Out

The French have long been known for their cuisine. Any time a storywriter wants to indicate fine dining, the French restaurant is invoked, along with its expense. However, French food is rather rich and contains a lot of dairy products, which are known to be problematic, especially for certain groups of people. On the other hand, Thai food, which is much less expensive, actually offers a much healthier choice. Thai food contains simple ingredients that provide good nutrition without challenging the body's ability to process unnatural foods or draining anyone's bank account.

Some of the vegetables used in Thai restaurants in the West are eggplant, broccoli, beans, bamboo shoots, tomatoes, cucumbers, Chinese kale, sweet potatoes, squash, cabbage, and mushrooms. Fruits are customarily served after a meal. These might include papaya, mango, pineapple, rose apples, durian, and Burmese grapes. These commonly used ingredients afford many diners a nutritious, low-calorie, slightly exotic, and economic alternative to other types of famous cuisine.

1. Which of these statements sums up the main idea of the passage?
- **a.** The more expensive the food, the better it is.
- **b.** The quality of food isn't always directly related to its cost.
- **c.** Thai food is better than French food.
- **d.** French food is better than Thai food.

2. What is the meaning of the word *process* as it is used in the passage?
- **a.** interpret
- **b.** accumulate
- **c.** digest
- **d.** accept

3. What are some of the vegetables that might appear in a dish you order at a Thai restaurant?
- **a.** cabbage, beans, and bamboo shoots
- **b.** broccoli, pineapple, and tomatoes
- **c.** squash, cauliflower, and Chinese kale
- **d.** onions, sweet potatoes, and mushrooms

4. Cuisines are often associated with particular
- **a.** price points.
- **b.** countries.
- **c.** ingredients.
- **d.** all of the above.

Read the following passage and answer the questions that follow.

Continental Drift

Humans have always been plagued by earthquakes and volcanoes, but geologists haven't always understood what causes them. Way back in 1912, Alfred Wegener advanced the theory of continental drift, which says that the continents are slowly moving. While some scientists took Wegener's ideas seriously, many did not, mainly because Wegener was a meteorologist, and so they thought he couldn't possibly know what he was talking about.

When this theory was presented in 1912, Wegener argued that all of the continents had been joined together at one time. He supported this theory by an examination of rock types, geological structures, and fossils, all of which demonstrated a significant match between the lands on the two sides of the Atlantic Ocean. If you look at a map of the world, you can see that the East Coast of the Americas fits the western side of the land mass on the other side of the Atlantic Ocean. But most geologists thought that the continents could not possibly be moving and therefore paid little attention to the supporting evidence that proposed this slow shifting of the continents.

In 1943, Wegener's theory was vehemently attacked by George Gaylord Simpson, who then put forth his own views contradicting the theory. His influence was so powerful that even those who had previously leaned in the direction of accepting Wegener's views began inclining in the opposite direction. But the hard evidence kept mounting, and by the 1950s this theory began to be accepted. Only since the 1960s has it been taught as factual. Today this theory is known as plate tectonics, and it is now possible to measure continental drift with the Global Positioning System.

The top layer of the Earth is called the crust. Below the crust is a viscous layer called the mantle. The mantle consists of the asthenosphere, composed of flowing rock, and the lithosphere, composed of rigid rock. The lithosphere is broken up into tectonic plates. There are approximately seven major plates and many minor plates. Where the plates meet, activity such as earthquakes and volcanoes occur because of the way the plates bump into each other. The plate boundaries help to shape mountains because of the interaction between the plates. These boundaries are also the site of mid-ocean ridges, such as the mid-Atlantic ridge.

In a given area, a long time can pass between events such as earthquakes, and thus many people aren't aware that they are living in a geologically active zone where such future events are inevitable.

5. Earth's mantle
   a. is liquid.
   b. is rigid.
   c. has a thick, sticky consistency between solid and liquid.
   d. is deep inside the Earth.

6. What is the meaning of the word *plate* as discussed in this passage?
   a. one of several rigid pieces of the Earth's lithosphere that together make up the layer just below the Earth's surface
   b. the Earth's crust
   c. pieces of rock inside the asthenosphere
   d. the land mass of the Earth that shows above water

7. Why did many scientists reject Wegener's theory about continental drift?
   a. They weren't open-minded.
   b. They didn't trust someone who was a meteorologist and not a geologist.
   c. Wegener didn't offer any evidence to support his theory.
   d. **a** and **b**, but not **c**

8. Where do earthquakes usually happen?
   a. in areas where the rocks in the Earth are weak
   b. in areas where earthquakes have never happened before
   c. at the surface of the Earth
   d. where the plates come together

9. What is the closest meaning to *vehemently*?
   a. maliciously
   b. secretly
   c. erroneously
   d. strongly

10. What is the closest meaning to *inevitable*?

    a. avoidable

    b. certain to happen

    c. unknown

    d. powerful

Daniel is an airline pilot with Bigelow Airlines. He received the following air travel schedule for the upcoming work week. Look at the schedule, then answer questions 11–15.

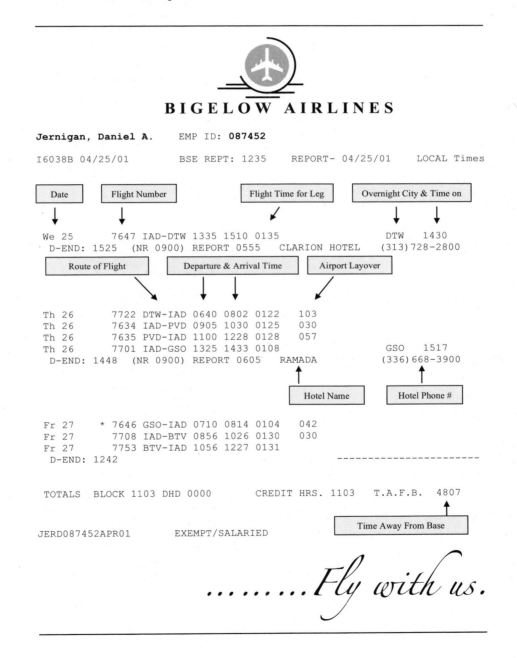

BIGELOW AIRLINES

Jernigan, Daniel A.   EMP ID: **087452**

I6038B 04/25/01   BSE REPT: 1235   REPORT- 04/25/01   LOCAL Times

| Date | Flight Number | | Flight Time for Leg | | Overnight City & Time on | |

We 25   7647 IAD-DTW 1335 1510 0135   DTW   1430
  D-END: 1525   (NR 0900) REPORT 0555   CLARION HOTEL   (313)728-2800

| | Route of Flight | | Departure & Arrival Time | | Airport Layover | |

Th 26   7722 DTW-IAD 0640 0802 0122   103
Th 26   7634 IAD-PVD 0905 1030 0125   030
Th 26   7635 PVD-IAD 1100 1228 0128   057
Th 26   7701 IAD-GSO 1325 1433 0108   GSO   1517
  D-END: 1448   (NR 0900) REPORT 0605   RAMADA   (336)668-3900

Hotel Name   *Hotel Phone #*

Fr 27   * 7646 GSO-IAD 0710 0814 0104   042
Fr 27   7708 IAD-BTV 0856 1026 0130   030
Fr 27   7753 BTV-IAD 1056 1227 0131
  D-END: 1242   ----------------------

TOTALS   BLOCK 1103 DHD 0000   CREDIT HRS. 1103   T.A.F.B.   4807

Time Away From Base

JERD087452APR01   EXEMPT/SALARIED

..........Fly with us.

11. What is the phone number of the hotel where Daniel will be staying the night of April 25?
   a. (336) 668-3900
   b. (313) 728-2800
   c. (710) 814-0104
   d. (800) 335-1510

12. What are the total credit hours Daniel will earn for this week?
   a. 1,103
   b. 4,807
   c. 1,448
   d. 1,242

13. Daniel's third flight route on Thursday will be
   a. DTW-IAD.
   b. IAD-BTV.
   c. PVD-IAD.
   d. GSO-IAD.

14. Most likely, the number 087452 is Daniel's
   a. employee number.
   b. flight number.
   c. license number.
   d. telephone number.

15. Which of the following would likely NOT be a reason why Daniel would need to know his T.A.F.B.?
   a. He may need to decide if he packed enough clothing.
   b. He may want to plan a little sightseeing in the city where he has a layover.
   c. He may need to take care of personal business within the week back home.
   d. He may wish to have surgery while away.

Read the poem by William Blake, then answer questions 16–20.

Love's Secret

Never seek to tell thy love,
Love that never told can be;
For the gentle wind does move
Silently, invisibly.

I told my love, I told my love,
I told her all my heart;
Trembling, cold, in ghastly fears,
Ah! she did depart!

Soon as she was gone from me,
A traveler came by,
Silently, invisibly
He took her with a sigh.

16. The tone of this poem is
   a. gleaming.
   b. pessimistic.
   c. joyful.
   d. elementary.

17. Blake seems to be saying that
   a. he has not experienced real love.
   b. unspoken love has a better chance of not being rejected.
   c. love is a burden.
   d. love is overrated.

18. According to the poem, the speaker's love for the other can live on if
   a. it is not told to the other.
   b. it is refused.
   c. it is denied as real.
   d. it occurs in adolescence.

19. The mood of this poem can best be described as
a. melancholy.
b. reverent.
c. intense.
d. scornful.

20. The idea of never revealing one's love to another to avoid emotional pain is
a. an opinion.
b. a fact.
c. neither a fact nor an opinion.
d. irrelevant.

Read the following conversation, then answer questions 21–25.

The Interview
Setting: Administrator's office in a community bank

BOURNE: Mr. Miller, I see you're right on time. That's a good start. (*They shake hands.*)

MILLER: Thank you for inviting me to the interview today.

BOURNE: Sit down. (*He sits in the chair in front of her desk; she sits behind the desk.*) So you're about to finish college, are you? I remember that time in my own life—exciting and scary.

MILLER: It's definitely both for me. I'm particularly excited about the job here at Community Savings and Loan.

BOURNE: (*smiles*) Then there's a mutual interest. We had a lot of applications, but we're interviewing only eight candidates. What I'd like to do is get a sense of your interests and tell you about our managerial trainee program here, so that we can see if the fit between us is as good as it looks on paper. How does that sound to you?

MILLER: Great.

BOURNE: Let me start by telling you about a rather common problem we've had with our past managerial trainees. Many of them run into a problem—something they have trouble learning or doing right. That's normal enough—we expect that. But a lot of trainees seem to get derailed when that happens. Instead of finding another way to approach the problem, they get discouraged and give up. So I'm very interested in hearing what you've done when you've encountered problems or roadblocks in your life.

MILLER: Well, I can remember one time when I hit a real roadblock. I was taking an advanced chemistry course, and I just couldn't seem to understand the material. I failed the first exam, even though I'd studied hard.

BOURNE: Good example of a problem. What did you do?

MILLER: I started going to all the tutorial sessions that the grad assistants offered. That helped a little, but I still wasn't getting the materials the way I should have. So I organized a study team and offered to pay for pizzas so that students who were on top of the class would have a reason to come.

BOURNE: (*nodding with admiration*) That shows a lot of initiative and creativity. Did the study team work?

MILLER: (*smiling*) It sure did. I wound up getting a B in the course, and so did several other members of the study team who had been in the same boat I was in early in the semester.

BOURNE: So you don't mind asking for help if you need it?

MILLER: I'd rather do that than flounder, but I'm usually pretty able to operate independently.

BOURNE: So you prefer working on your own to working with others?

MILLER: That depends on the situation or project. If I have all that I need to do something on my own, I'm comfortable working solo. But there are other cases in which I don't have everything I need to do something well—maybe I don't have experience in some aspect of the job or I don't have a particular skill or I don't understand some perspectives on the issue. In cases like that, I think teams are more effective than individuals.

BOURNE: Good. Banking management requires the ability to be self-initiating and also the ability to work with others. Let me ask another question. As I was looking over your transcript and resume, I noticed that you changed your major several times. Does that indicate you have difficulty making a commitment and sticking with it?

MILLER: I guess you could think that, but it really shows that I was willing to explore a lot of alternatives before making a final commitment.

BOURNE: But don't you think that you wasted a lot of time and courses getting to that commitment?

MILLER: I don't think so. I learned something in all of the courses I took. For instance, when I was a philosophy major, I learned about logical thinking and careful reasoning. That's going to be useful to me in management. When I was majoring in English, I learned how to write well and how to read others' writing critically. That's going to serve me well in management, too.

BOURNE: So what led you to your final decision to double-major in business and communication? That's an unusual combination.

MILLER: It seems a very natural one to me. I wanted to learn about business because I want to be a manager in an organization. I need to know how organizations work, and I need to understand different management philosophies and styles. At the same time, managers work with people, and that means I have to have strong communication skills.

21. What is likely to be the author's purpose for writing this conversation?
    a. to rid the bank of possible thieves
    b. to show the importance of good interviewing skills
    c. to explain how Community Savings and Loan's managerial trainee program works
    d. to meet a hiring deadline

22. According to the answers given by Miller, the reader can assume that he was
    a. scared.
    b. confident.
    c. unsure.
    d. obnoxious.

23. It seems likely that the reason Miller got an interview was because of his
    a. resume.
    b. good looks.
    c. father's phone calls to the bank.
    d. teacher's recommendation.

24. Comparing Miller and Bourne, the reader could conclude that _____ worked at a bank.
    a. neither Miller nor Bourne has ever
    b. both Miller and Bourne have
    c. Bourne has never
    d. Miller has never

25. Based on this conversation, do you think Miller was offered a position at the bank?

  a. No. He was too nervous.

  b. No. He was too sure of himself.

  c. Yes. He took challenging questions and answered them to his advantage.

  d. Yes. He was probably well dressed for the interview.

Read the following passage and answer the questions that follow.

A Day She Will Never Forget

(1)

April 20, 1984 began not unlike any other spring day. Beverly was doing her daily rituals at her job as a court reporter at the courthouse. She knew a chance of severe weather was a threat, but the things that happened that day were events neither she nor anyone else in the small, rural town would ever be ready to endure. "I've never experienced anything like it," she is often quoted as saying.

(2)

Around lunchtime, the first of two warnings was announced. The first event moved through the outskirts of town like children playing hopscotch. "Telephone poles along Route 20 were snapped like toothpicks," Beverly recalls. It uprooted trees, destroyed a few barns, and made new paths in the farmers' fields. Electricity throughout the region was interrupted with travelers in vehicles unsure of whether to "stop or go" at non-working traffic lights. Children at the community school hunkered down in hallways, covering their heads with books, backpacks, and jackets. "The teachers did such a good job at comforting those children," Beverly says.

(3)

Approximately half an hour after the first event was announced, a second one was spotted. It traveled straight through the middle of town and spanned a good mile in width. The local Piggly Wiggly was destroyed, the town's oldest historic home lost its roof, and the youth baseball facilities were razed. Luckily, the destruction missed the school children and did no damage to the school. Yet seven people in that small town did lose their lives that day. "We lost some really good people that day," says Beverly.

(4)

A memorial fountain was erected in the downtown area. Here, people come together to read the names of those who perished and toss a penny into the fountain as a means of good wishes for the future of the town. The fountain is one town attraction that Beverly wished had never been built. After all, she says, "That was a day I will never forget."

(5)

Indeed, Beverly will always recall that day. Though her office was left untouched, her spirit was forever damaged. "I have the utmost respect for the weather more than I used to," she says. She saw what a change in weather could do in such a short amount of time. One of those who perished was a former classmate of hers. The victim was a community leader who was looking forward to the arrival of her first grandchild.

26. The style of this essay could BEST be described as

  a. literary.

  b. technical.

  c. operational.

  d. conversational.

27. In the context of this essay, the word *rituals*, in paragraph one, would be better worded as
  a. spells.
  b. beliefs.
  c. routines.
  d. cleaning.

28. The best paragraph order for the above essay is
  a. 2, 4, 1, 5, 3.
  b. 3, 5, 4, 1, 2.
  c. 1, 2, 3, 5, 4.
  d. 4, 2, 1, 3, 5.

29. Even though the word is never used in the essay, the supporting evidence in the essay implies that the events that occurred were
  a. tornadoes.
  b. hurricanes.
  c. snow storms.
  d. flash floods.

30. According to the passage, how many weather events happened that day?
  a. one
  b. two
  c. three
  d. four

Look at the following advertisement and answer the questions that follow.

Academic School Tours, Inc.
—We believe experience is the key to a good education!—

Tour Option 1 $299*
June 3–5
– 3 days/2 nights Accommodations
– Ground Transportation
– All Inclusive Meals
– Tour Admissions

Tour Option 2 $449*
July 7–10
– 4 days/3 nights Accommodations
– Rail Transportation
– 3 dinners/4 lunches
– Tour Admissions

Tour Option 3 $699*^
July 22–26
– 5 days/4 nights Accommodations
– Air Transportation
– All Inclusive Meals
– Tour Admissions

*Per Person
^ Optional Travel Insurance: $49

Washington, D.C. Summer Tours
Sponsored by
Ingram-Stanhope High School PTA

• History in Action
• Wonderful Accommodations
• Student-Focused
• Fine Dining
• Experienced Tour Guides

Need more information or want to register?
Phone (877) 587-9832
or check out our website at
www.studenttours.com

31. The term *accommodations* in the tour advertisement refers to
   a. hotels.
   b. trains.
   c. airplanes.
   d. taxis.

32. How will participants who choose option 2 be traveling?
   a. by bus
   b. by car
   c. by train
   d. by airplane

33. If a student chooses option 3 with travel insurance, what would his or her tour price be?
   a. $499
   b. $548
   c. $699
   d. $748

34. Why would the reader most likely assume this company has done tours in the past?
   a. The company believes students must experience things as part of their education.
   b. The company says that it is student-focused.
   c. The company has experienced tour guides.
   d. The company has a website.

35. Which of the following groups of people would probably NOT be interested in this advertisement?
   a. teachers
   b. dentists
   c. parents
   d. students

Read the following passage and answer the questions that follow.

The British Monarchy

The succession to the throne is regulated not only through descent but also by parliamentary statute. The order of succession is the sequence of members of the Royal Family according to the order in which they stand in line to the throne.

The basis for the succession was determined in the constitutional developments of the seventeenth century, which culminated in the Bill of Rights (1689) and the Act of Settlement (1701). When James II fled the country in 1688, Parliament held that he had "abdicated the government" and that the throne was vacant. The throne was then offered, not to James's young son, but to his daughter Mary and her husband William of Orange, as joint rulers.

It therefore came to be established not only that the sovereign rules through Parliament but that the succession to the throne also can be regulated by Parliament, and that a sovereign can be deprived of his title through misgovernment. The succession to the throne is regulated not only through descent but also by statute; the Act of Settlement confirmed that it was for Parliament to determine the title to the throne. The Act laid down that only Protestant descendants of Princess Sophia—the Electress of Hanover and granddaughter of James I—are eligible to succeed. Subsequent Acts have confirmed this.

Parliament, under the Bill of Rights and the Act of Settlement, also laid down various conditions that the sovereign must meet. Roman Catholics are not allowed to succeed the throne, nor may the sovereign marry a Roman Catholic. The sovereign must, in addition, be in communion with the Church of England and must swear to preserve the established Church of England and the established Church of Scotland. The sovereign must also promise to uphold the Protestant succession.

Unlike succession to the throne, which is regulated not only through descent but also by parliamentary statute, precedence of the Royal Family at Court is determined by law as well as traditions and customs. Precedence of members of the Royal Family at private events is a matter of the Queen's discretion. The Queen decides which members of her family are accorded the status of members of the Royal Family and also, from time to time, approves their precedence. The Queen determines both separate precedence (for ladies and gentlemen) and also joint precedence.

Generally speaking, the children, grandchildren, and great-grandchildren of a sovereign, as well as their spouses, are members of the Royal Family. First cousins of the monarch may also be included. Children are included on coming of age or after they have completed their education.

Precedence of the Royal Family at Court does not follow the line of succession. Thus, the Duke of Edinburgh takes precedence immediately after the Queen.

36. The OPPOSITE of the word *succession* as used in the above essay is
   a. retribution.
   b. recession.
   c. election.
   d. intervention.

37. When the writer states that the sovereign is required to "be in communion with the Church of England," the term *in communion with* DOES NOT mean
   a. in agreement with.
   b. opposed to.
   c. devoted to.
   d. married in.

38. According to the passage, what factors determine succession?
   a. descent
   b. parliamentary statute
   c. popular vote
   d. both descent and parliamentary statute

39. George, Duke of Kent, was an uncle of the current Queen of England, Elizabeth II. Based on the passage, we can safely assume that the following is true about his three children, Edward, Alexandra, and Michael.
   a. They are members of the Royal Family.
   b. They are not allowed to marry someone who is Roman Catholic.
   c. Both **a.** and **b.**
   d. None of the above.

40. The passage suggests that which of the following is affiliated with Protestantism?
   a. Roman Catholic Church.
   b. Church of Scotland.
   c. William of Orange.
   d. First cousins of the Queen.

Read the following, then answer the questions that follow.

The manager of Rambo's Building Supply and Home Entertainment Center asked Fred, an associate in the tools department, and Jackson, an associate in the computers department, to work on Christmas Eve. This particular date fell on a day of the week that both were usually not scheduled to work. Neither of the employees was very excited to hear that he was being asked to come in on this day. Both were contacted by email, and the following responses were logged in the manager's email system.

Fred: *I DO NOT WANT TO WORK ON CHRIST-MAS EVE! This company is run by a load of jerks. I have a plane to catch on that day at 12:30 in Monroe. How do you expect me to work and get to the airport on time? You should have asked me before now. I can't get my money back for the ticket, either. Get somebody else?!?!?!?!?. . . . . Please!*

Jackson: *I understand that more help is needed on this busy shopping day. Yet, I regret I am scheduled to fly out of Monroe at 12:30 in order that I can make the 3-hour flight to have Christmas Eve dinner with my family. Had I known earlier that I might be asked to work, I would have gladly made other flight arrangements. I am concerned because my plane ticket is non-refundable. Would it be acceptable if I asked another coworker to work in my place? I appreciate your working with me as we try to reach a compromise.*

---

41. The tone of the first email appears to be one of
   a. happiness.
   b. disgust.
   c. neutrality.
   d. curiosity.

42. Based on Jackson's response, the manager would most likely describe Jackson as a
   a. disgruntled worker.
   b. former employee.
   c. selfish individual.
   d. team player.

43. Suppose the manager wrote back to Fred with a demand that Fred correct his attitude and report to work as asked. Fred's disposition would MOST LIKELY be one of
   a. agreement.
   b. partiality to the company.
   c. resentment.
   d. fear.

44. Why can the reader assume that both Fred and Jackson had plane reservations for 12:30 in the afternoon, rather than 12:30 in the morning?
   a. Jackson mentioned that he was trying to get to a dinner, and a building supply store would not typically be open at 12:30 in the morning.
   b. Fred said that he was flying during the day, and Jackson only works days.
   c. Both Fred and Jackson made it clear that their tickets were non-refundable.
   d. Fred was not afraid of the manager's response.

45. Assume that in the end Jackson was granted the day off. If he were asked by friends about his work environment, Jackson would probably respond that it is
   a. pleasant.
   b. burdensome.
   c. unfair.
   d. dramatic.

The following is an excerpt from the bylaws of a local Daughters of the American Revolution chapter. Study the excerpt and answer questions 46–50.

Article III

Members

Section 1. Eligibility. Any woman is eligible for membership in the National Society of the Daughters of the American Revolution who is not less than eighteen years of age, and who is lineally descended from a man or woman who, with unfailing loyalty to the cause of American Independence, served as a sailor, or soldier, or civil officer in one of the several Colonies or States, or in the United Colonies or States or as a recognized patriot or rendered material aid thereto, provided the applicant for Chapter membership is personally acceptable to the Chapter.

Section 2. Admission. An applicant for membership through this Chapter shall be endorsed by two members of the Chapter who are in good standing and to whom the applicant is personally known. The Chapter may not discriminate against the applicant on the basis of race or creed. The acceptability of the applicant for Chapter membership shall be by a majority vote by ballot of the Chapter at a regular meeting. Upon favorable action, the applicant shall be given the official application papers for membership in the National Society. Within one year, unless granted extension by the Chapter, the applicant shall return to the Chapter all required documents, prepared in accordance with instructions established and distributed by the National Society, and accompanied by the prescribed fees and dues. [NSDAR Bylaws Article III. Section 2 (a)]

Section 3. Transfers. A member desiring to unite with the chapter by transfer, either from another chapter or member-at-large, shall be proposed and accepted by the Chapter in the same manner as a new member.

Section 4. Resignations. A member desiring to resign shall present her resignation in writing to the Chapter Registrar, who shall immediately report the resignation to the Office of the Organizing Secretary General. A member whose dues are delinquent shall not be entitled to resign from membership. [NSDAR bylaws article IV. Section 2 (e) (4).]

46. In the phrase *lineally descended from a man or woman*, the words *lineally descended from* could also be written as
a. cousins of.
b. church members with.
c. direct descendants of.
d. siblings of.

47. To whom must a person first submit her wish to resign her membership?
a. Chapter President
b. Chapter Registrar
c. Chapter Membership Chair
d. Secretary General

48. Which of the following is NOT a requirement for membership?
a. being age 18 or older
b. being a descendant of someone who was actively connected to the American Revolution
c. receiving a majority vote of chapter members
d. being Caucasian

49. According to the passage, in which of the following situations is a member not allowed to resign?
   a. She's deceased.
   b. She owes membership dues.
   c. There's a majority vote against her resignation.
   d. She didn't follow the rules of her chapter.

50. Suppose a woman who is a member of a chapter in another state wishes to become a member of the local chapter. In which section of the bylaws is she instructed what to do AND what process must she follow?
   a. Section 4; follow same process as a new member
   b. Section 3; follow same process as a new member
   c. Section 1; follow same process as a National member
   d. Section 2; follow same process as a National member

Language

1. Choose the sentence that contains a subjective pronoun.
   a. The coach ordered them to stop practicing.
   b. My cousin and me went to the movies last night.
   c. The group of tourists did not understand him.
   d. She talked to her brother on the phone yesterday.

2. Choose the sentence that contains an objective pronoun that is used correctly.
   a. After lunch, Dana and she went to a movie.
   b. Cousin Fred gave me a mysterious box.
   c. Sam and her are both good athletes.
   d. Cousin Del has been very kind to Dana and I.

3. Choose the sentence that contains a possessive pronoun.
   a. This is the book that the president wrote himself.
   b. When asked to select an apple, Dan chose the greenest one.
   c. The red bike belongs to both Jenny and her sister.
   d. Which coats are on the bench?

4. Choose the sentence that contains a relative pronoun that is used correctly. Do not consider informal usage.
   a. Give it to whoever wants it.
   b. He knows he is a controversial person whom people either love or hate.
   c. Finn is the dog that came to the assisted living home yesterday to play with the residents.
   d. People are looking for a strong president which will move this country forward.

5. Choose the sentence that correctly uses a reflexive pronoun.
   a. I saw me in the mirror.
   b. Why do you blame yourself?
   c. He accomplished the feat hisself.
   d. They cannot look after theirselves.

6. Choose the sentence that contains a demonstrative pronoun that is used correctly.
   a. These book is considered a classic.
   b. Especially with the recent recession, this are bad times.
   c. Did your last orange taste as good as this one?
   d. Do you really like these pictures over there?

7. Select the sentence that contains subject-pronoun agreement.
  a. If a person wants to succeed in life, you have to know the rules of the game.
  b. All students must have their pencils available.
  c. If they want to succeed in life, he has to know the rules of the game.
  d. If anybody wants to succeed in life, they have to know the rules of the game.

8. Choose the sentence that contains a present tense verb that is used correctly.
  a. We studied the results of the test tomorrow.
  b. We takes medicine when we are sick.
  c. I will eat fish for my dinner yesterday.
  d. Please bring me the hammer from the tool bench.

9. Select the sentence that contains a past tense verb that is used correctly.
  a. I get up every day at 6:30 A.M.
  b. Joan practices very hard yesterday.
  c. The children swam in the pool all day.
  d. They will be here very soon.

10. Select the sentence that contains a future tense verb that is used correctly.
  a. Joseph will take his dog for a walk after work today.
  b. Del will goes to the store tomorrow.
  c. Kaya went through all the possible combinations.
  d. You are there every day on a regular basis.

11. Select the sentence that contains a present perfect tense verb that is used correctly.
  a. Jack lived in Boston for five years and still lived there.
  b. We saw three movies last week.
  c. My uncle has crashed his car last year.
  d. I have seen that play already.

12. Select the sentence that contains a progressive tense verb that is used correctly.
  a. The children are playing hide and seek with their dog Rover.
  b. Finding a needle in a haystack is not easy.
  c. The little dog started barking furiously.
  d. I have run several marathons this year.

13. Choose the sentence with correct subject-verb agreement.
  a. The group are going to present a demonstration later.
  b. Neither Brady nor his sister are going to the ceremony.
  c. My chorus consists of twelve members.
  d. The group of students were blocking the hallway.

14. Select the underlined verb that is used correctly based on the meaning of the rest of the sentence.
  a. Patrick <u>inferred</u> that he had gotten the promotion when he gave me a thumbs-up sign and a wink.
  b. He asked, "<u>May</u> I take your coat?"
  c. They <u>adapted</u> a child from Vietnam last year.
  d. The twins <u>immigrated</u> from Canada last year.

15. Choose the sentence that uses a comparative adjective correctly.
   a. Rating the Three Stooges, I believe Larry is the funnier.
   b. Of the two dishes, this one is the worst.
   c. Sofia's cottage is farther from the lake than mine is.
   d. Of the two drinks, which one do you think is the sweetest?

16. Choose the sentence that uses a superlative adjective correctly.
   a. That painting is more darker than all the rest of the paintings.
   b. I asked all of them, "Who is the best skier?"
   c. She is the more beautiful of all the statues.
   d. This is my most happiest moment of the entire day.

17. Choose the sentence that uses a comparative adverb correctly.
   a. Of the two sports cars, which do you think goes fast?
   b. Of the four assistants, Josh works more carefully.
   c. I took the class more seriously than Dan did.
   d. The florist works hardest than his competitors.

18. Choose the sentence that uses a superlative adverb correctly.
   a. Of all the students in the class, she plays the best.
   b. He plays best in front of the fans than he does in practice.
   c. The sun shines more brightly than the moon.
   d. I wanted to tell you that next Friday is the most soonest we can arrive.

19. Choose the sentence that correctly uses a modifier, either an adjective or an adverb.
   a. He asked how the team played at last night's game, and I answered, "We played good."
   b. She walked slow down the block holding her granddaughter's hand.
   c. I have seen her perform in concert, and she sings beautifully.
   d. I have seen her perform in concert, and she sings beautiful.

20. Choose the sentence that uses a negative correctly.
   a. We were not barely able to see the stage because we were so high up in the balcony.
   b. I do not want no second helpings.
   c. My cat will not let no one pet him but my Dad and me.
   d. The supervisor said that I cannot do anything right.

21. Choose the complete, correct sentence.
   a. Alex is very smart, he began reading when he was seven years old.
   b. After Mary ate half a box of Twinkies.
   c. To catch butterflies for the biology class.
   d. Daniel watched in dismay as Lou poured the rest of the soup down the kitchen sink.

22. Select the choice that combines the clauses into the most readable, logical sentence.
   a. The waves were almost 15 feet tall, and we decided not to surf.
   b. The comic book convention was the first ever, and it lasted all day, and several super heroes appeared in costume.
   c. She was our Spanish teacher when we were in high school, but she was a birdlike, unfriendly woman who had sparkling eyes.
   d. Mr. Sam Sunshine, the principal of my elementary school, was a short, pudgy man.

23. Select the compound sentence that is punctuated correctly.
   a. The man entered the store dressed in a gorilla costume, the clerk was not amused.
   b. The man entered the store dressed in a gorilla costume the clerk was not amused.
   c. The man entered the store dressed in a gorilla costume and the clerk was not amused.
   d. The man entered the store dressed in a gorilla costume, and the clerk was not amused.

24. Select the choice that shows two independent clauses combined correctly.
   a. We were late because of car trouble so we missed the first act of the play.
   b. The bushes were trimmed, and the grass was mowed.
   c. During holidays, the school is deserted.
   d. My uncle likes to eat at fancy restaurants and visiting museums.

25. Select the sentence that uses correct punctuation.
   a. My cousin, who is 10 years old has very strange ears.
   b. Even though the bowl was filled with popcorn Alana refused to eat it.
   c. My brother Trevor loved to sit on the dock, which was shaded by a large tree.
   d. When a six-foot snake slithered across the sidewalk Rhonda screamed.

26. Select the most clearly written sentence.
   a. Less attention is paid to commercials that lack human interest stories than to other types of commercials.
   b. Tanya worked in a medical lab last summer, which may be her career choice.
   c. Freshman college students must make many choices, and sometimes you get confused.
   d. Because of the growing use of computers to store and process information, sales of computers are growing exponentially.

27. Select the sentence that shows parallel structure.
   a. Sean likes to hike, to swim, and riding a bike.
   b. The dictionary can be used to find the following: meanings, pronunciations, correct spellings, and looking up irregular verbs.
   c. Nicolas not only dislikes contests but also refuses to enter them.
   d. The students were asked to write their reports quickly, accurately, and in a detailed manner.

28. Select the sentence that is concise and does not contain repetition.
   a. Balancing the budget by Friday is impossible without extra help.
   b. It goes without saying that we are acquainted with your policy on filing tax returns, and we have every intention of complying with the regulations that you have mentioned.
   c. Emission allowances are issued every year on an annual basis.
   d. I think we should postpone that decision until later.

29. Which of the following sentences would function as the best topic sentence of a paragraph or essay?
   a. My brother always seemed to find ways to get hurt.
   b. I am going to write about my brother.
   c. My brother could be a perfect angel.
   d. And my brother's new crew cut isn't my idea of fabulous.

30. In the choices below, the first sentence is a topic sentence. Choose which one is followed by an appropriate supporting sentence.
   a. Wanda loves cars. Wanda likes to travel.
   b. Sam really enjoys some sports. He loves to play tennis every afternoon.
   c. Sharks can be dangerous. Many sea creatures can be dangerous.
   d. The library is a great place to study. The school has a variety of places where students can study.

31. Choose which paragraph presents a series of events or describes a process in a logical order.
   a. (1) There is no harm in putting a special treat in your child's lunchbox. (2) Usually, healthy snacks are defined as foods with low sugar and fat content. (3) Some examples include carrot and celery sticks and granola bars. (4) However, in general it is a much better idea to provide healthy snacks.
   b. (1) The reasons for so many deaths is that cars can generate a great deal of heat. (2) Firefighters know that the dangers of car fires are too often overlooked. (3) In the U.S., one out of five fires involves cars, causing many deaths and injuries to civilians and firefighters.
   c. (1) Indeed, most gardeners can fit irises into their scheme to add beauty without a lot of effort. (2) Irises are colorful flowers that grow in moist soil. (3) They are common all over America and make a wonderful choice for any yard.
   d. (1) My friend Jackson is an excellent example of reliability. (2) He always keeps his word, even when it becomes inconvenient for him. (3) Once, Jackson promised to drive two and a half hours to pick me up when my battery died, and there he was, right on time. (4) This is the secret of being reliable: always do what you say you'll do.

32. Read the following paragraph and choose the sentence that does not belong.

(1) Lighting in a hospital room is important. (2) Each room usually has an overhead light and a bed lamp. (3) Hospital sheets are usually white. (4) The lighting should be adjusted so each patient in the room has sufficient light.

   a. Sentence 1
   b. Sentence 2
   c. Sentence 3
   d. Sentence 4

33. Choose the sentences that contain the correct transitional phrase.
   a. She won the lottery. However, she has much more money than she used to have.
   b. Reggie has two dogs and three cats in his home. In addition, he has several rare birds.
   c. The town had rain for several days. In spite of this, there was flooding in several areas.
   d. Scott is very bright. Furthermore, his grades are very poor.

34. Select the sentence or sentences that contain correct capitalization.
   a. The play was a hit, but Oh, how frightened I was!
   b. Oh dear! i think i've lost my watch.
   c. Oh, Sal! I've won a trip to California!
   d. Please listen carefully while I read the letter to Him.

35. Select the sentence that contains correct capitalization.
   a. Homer was a very famous Poet.
   b. The Princess secretly hoped that King Abboud would step down and she could become Queen.
   c. In the play, she had the role of Athena, a Greek goddess.
   d. We were studying about a famous russian tsar.

36. Select the sentence that contains correct capitalization.
   a. On thursday, it will be the first day of Spring.
   b. Roland and Phyl played with their dog at the park on friday.
   c. We went to the movies on saturday.
   d. The shop is open two Sundays a month.

37. Select the sentence that contains correct capitalization.
   a. My birthday is in the same month as Samantha's: june.
   b. Independence Day is usually called the fourth of july.
   c. One of the poems I had to learn mentions "the merry month of May."
   d. My birthday is in the month of december.

38. Select the sentence that contains correct capitalization.
   a. The hills West of Perth, Australia, are magnificent.
   b. To get to New York by car, you can take Route 95.
   c. To get there, take a left at the big rock South of town.
   d. On our trip to the middle east, we visited many countries.

39. Select the sentence that contains correct capitalization.

    a. When I was young, I thought I would become a Doctor.

    b. Wilson Smith is a Vice President at the company.

    c. My aunt, General Patricia Underwood, has written that she will be unable to attend my party.

    d. I have an Uncle whose first name is Stanley.

40. Choose the sentence that is correctly punctuated.

    a. The teacher asked why Maria had left out the easy exercises?

    b. Yes, but what if a hurricane strikes.

    c. My cousin worked for N.A.T.O.

    d. Hand in the poster essays on Friday.

41. Choose the sentence that is correctly punctuated.

    a. How much money did you transfer?

    b. You are Swedish, are you not.

    c. The waiter asked us if we would like to order an appetizer?

    d. The waiter asked us, if we would like to order an appetizer.

42. Choose the sentence that is correctly punctuated.

    a. I demand that you stop immediately!

    b. What are you doing?, he shouted excitedly.

    c. We have some really(!) low-priced rugs on sale this week.

    d. "Good heavens" he said, "I did not know that."

43. Choose the sentence that is correctly punctuated.

    a. The scientist was well-known for his experiments, but few people knew that he never made much money during his lifetime.

    b. The critics hated the play yet it ran for two years.

    c. Aracella was at the movies, while the rest of us were at the game.

    d. Xavier Smith who likes animals wants to be a veterinarian.

44. Choose the sentence with a correctly punctuated series.

    a. Would you like me to paint your bedroom walls green blue gray or white?

    b. This morning I woke up, got dressed, brushed my teeth, and ate breakfast.

    c. The street was filled with angry protesters, shouting spectators and police.

    d. This Italian restaurant serves the best spaghetti and meatballs, and pizza in town.

45. Choose the sentence that is correctly punctuated.

    a. Stop jumping on the bed boys.

    b. What I said Liv and John was to stop making noise!

    c. I told Dad not to wait up for me tonight.

    d. It was a pleasure to meet you Sir.

46. Choose the sentence that is correctly punctuated.

    a. Well the rain has played its part in the playing of the game.

    b. Yes it is 100% guaranteed.

    c. Well, I know it seems impossible, but our office can process 400 applications a day.

    d. I never even thought about stealing the coat, and no I didn't do it.

47. Select the sentence that punctuates an appositive correctly.
  a. A man of integrity Mr. Smith is the most honest man I know.
  b. Danielle, a star student, will surely go to college.
  c. Robert Dolan CEO will be our featured speaker.
  d. My cousin, who received a scholarship, will go to Harvard.

48. Choose the sentence that is correctly punctuated.
  a. At the end of the road on the west side of the train station an elderly couple sold apples each autumn.
  b. To buy this vehicle you must pay a $5,000.00 deposit
  c. Adam turned left, when he reached the stop sign.
  d. Her head hanging on her chest, the runner admitted defeat.

49. Choose the sentence that is correctly punctuated.
  a. It is the spirit of the dancer not the dance that counts.
  b. He did not however keep his promise.
  c. The fruit fly, for example, can breed up to 10 times in an hour.
  d. The tortoise, as far as we know has been on earth for thousand of years.

50. Choose the sentence that uses commas and/or semicolons correctly.
  a. Danica did as she was told, however, she grumbled constantly.
  b. Anne plans to invite student council members Eva Tyler; Jamal White; and Sam Stark.
  c. The test will be given on Wednesday, June 6; and Thursday, June 7.
  d. The conference has registered people from Salem, Massachusetts; San Francisco, California; and Miami, Florida.

51. Choose the sentence that uses quotation marks and punctuation correctly.
  a. Zelda said that "she was going to Trenton on Saturday."
  b. My favorite song is "Tonight" from *West Side Story*.
  c. Jody said, "We should hurry." "The last feature has started."
  d. He whispered, "Please do not tell the coach.

52. Choose the sentence that uses quotations correctly.
  a. Albert Einstein once said "imagination is more important than knowledge."
  b. Albert Einstein once said, "imagination is more important than knowledge."
  c. Mr. Jones, who was working in his field that morning, said, "the alien spaceship appeared right before my eyes."
  d. When accused, President Richard Nixon maintained that he was "not a crook."

53. Choose the sentence that uses quotations correctly.

    a. "I love the beach," Kevin said, "especially when it's not too windy."

    b. My father always said "Be careful what you wish for."

    c. As I feared, Mr. Lambeth announced "Close your books for today's quiz."

    d. "Have it your way" Alberta added "if that's how you feel."

54. Choose the sentence that uses quotation marks and punctuation correctly.

    a. Have you read the assigned short story, "Foxfire"?

    b. I used to sing a song called "Where Have All the Flowers Gone"?

    c. As I feared, Mr. Smith announced that, "Marcus will be the chaperone of the spring break trip."

    d. "Diane," she said, "put the book down and go outside for a little while".

55. Choose the sentence that correctly uses apostrophes.

    a. Whose playing today, the Red Sox or the Yankees?

    b. Lets go down to the river and fish.

    c. You're the boss of the entire organization.

    d. She was'nt there at 3:00 P.M.

Language Mechanics

For questions 1–3, choose the complete sentence that contains an infinitive phrase.

1. a. For vacations, I go to my house in the mountains.

    b. We intended to leave early.

    c. To break a piece of wood with his bare hands.

    d. To catch flies for their biology experiment.

2. a. "To dream the impossible dream."

    b. To delete the word *very* in your writing.

    c. My friend helped in the building of the model airplane.

    d. To win at bridge takes much concentration.

3. a. They gave the award to Senator Smith.

    b. For example, pens and candy wrappers were in the desk.

    c. They wanted to join the photography club.

    d. Only to watch as the boat slowly sank beneath the waves.

For questions 4–6, each of the sentences may contain an appositive. Choose the sentence that contains an appositive and is correctly punctuated.

4. a. They gave the award to Senator Smith.

    b. For example, pens and candy wrappers were in the desk.

    c. Mexico City, the largest city in the world, has many interesting sights.

    d. Only to watch as the boat slowly sank beneath the waves.

5. a. My cousin, an excellent basketball player is also a musician.
   b. This idea, the appositive can be a tricky part of grammar.
   c. Amanda Sanchez, a professional guide, led the children on a nature hike.
   d. I read a book about Ben Franklin, who is known as a famous inventor and diplomat.

6. a. I once saw John Farrell, the manager of the Boston Red Sox, in a restaurant.
   b. My cousin that lives at home, drives a company car.
   c. I took a bell from the court jester's hat for my cat.
   d. The altitude of the capital of Tibet exceeds 12,000 feet.

For questions 7–9, choose the sentence that does not contain a misplaced or dangling modifier.

7. a. On her way home, my sister found a gold man's watch.
   b. The child ate a cold bowl of oatmeal for breakfast.
   c. The dealer sold the Chevrolet to the buyer with leather seats.
   d. My mother enrolled in medical school when I was nine years old.

8. a. Having so much gardening to do, it was extremely tiring.
   b. After playing tennis all day, she had very sore legs.
   c. Having eaten three desserts, his pants soon did not fit.
   d. They saw a fence behind the house made of barbed wire.

9. a. Having been fixed the day before, Dana was able to use the car.
   b. Walking to the movies, the sudden storm drenched the group.
   c. Looking toward the west, I saw a line of thunderstorms moving rapidly.
   d. Upon reaching the station, the sun came out.

For questions 10–12, select the sentence that correctly uses a prepositional phrase.

10. a. Four armed men held up the bank.
   b. Larry went to lunch today with Tom and I.
   c. When Mikayla called me, she did not tell me where she was at.
   d. Swimming in the ocean at high tide can be a strenuous activity.

11. a. You will gain proficiency practicing the piano daily.
   b. She fell down and hurt her palm.
   c. Who did you send the memo to?
   d. Putting your coat down on the kitchen table is fine if you don't mind the crumbs.

12. a. Yesterday we ordered Indian take-out.
   b. Thinking we had more money, we ran up the bill.
   c. Steve was having volume control problems with the new television.
   d. I thought we would never pull through the mud and get home safely.

For questions 13 and 14, choose the sentence that contains a subordinate clause before the independent clause.

13. **a.** Because I had an accident, I got sent to the supervisor's office.
   b. I did not get the prize even though I had the highest mark.
   c. The music was extremely loud when we studied in the cafeteria.
   d. My neighbors will be evicted if they do not pay their rent.

14. **a.** I will show you the book when Ashley arrives.
   b. The battery that I bought last week is not working.
   c. While waiters served beer, a band of musicians entertained the crowd of tourists.
   d. I know the person who owns that store.

For question 15, choose the sentence that introduces the independent clause before the subordinate clause.

15. **a.** If you need me, I will help you.
   b. The friend who is visiting Jeremy makes terrific lasagna, although it contains too much spinach for my taste.
   c. When you reach the end of the hallway, turn right.
   d. Whenever you dust the furniture, I sneeze.

For question 16, choose the sentence that contains a subordinate clause.

16. **a.** I had to run all the way to school.
   b. Jim read a book; he really enjoyed the characterization.
   c. Because I missed the bus, I was late for work.
   d. The cat is in the bedroom at the end of the hall.

For question 17, choose the sentence that introduces the independent clause before the subordinate clause.

17. **a.** Because the water was clear, the tourists could see the shark.
   b. Jan was wearing the dress with the beautiful material and stripes.
   c. The class enjoyed the book because it was about contemporary sports figures.
   d. My cousins saw a movie last night; they really enjoyed the show.

For question 18, choose the sentence that contains a prepositional phrase.

18. **a.** Last year, we went abroad.
   b. I saw the book jammed behind the couch.
   c. Please sit down and enjoy the music.
   d. I said, "Put down the toy."

For question 19, choose the sentence that does not contain a dangling or misplaced modifier.

19. **a.** We ate the lunch that we had brought slowly.
   b. At eight years old, my father gave me a bicycle.
   c. The torn student's book lay on the desk.
   d. After reading the outstanding novel, the students thought the upcoming movie based on it would be exciting.

For question 20, each sentence contains an appositive. Choose the sentence that is correctly punctuated.

20. **a.** Patricia an excellent student is also a chemist.
   b. John was surprised when he saw his former roommate Fred, at the dance.
   c. This ring, an heirloom was given to me by a friend.
   d. One of my dogs, Dolly, is about to have puppies.

Vocabulary

For questions 1–8, choose the word or phrase that means the same, or almost the same, as the underlined word.

1. repudiated belief
   a. rejected as untrue
   b. controversial
   c. unknown
   d. enjoyed for its popularity

2. acerbic conversation
   a. random
   b. complimentary
   c. harsh
   d. ethical

3. defunct charge account
   a. inactive
   b. competitive
   c. small
   d. undesirable

4. genteel manners
   a. uncouth
   b. engrained
   c. passive
   d. refined

5. taut guitar string
   a. loose
   b. expensive
   c. tight
   d. cheap

6. laudable trait
   a. questionable
   b. evasive
   c. praiseworthy
   d. uncouth

7. obscure point
   a. unclear
   b. blatant
   c. parallel
   d. corrosive

8. looking barbaric
   a. tasteful
   b. uncivilized
   c. confused
   d. agreeable

For questions 9–12, read the sentences, and then choose the word that best completes BOTH sentences.

9. The theater department will _____ the performance.

   The little girl decided to _____ a "lost dog" poster on the telephone pole.

   a. advertise
   b. present
   c. tape
   d. staple

10. The Victorian man and woman in the story were encouraged to _____ each other by their families.

    A _____ hearing has been scheduled for the case against the accused criminals.

    a. public
    b. focus
    c. romance
    d. court

11. The person at the center of the investigation is known to have a _____ past.

Our grandmother collects quilts that have a _____ pattern.

    a. geometrical
    b. popular
    c. checkered
    d. troubled

12. The television _____ takes up one floor of a high-rise office building.

Can you _____ the television on top of the chest of drawers?

    a. control
    b. station
    c. antenna
    d. anchor

For questions 13–16, read the following paragraph, which has four missing words. Then fill in each empty spot by choosing the word that makes the most sense in terms of grammar and meaning.

The Department of Corrections is under the control of the state government. **(13)** individuals are housed in prisons located in rural areas throughout the state. Individuals sentenced to prison for **(14)** crimes are sent to a much more secure facility in the southern part of the state. Individuals sentenced for lesser types of crimes are housed in less secure **(15)** in other locations. Information on **(16)** individuals within the state is available on the Department of Corrections' website.

13. **a.** Convicted
    b. Emancipated
    c. Curtailed
    d. Independent

14. **a.** heinous
    b. harassed
    c. trivial
    d. irrelevant

15. **a.** faculties
    b. bunks
    c. facilities
    d. hotels

16. **a.** implemented
    b. inundated
    c. irritable
    d. incarcerated

For questions 17–20, read the following paragraph, which has four missing words. Then fill in each empty spot by choosing the word that makes the most sense in terms of grammar and meaning.

W.C. Handy, known as "Father of the Blues," was born in Florence, Alabama, in 1873. The **(17)** of music performed by Handy is celebrated each year at a summer street festival in Florence. Mr. Handy **(18)** many famous songs. One well-known song **(19)** to Handy is "Memphis Blues." This song **(20)** Handy's time in Memphis, Tennessee.

17. **a.** symbol
    b. issue
    c. catechism
    d. genre

18. **a.** composed
    b. attributed
    c. retorted
    d. discovered

19. **a.** deducted
    b. credited
    c. charged
    d. arranged

20. a. rescinded
   b. recalls
   c. appoints
   d. created

Spelling

For questions 1–10, choose the word that is spelled correctly and best completes the sentence.

1. It is _____ that the uniforms did not arrive in time for the first game.
   a. ridiculous
   b. redikulous
   c. redicculous
   d. redickulous

2. We _____ will be attending the reunion at the end of the month.
   a. defunatley
   b. definately
   c. defanitely
   d. definitely

3. She is _____ stronger than the other players.
   a. inheruntly
   b. inherentley
   c. inherently
   d. inherantly

4. Wasn't that a brilliant _____ mentioned in our meeting earlier today?
   a. suggestun
   b. sugesstion
   c. sugestion
   d. suggestion

5. The chef will need to _____ the egg yolks from the egg whites carefully to make the meringue.
   a. seperate
   b. separate
   c. sepurate
   d. sepirate

6. Do you ever consider the _____ of UFOs in our world?
   a. existence
   b. exestence
   c. exastence
   d. exustence

7. The management team will _____ the needs of the client.
   a. accomodate
   b. acommodate
   c. accommodate
   d. accomidate

8. Tim and Tina should be able to _____ the lawnmower onto the truck bed.
   a. load
   b. lowed
   c. lode
   d. loaud

9. Many people at the convention found the candidate's speech _____.
   a. distastefull
   b. distasting
   c. untasted
   d. distasteful

10. The _____ set of cookware will be going on sale next weekend.
   a. eligant
   b. elegent
   c. elegint
   d. elegant

For questions 11–20, read the phrases or sentences. Find the underlined word that is NOT spelled correctly in the context of the sentence.

11. **a.** dull <u>scissors</u>
  b. narrow <u>point</u>
  c. sharp <u>nife</u>
  d. small <u>crawlspace</u>

12. **a.** <u>residence</u> of an apartment complex
  b. <u>tenants</u> of an apartment complex
  c. <u>owners</u> of an apartment complex
  d. <u>inhabitants</u> of an apartment complex

13. **a.** <u>purposefully</u> recited speech
  b. <u>vicariously</u> imagined vacation
  c. <u>hurredly</u> spoken argument
  d. <u>respectfully</u> spoken marriage vows

14. **a.** <u>committed</u> relationship
  b. <u>benefitting</u> factor
  c. <u>financially</u> secure
  d. <u>meaningful</u> sermon

15. **a.** Ted will <u>comb</u> the horse's hair.
  b. Jamie still <u>mourns</u> the death of her bird.
  c. We will <u>suround</u> the house with a few new bushes.
  d. New <u>possibilities</u> arrive daily.

16. **a.** <u>participents</u> attend
  b. Suzette <u>interprets</u>
  c. Chung So <u>contracts</u>
  d. infants <u>sleep</u>

17. **a.** <u>foul</u> ball
  b. <u>least</u> vehicle
  c. <u>minor</u> league
  d. <u>physical</u> plant

18. **a.** <u>outrageous</u> smell
  b. <u>perpetual</u> motion
  c. <u>sheer</u> fabric
  d. <u>caushus</u> behavior

19. **a.** <u>noninterested</u> party
  b. <u>biweekly</u> deposit
  c. <u>interstate</u> transfer
  d. <u>semiprecious</u> stone

20. **a.** <u>regrettable</u> mistake
  b. <u>imbarrassed</u> child
  c. <u>effectual</u> solution
  d. <u>intellectually</u> stimulating

Mathematics Computation

1. Evaluate $(-3)(7)(-4)$.
  a. 84
  b. −84
  c. 63
  d. −49

2. Evaluate $135 - 201$.
  a. 66
  b. −66
  c. −76
  d. 76

3. Evaluate $(-48) + (-110) + 27$.
  a. −185
  b. 185
  c. 131
  d. −131

4. Evaluate $69{,}496 \div (-1{,}022)$.
  a. 68,474
  b. 68
  c. −68
  d. −608

5. At 9 A.M., the outside temperature was 68°F. At 2 P.M. that same day, the temperature had increased by 25°F. What was the temperature at 2 P.M.?
   a. 83°F
   b. 92°F
   c. 93°F
   d. 94°F

6. Linda has one year to pay off a $900 loan. What is her monthly payment if she wants to take the full year to pay it off?
   a. $55
   b. $65
   c. $75
   d. $90

7. There are 5,280 feet in one mile. How many feet are in 13 miles?
   a. 68,380 feet
   b. 68,640 feet
   c. 21,120 feet
   d. 15,840 feet

8. Evaluate $-37 - (-9)$.
   a. -46
   b. -42
   c. -28
   d. 28

9. You are making chocolate chip cookies. The original recipe calls for 1 cup of sugar and $1\frac{3}{4}$ cups of flour. If you are tripling the recipe, how much flour do you need?
   a. $3\frac{3}{4}$ cups
   b. 3 cups
   c. $3\frac{1}{2}$ cups
   d. $5\frac{1}{4}$ cups

10. Evaluate $\frac{2}{3} + \frac{1}{4}$.
   a. $\frac{1}{6}$
   b. $\frac{3}{12}$
   c. $\frac{3}{7}$
   d. $\frac{11}{12}$

11. Evaluate $\frac{4}{7} \div \frac{7}{8}$.
   a. $\frac{32}{49}$
   b. $\frac{28}{56}$
   c. $\frac{11}{15}$
   d. $\frac{4}{8}$

12. Ava purchased $\frac{3}{4}$ yard of fabric. She used $\frac{1}{3}$ yard for her project. How much of the fabric is left?
   a. $\frac{5}{12}$ yard
   b. $\frac{1}{4}$ yard
   c. $\frac{4}{7}$ yard
   d. 2 yards

13. Christian purchased three parcels of land measuring $1\frac{3}{4}$ acres, $\frac{5}{8}$ acre, and $2\frac{1}{2}$ acres. How many total acres did Christian purchase?
   a. $2\frac{9}{14}$ acres
   b. $3\frac{5}{8}$ acres
   c. $4\frac{7}{8}$ acres
   d. $5\frac{1}{8}$ acres

14. Evaluate $2\frac{2}{9} \times 7\frac{1}{5}$.
   a. $14\frac{3}{14}$
   b. $14\frac{2}{45}$
   c. 15
   d. 16

15. Evaluate $1\frac{3}{5} \div 2\frac{2}{3}$.
   a. $\frac{64}{15}$
   b. $\frac{3}{5}$
   c. $\frac{11}{13}$
   d. $\frac{5}{3}$

16. Evaluate $3\frac{2}{3} - 1\frac{4}{5}$.

    a. $1\frac{2}{15}$

    b. -1

    c. $2\frac{13}{15}$

    d. $1\frac{13}{15}$

17. You are earning a wage of $9.02 per hour. If you work an 8-hour shift on Monday and 8 hours on Tuesday, what is your total gross pay for those two days?

    a. $170.02

    b. $25.02

    c. $72.16

    d. $144.32

18. Alexandre purchased three textbooks for college. They cost $43.95, $120, and $74.99. Find the total cost of the books before tax.

    a. $237.84

    b. $238.94

    c. $138.94

    d. $106.94

19. Gary has $1,895.51 in his checking account. He then wrote a check for $68.74. How much money does Gary currently have in his account?

    a. $1,726.77

    b. $1,826.77

    c. $1,836.73

    d. $1,806.73

20. Evaluate $197.4 + 0.72 + 17.43 + 0.286$.

    a. 215.836

    b. 407.5

    c. 2,158.36

    d. 4,075

21. Evaluate $2.068 - (-38.7)$.

    a. 16.81

    b. -36.632

    c. 428.06

    d. 40.768

22. Adam has a summer job for 11 weeks. At the end of the summer, he will have earned $1,381.93. How much does he earn each week?

    a. $123.82

    b. $125.63

    c. $126.18

    d. $138.19

23. Evaluate 0.00076×0.009.

    a. 0.000684

    b. 0.000608

    c. 0.0000608

    d. 0.00000684

24. Reduce to lowest terms: $\dfrac{6(2) - 12 \div 6}{2^3 + \sqrt{49}}$.

    a. 0

    b. $\frac{10}{11}$

    c. $\frac{2}{3}$

    d. $\frac{2}{5}$

25. Evaluate $7 + 3(5^2 + \sqrt{16}) - 49$.

    a. 0

    b. 45

    c. 57

    d. 241

26. Evaluate $4 + 7(3 - 9) + 6(3^2)$.

    a. -12

    b. -2

    c. 16

    d. 100

27. 80% of 125 is what number?
   a. 100
   b. 45
   c. 1,000
   d. 625

28. 72 is what percent of 160?
   a. 25%
   b. 45%
   c. 55%
   d. 75%

29. 4.7 is 1% of what number?
   a. 4.7
   b. 47
   c. 470
   d. 4,700

30. Solve for x: $4x - 4 = 20$.
   a. 4
   b. 20
   c. 64
   d. 6

31. Solve for x: $3x - 12 = 24 - 9x$.
   a. -2
   b. 12
   c. 3
   d. 24

32. Simplify $4x^2 + 3x^2 + 2x$.
   a. $9x^5$
   b. $12x^4 + 2x$
   c. $7x^2 + 2x$
   d. $4x^2 + 5x$

33. Evaluate $\sqrt{36} + \sqrt{64}$.
   a. 10
   b. 14
   c. 24
   d. 50

34. Evaluate $4^3 + 3^4$.
   a. 24
   b. 38
   c. 76
   d. 145

35. Evaluate $-(4^2) + 2^3 + (-1)^4$.
   a. -8
   b. -7
   c. 23
   d. 25

36. Evaluate $\sqrt[3]{125} + \sqrt[5]{32}$.
   a. 35
   b. 17
   c. 7
   d. 3

37. Simplify $3xy + 2x^2y + 5xy + 7x^2y$.
   a. $17x^6y^4$
   b. $5xy + 12x^2y$
   c. $8xy + 9x^2y$
   d. $8x^2y^2 + 9x^4y^2$

38. Solve for w: $6w + 2 = 5w - 4 + 9$.
   a. 1
   b. 3
   c. 7
   d. 11

39. Evaluate $(4x^3y^5)^2$.
   a. $16x^6y^{10}$
   b. $8x^5y^7$
   c. $4x^6y^{10}$
   d. $4x^5y^7$

40. Simplify $-4(5y - 1) + 7y$.
   a. $-2y - 1$
   b. $12y + 4$
   c. $-13y + 4$
   d. $27y + 1$

Applied Mathematics

1. Use front-end rounding to estimate the product of 987 × 215.

    a. 180,000

    b. 200,000

    c. 270,000

    d. 300,000

2. Use front-end rounding to estimate the difference of 311 − 658.

    a. −200

    b. −300

    c. −400

    d. −500

3. Round 13,715 to the nearest thousand.

    a. 10,000

    b. 13,000

    c. 13,700

    d. 14,000

4. Round 427.5192 to the nearest hundredth.

    a. 427.5

    b. 427.52

    c. 427.519

    d. 400.5192

5. Convert 54,970 to scientific notation.

    a. 5.497×10^5

    b. 5.497×10^4

    c. 54.97×10^3

    d. 0.5497×10^5

6. If three gallons of paint cover 950 square feet, how many gallons of paint will Jennifer need to paint 3,800 square feet of wall surface?

    a. 4 gallons

    b. 9 gallons

    c. 11 gallons

    d. 12 gallons

7. Which of the choices is NOT equivalent to $\frac{2}{3}$?

    a. 4:6

    b. $0.6\overline{6}$

    c. $66\frac{2}{3}\%$

    d. $\frac{6}{7}$

8. Convert $\frac{4}{25}$ to a percent.

    a. 0.16%

    b. 1.6%

    c. 16%

    d. 160%

9. Find 33% of 1,592.

    a. 52.536

    b. 525.36

    c. 54.128

    d. 541.28

10. Which number is divisible by three?

    a. 152,113

    b. 154,320

    c. 217,900

    d. 321,806

11. Find the least common multiple of 14, 28, and 42.

    a. 2

    b. 14

    c. 84

    d. 168

12. Find the greatest common factor of 132, 140, and 252.

    a. 2

    b. 4

    c. 12

    d. 28

13. Evaluate $4^3 + 7^2 + 3^0$.
   a. 113
   b. 114
   c. 116
   d. 118

14. Find the next number in the following pattern:

   7, 15, 23, 31, 39, . . .

   a. 41
   b. 43
   c. 45
   d. 47

15. Find the next entry in the following pictorial pattern:

   ○, ■, ★ ★, ○○○, ■■■■■, . . .

   a. ★★★
   b. ★★★★
   c. ★★★★★
   d. ★★★★★★★

16. Simplify the following expression:
   $2(2x + 5) - 3(x - 1)$.
   a. $x + 7$
   b. $x + 13$
   c. $7x + 13$
   d. $13x$

17. Solve the following inequality: $-3x + 4 \geq 31$.
   a. $x \geq -9$
   b. $x \geq 9$
   c. $x \leq -9$
   d. $x \leq 9$

18. Evaluate $y = 3x - 7$ for $x = 4$.
   a. 0
   b. 5
   c. 12
   d. 19

19. Given $y = \frac{1}{2}x - 7$, find x when $y = 4$.
   a. -5
   b. 5
   c. 22
   d. 24

20. Sofia has a rectangular garden that measures 6 feet by 8 feet. She wishes to put a fence around her garden. How much fencing will she need?
   a. 14 ft.
   b. 20 ft.
   c. 28 ft.
   d. 48 ft.

21. One wall of a room is to be painted purple; however, the door on that wall is not to be painted. The wall measures 9 feet by 12 feet. The door measures 48 inches by 7 feet. How many square feet are to be painted?
   a. 80 sq. ft.
   b. 108 sq. ft.
   c. 129 sq. ft.
   d. 136 sq. ft.

22. Find the area of a circle with the diameter of 10 in. Use 3.14 for π.
   a. 15.7 sq. in.
   b. 31.4 sq. in.
   c. 78.5 sq. in.
   d. 84.7 sq. in.

23. Find the circumference of a circle with a radius of seven inches. Use 3.14 for π.
   a. 22.19 in.
   b. 43.96 in.
   c. 117.84 in.
   d. 153.86 in.

24. George drove 75 miles per hour on the highway for three hours without stopping. How many miles did he travel?
- **a.** 165 miles
- **b.** 195 miles
- **c.** 225 miles
- **d.** 255 miles

25. Sarah went on a two-hour hike. She covered 6.5 miles of terrain. On average, how fast was Sarah walking?
- **a.** 3.25 mph
- **b.** 4 mph
- **c.** 9 mph
- **d.** 13 mph

26. Find the volume of a box that measures 13 inches long, 8 inches wide, and 3 inches deep.
- **a.** 126 cu. in.
- **b.** 143 cu. in.
- **c.** 288 cu. in.
- **d.** 312 cu. in.

27. For which equation is the point $(14, -2)$ a solution?
- **a.** $y = (-\frac{1}{2})x - 5$
- **b.** $y = \frac{1}{2}x + 5$
- **c.** $y = (-\frac{1}{2})x + 5$
- **d.** $y = \frac{1}{2}x - 5$

28. Marisa's age is 13 years more than Liliana's age. The sum of their ages is 145. Create an equation that models this situation.
- **a.** $x + 13 = 145$
- **b.** $2x - 13 = 145$
- **c.** $(x + 13) + x = 145$
- **d.** $13x + x = 145$

29. Alexandre has $427 in his savings account. This amount is eight dollars less than three times the amount Zach has in his savings account. Find an equation that models this situation.
- **a.** $3x - 8 = 427$
- **b.** $3(x - 8) = 427$
- **c.** $8 - 3x = 427$
- **d.** $8x - 3 = 427$

30. Twice the sum of a number and ten is 42. Find the number.
- **a.** 9
- **b.** 11
- **c.** 16
- **d.** 30

31. The product of five and a number is decreased by 12. The result is twice the number. Find the number.
- **a.** 20
- **b.** 17
- **c.** 9
- **d.** 4

32. Olivia earned $250 a week plus 5% commission on all sales over $1,500. How much did she earn the week she sold $3,500 worth of merchandise?
- **a.** $350
- **b.** $425
- **c.** $1,250
- **d.** $1,750

33. A local clothing store is having a sale on jeans. A pair of boot cut jeans that regularly sells for $75 is now on sale for 30% off. What is the new price of the jeans before tax?
- **a.** $52.50
- **b.** $49.50
- **c.** $45.00
- **d.** $22.50

34. Pamela and Carla sold $672 of baked goods at a local farmer's market. Eight percent of their earnings went to cover their expenses. The rest was profit to be split equally between them. How much cash did each woman receive?

a. $268.80
b. $309.12
c. $336.00
d. $342.72

35. At a high school soccer tryout, $\frac{3}{4}$ of the students trying out earned a spot on a team. If 36 players were chosen for the team, how many students tried out?

a. 40
b. 48
c. 72
d. 81

36. Pete's Exotic Fish Emporium sells 75 varieties of exotic fish. Of those varieties, $\frac{1}{3}$ are saltwater fish. Of those saltwater fish, $\frac{2}{5}$ are classified as aggressive. How many of the varieties of fish are aggressive saltwater fish?

a. 10
b. 15
c. 25
d. 30

37. At a local Italian restaurant, customers have the choice of ordering off the menu or visiting the buffet. Menu orders account for $\frac{3}{10}$ of all dinner sales. If 120 customers are currently in the restaurant, how many visited the buffet?

a. 36
b. 75
c. 84
d. 100

38. A survey of student's favorite summer activities was conducted at school. The researcher collecting the data wishes to display the results as categories, without displaying individual results or percentages. Which data display should the researcher choose?

a. line graph
b. bar graph
c. box plot
d. stem-and-leaf plot

39. Estimate the temperature for the coldest day in June.

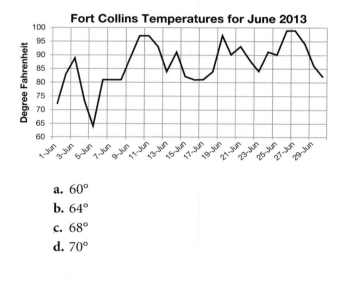

a. 60°
b. 64°
c. 68°
d. 70°

40. A group of people were asked to choose their favorite ice cream flavor from vanilla, chocolate, strawberry, and chocolate chip mint. Using the circle graph below, which flavor received the most votes?

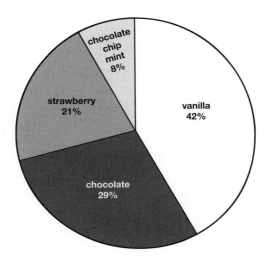

a. Chocolate
b. Chocolate chip mint
c. Strawberry
d. Vanilla

41. Lydia made an inventory of her shoes. The results are displayed in the chart below. How many boots does Lydia have?

Athletic	II
Boots	IIII
Casual shoes	IIII III
Heels	IIII
Sandals	IIII II

a. 4
b. 5
c. 7
d. 8

42. Find the mean wages in Tacoma for all four medical office professionals.

Medical Office Professionals	WA 2006	Tacoma 2006	WA # workers 2004	WA # workers 2014
Medical Assistants	$15	$13	9,690	11,650
Medical Records Technicians	$14	$15	5,140	6,130
Medical Secretaries	$15	$15	13,740	16,590
Medical Transcriptionists	$16	$16	2,570	3,180

a. $14.75
b. $15.00
c. $3.00
d. $14.00

43. A bag of marbles contains three red marbles, five green marbles, and seven blue marbles. What is the probability of pulling out a red marble?

a. $\frac{1}{5}$

b. $\frac{3}{14}$

c. $\frac{3}{5}$

d. $\frac{4}{5}$

44. A fair coin is tossed three times. The possible outcomes are heads or tails. What is the probability that two tosses will come up heads?

a. $\frac{1}{4}$

b. $\frac{3}{8}$

c. $\frac{1}{2}$

d. $\frac{5}{8}$

45. Find the mean of the following data set: 69, 75, 80, 75, 91.

a. 75

b. 78

c. 80

d. 83

46. Find the median of the following data set: 33, 58, 27, 46, 15, 21.

a. 30

b. 33

c. 36.5

d. 43

47. Which of the following is best described as part of a line that begins at an endpoint and extends endlessly in one direction?

a. angle

b. ray

c. segment

d. plane

48. Find the slope of the line that passes through the points $(-4,3)$ and $(2,7)$.

a. $-\frac{3}{2}$

b. $\frac{3}{2}$

c. $-\frac{2}{3}$

d. $\frac{2}{3}$

49. What part of the circle centered at P is defined by the center line on the image below?

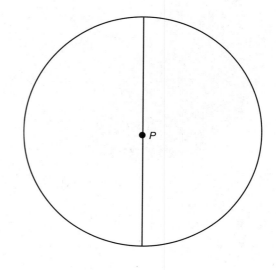

a. arc

b. radius

c. circumference

d. diameter

50. If the rectangle *PQRS* is dilated by a factor of two, what is its new location?

a.

b.

c.

d.

Answers and Explanations, Test 1

Reading

1. b. Choice **a** is incorrect. It directly contradicts the main idea of the passage. Choice **b** is the correct answer. This states the main idea of the passage. Choice **c** is incorrect. Although this conclusion may possibly be drawn by some, it is not the main idea of the passage. Choice **d** is incorrect. There is no basis for such a conclusion.
Section: Construct Meaning
Subsection: Main Idea

2. c. Choice **a** is incorrect. In this context, *process* means to *digest*. Choice **b** is incorrect. In this context, *process* means to *digest*. Choice **c** is the correct answer. In this context, *process* refers to *the body's ability to digest* food. Choice **d** is incorrect. In this context, *process* means to *digest*.
Section: Words in Context
Subsection: Appropriate Word

3. a. Choice **a** is the correct answer. These three items were listed as vegetables used in Thai restaurants. Choice **b** is incorrect. Pineapple is not a vegetable and was listed as a fruit. Choice **c** is incorrect. Cauliflower was not listed in the passage. Choice **d** is incorrect. Onions were not listed in the passage.
Section: Recall Information
Subsection: Sequence

4. d. Choice **a** is incorrect. In the passage, the writer makes a connection between cost and cuisine. Choice **b** is incorrect. French food comes from France, the European country. Thai food comes from Thailand, the Southeast Asian country. Choice **c** is incorrect. The writer mentions specific ingredients associated with both types of food (for example, dairy products in French food, and certain fruits and vegetables in Thai food). Choice **d** is the correct answer. It includes choices **a**, **b**, and **c**, all of which are true.
Section: Evaluate/Extend Meaning
Subsection: Generalizations

5. c. Choice **a** is incorrect. The passage states that the mantle is a viscous layer, and the definition of *viscous* is not *liquid*. Choice **b** is incorrect. The passage states that the mantle is a viscous layer, and the definition of *viscous* is not *rigid*. Choice **c** is the correct answer. The passage states that the mantle is a viscous layer, and *viscous* means that it has a thick, sticky consistency between solid and liquid. Choice **d** is incorrect. The passage states that the mantle is below the crust, not deep inside the Earth.
Section: Words in Context
Subsection: Appropriate Word

6. a. Choice **a** is the correct answer. This is exactly what is stated in the passage. Choice **b** is incorrect. The plates exist below the Earth's crust. Choice **c** is incorrect. This is not stated in the passage, and it actually contradicts what is stated in the passage. Choice **d** is incorrect. This is not stated in the passage, and it actually contradicts what is stated in the passage.
Section: Words in Context
Subsection: Same Meaning

7. d. Choice **a** is incorrect. Although this is true, it is not the complete answer. Choice **b** is incorrect. Although this is true, it is not the complete answer. Choice **c** is incorrect. It directly contradicts what is stated in the passage. Choice **d** is the correct answer. It says that **a** and **b** are true but that **c** is not, and that is so.
Section: Recall Information
Subsection: Sequence

8. d. Choice **a** is incorrect. This is invented material that was not stated in the passage. Choice **b** is incorrect. This is invented material that was not stated in the passage. Choice **c** is incorrect. This is invented material that was not stated in the passage. Choice **d** is the correct answer. This is stated in the passage.
Section: Recall Information
Subsection: Stated Concepts

9. d. Choice **a** is incorrect. *Vehemently* is not defined as *maliciously*. Choice **b** is incorrect. *Vehemently* is not defined as *secretly*. Choice **c** is incorrect. *Vehemently* is not defined as *erroneously*. Choice **d** is the correct answer. *Vehemently* is defined as *showing strong feeling, forceful, passionate,* or *intense*.
Section: Words in Context
Subsection: Same Meaning

10. b. Choice **a** is incorrect. *Inevitable* means *unavoidable*, not *avoidable*. Choice **b** is the correct answer. *Inevitable* means *certain to happen, unavoidable*. Choice **c** is incorrect. *Inevitable* does not mean *unknown*. Choice **d** is incorrect. *Inevitable* does not mean *powerful*.
Section: Words in Context
Subsection: Same Meaning

11. b. Choice **a** is incorrect. This is the hotel phone number for the stay of April 26. Choice **b** is the correct answer. The phone number is listed to the right of the date. Choice **c** is incorrect. This phone number is not listed anywhere on the chart. Choice **d** is incorrect. This phone number is not listed anywhere on the chart.
Section: Recall Information
Subsection: Sequence

12. a. Choice **a** is the correct answer. The total number of hours is listed at the bottom of the form. Choice **b** is incorrect. This is the number of hours away from base. Choice **c** is incorrect. This number is associated with April 26 only. Choice **d** is incorrect. This number is associated with April 27 only.
Section: Recall Information
Subsection: Sequence

13. c. Choice **a** is incorrect. This is his first flight on Thursday. Choice **b** is incorrect. This is his second flight on Friday. Choice **c** is the correct answer. He will be traveling from PVD to IAD. Choice **d** is incorrect. This is his first flight on Friday.
Section: Interpret Graphic Information
Subsection: Reference Sources

14. a. Choice **a** is the correct answer. It can be assumed that the "EMP ID" number after Daniel's name would be his employee number with Bigelow Airlines. Choice **b** is incorrect. It cannot be assumed that the number after his name would be a flight number with Bigelow Airlines. Choice **c** is incorrect. It cannot be assumed that the number after his name would be a license number. Choice **d** is incorrect. It cannot be assumed that the number after his name would be a telephone number.
Section: Interpret Graphic Information
Subsection: Reference Sources

15. d. Choice **a** is incorrect. This could be a reason a pilot needs to know his T.A.F.B. Choice **b** is incorrect. This could be a reason a pilot needs to know his T.A.F.B. Choice **c** is incorrect. This could be a reason a pilot needs to know his T.A.F.B. Choice **d** is the correct answer. A pilot would probably not schedule a surgical procedure while he was on a flight layover.
Section: Interpret Graphic Information
Subsection: Reference Sources

16. b. Choice **a** is incorrect. The tone of the poem is not gleaming. Choice **b** is the correct answer. The tone of the poem is pessimistic, as the writer shares his recommendation that one should never share one's feelings of love with the beloved. Choice **c** is incorrect. The tone of the poem is not joyful. Choice **d** is incorrect. The tone of the poem is not elementary.
Section: Evaluate/Extend Meaning
Subsection: Effect/Intention

17. b. Choice **a** is incorrect. Blake says he did love the woman mentioned in the poem. Choice **b** is the correct answer. Blake believes that it's better to keep secret one's feelings of love for someone else. Choice **c** is incorrect. Blake is not saying love is a burden. Choice **d** is incorrect. Blake is not saying love is overrated.
Section: Evaluate/Extend Meaning
Subsection: Fact/Opinion

18. a. Choice **a** is the correct answer. Blake seems to believe that you risk rejection if you open up. Choice **b** is incorrect. The writer does not say the individual's love for the other can live on if it is refused. Choice **c** is incorrect. The writer does not say the individual's love for the other can live on if it is denied as real. Choice **d** is incorrect. The writer does not say the individual's love for the other can live on if it occurs in adolescence.
Section: Construct Meaning
Subsection: Main Idea

19. a. Choice **a** is the correct answer. The writer talks about a lost love and realizes that he made a mistake. Of the four choices, the word *melancholy* is most logical and best describes the mood of the poem. Choice **b** is incorrect. The mood of the poem is not reverent. Choice **c** is incorrect. The mood of the poem is not particularly intense. Choice **d** is incorrect. The mood of the poem is not scornful.
Section: Evaluate/Extend Meaning
Subsection: Effect/Intention

20. a. Choice **a** is the correct answer. While it may or may not be a good idea, this is the opinion of the writer. Choice **b** is incorrect. This is more of an opinion than a fact. Choice **c** is incorrect. This is more of an opinion than a fact. Choice **d** is incorrect. The idea is central to the poem.
Section: Evaluate/Extend Meaning
Subsection: Fact/Opinion

21. b. Choice **a** is incorrect. The writer's purpose was not to rid the bank of possible thieves. Choice **b** is the correct answer. The writer's purpose was to showcase proper interviewing skills. Choice **c** is incorrect. While Bourne alludes to the bank's managerial trainee program throughout the interview, it is Miller's skills, not the program, that are the central focus of the passage. Choice **d** is incorrect. The writer was not trying to meet a deadline.
Section: Evaluate/Extend Meaning
Subsection: Author Purpose

22. b. Choice **a** is incorrect. Miller did not appear to be scared. Choice **b** is the correct answer. Miller addressed each question with a positive, intelligent response. Choice **c** is incorrect. Miller did not seem unsure. Choice **d** is incorrect. Miller did not sound obnoxious.
Section: Construct Meaning
Subsection: Character Aspects

23. a. Choice **a** is the correct answer. Bourne makes reference to Miller's resume and seems to be consulting it during the interview. Also, more generally, sending a resume is a standard first step when applying for a job. Choice **b** is incorrect. This is not a logical answer. Choice **c** is incorrect. Miller's father is not mentioned in the interview. Furthermore, it is not typical for parents to call companies to help their children get a job. Choice **d** is incorrect. While a recommendation from a teacher may have been included in Miller's application, there is no mention of a teacher's recommendation in the passage.
Section: Construct Meaning
Subsection: Supporting Evidence

24. d. Choice **a** is incorrect. The reader can conclude that Bourne currently works at Community Savings and Loan. Choice **b** is incorrect. The reader can conclude that Bourne currently works at a bank (Community Savings and Loan), but not that Miller has. Choice **c** is incorrect. The reader can conclude that Bourne currently works at a bank. Choice **d** is the correct answer. It seems as though Miller has never worked at a bank.
Section: Construct Meaning
Subsection: Compare/Contrast

25. c. Choice **a** is incorrect. There is nothing in the transcript to suggest that Miller seemed nervous. His answers were worded in a clear, confident way. Choice **b** is incorrect. Although Miller talked about his accomplishments and best qualities in the interview, he seemed to take a thoughtful approach to Bourne's questions, not a cocky one. Furthermore, Bourne seemed pleased by his responses. Choice **c** is the correct answer. Miller was asked questions that some people would interpret as a way to play on one's weaknesses. He took these questions and turned them into answers that showed how he could make something positive out of something potentially negative. Choice **d** is incorrect. The reader cannot assume Miller was well-dressed for the interview.
Section: Evaluate/Extend Meaning
Subsection: Predict Outcomes

26. d. Choice **a** is incorrect. The style of the essay would not be best described as literary. Choice **b** is incorrect. The style of the essay would not be best described as technical. Choice **c** is incorrect. The style of the essay would not be best described as operational. Choice **d** is the correct answer. The writer tells the story in a conversational tone, using Beverly's personal recollections throughout.
Section: Evaluate/Extend Meaning
Subsection: Style Techniques

27. c. Choice **a** is incorrect. The word *spells* is not a good substitution. Choice **b** is incorrect. The word *beliefs* is not a good substitution. Choice **c** is the correct answer. The *rituals* that Beverly performed were part of the *routines* that she did every day in her job. Choice **d** is incorrect. The word *cleaning* is not a good substitution.
Section: Words in Context
Subsection: Appropriate Word

28. c. Choice **a** is incorrect. The essay should not begin with paragraph 2 nor end with paragraph 3. Choice **b** is incorrect. The essay should not begin with paragraph 3 nor end with paragraph 2. Choice **c** is the correct answer. Paragraph 4 would serve as a good conclusion to the story. Choice **d** is incorrect. The essay should not begin with paragraph 4.
Section: Construct Meaning
Subsection: Conclusion

29. a. Choice **a** is the correct answer. Statements such as *a second one was spotted* and *it traveled straight through the middle of town and spanned a good mile in width* imply that tornadoes are the weather events that struck the town. Choice **b** is incorrect. Evidence in the essay does not suggest hurricanes. Choice **c** is incorrect. Evidence in the essay does not suggest snow storms. Choice **d** is incorrect. Evidence in the essay does not suggest flash flooding.
Section: Construct Meaning
Subsection: Supporting Evidence

30. b. Choice **a** is incorrect. The passage references two weather events. Choice **b** is the correct answer. The passage references two tornadoes that passed in or near the town. Choice **c** is incorrect. The passage references two weather events. Choice **d** is incorrect. The passage references two weather events.
Section: Construct Meaning
Subsection: Summary/Paraphrase

31. a. Choice **a** is the correct answer. One of the definitions of *accommodations* is *lodging*, such as at a hotel, and that fits with the context of the ad. Choice **b** is incorrect. *Accommodations* refers to where a person stays, not transportation options. Choice **c** is incorrect. *Accommodations* refers to where a person stays, not transportation options. Choice **d** is incorrect. *Accommodations* refers to where a person stays, not transportation options.
Section: Words in Context
Subsection: Same Meaning

32. c. Choice **a** is incorrect. Option 2 does not mention bus travel. Choice **b** is incorrect. Option 2 does not mention car travel. Choice **c** is the correct answer. Rail transportation and train transportation are the same thing. Choice **d** is incorrect. Option 2 does not mention airplane travel.
Section: Evaluate/Extend Meaning
Subsection: Generalizations

33. d. Choice **a** is incorrect. The base price for tour option 3 is $699. According to the chart, optional travel insurance costs $49. The two numbers added together do not equal $499. Choice **b** is incorrect. The base price for tour option 3 is $699. According to the chart, optional travel insurance costs $49. The two numbers added together do not equal $548. Choice **c** is incorrect. The base price for tour option 3 alone is $699. Choice **d** is the correct answer. The base price for tour option 3 alone is $699. According to the chart, optional travel insurance costs $49. The two numbers added together equal $748.
Section: Interpret Graphic Information
Subsection: Reference Sources

34. c. Choice **a** is incorrect. The reader cannot assume the company has experience with student travel just because the company believes that students should learn through experience. Choice **b** is incorrect. The reader cannot assume the company has experience with student travel just because the company is student-focused. Choice **c** is the correct answer. This is the only choice that suggests that the company has conducted tours in the past. Choice **d** is incorrect. Though the company has a website, this does not guarantee that the company has done student travel in the past.
Section: Evaluate/Extend Meaning
Subsection: Generalizations

35. b. Choice **a** is incorrect. A teacher would likely be interested in student travel. Choice **b** is the correct answer. Dentists are not usually involved in student travel. Choice **c** is incorrect. A parent would likely be interested in student travel. Choice **d** is incorrect. A student would likely be interested in student travel.
Section: Interpret Graphic Information
Subsection: Reference Sources

36. c. Choice **a** is incorrect. The word *retribution* means *reward*. This term is not the opposite of the word *succession*. Choice **b** is incorrect. The word *recession* means *a withdrawing process*. This term is not the opposite of the word *succession*. Choice **c** is the correct answer. The monarchy is named, in part, based on birth rather than on popular vote. Choice **d** is incorrect. The word *intervention* means *something that comes between*. This term is not the opposite of the word *succession*.
Section: Words in Context
Subsection: Opposite Meaning

37. b. Choice **a** is incorrect. The term does mean *in communion*. Choice **b** is the correct answer. All the other choices mean the same or almost the same as *in communion*. Choice **c** is incorrect. The term does mean *in communion*. Choice **d** is incorrect. The term does mean *in communion*.
Section: Words in Context
Subsection: Opposite Meaning

38. d. Choice **a** is incorrect. Descent is only one factor. Choice **b** is incorrect. Parliamentary statute is only one factor. Choice **c** is incorrect. Popular vote is not a factor. Choice **d** is the correct answer. Paragraph one states that succession to the throne is based on both descent and parliamentary statute.
Section: Recall Information
Subsection: Sequence

39. d. Choice **a** is incorrect. The fact that their father was the Queen's uncle indicates that Edward, Alexandra, and Michael are first cousins of the Queen. The passage says that *first cousins of the monarch may also be included* in the Royal Family. This means that Edward, Alexandra, and Michael may be members of the Royal Family, but it's just a possibility. Choice **b** is incorrect. According to the passage, there are laws preventing a sovereign from marrying a Roman Catholic. There is no mention of rules for the sovereign's relatives. Choice **c** is incorrect. Since both **a** and **b** are wrong, **c** is also wrong. Choice **d** is the correct answer. None of the options are right.
Section: Construct Meaning
Subsection: Conclusion

40. b. Choice **a** is incorrect. It can be reasoned from the passage that the Roman Catholic Church is not affiliated with Protestantism, since a sovereign is required *not* to be Roman Catholic or to marry a Roman Catholic but is required to uphold the Protestant succession. Choice **b** is the correct answer. This is the best answer, since the passage says that the sovereign must swear to preserve the Church of Scotland as well as the Protestant succession. Choice **c** is incorrect. There is no mention of William of Orange's religious affiliations. Choice **d** is incorrect. It can be assumed that some first cousins of the Queen may have other religious affiliations.
Section: Evaluate/Extend Meaning
Subsection: Generalizations

41. b. Choice **a** is incorrect. Fred was not happy. Choice **b** is the correct answer. Fred appears to be upset with the request that has been made. Fred chose to respond using capital letters in the first sentence and ended his response with an exclamation point. This style suggests anger. Choice **c** is incorrect. Fred was not neutral. He expressed his feelings. Choice **d** is incorrect. Fred did not appear curious.
Section: Construct Meaning
Subsection: Compare/Contrast

42. d. Choice **a** is incorrect. The manager would probably not describe Jackson as disgruntled. Choice **b** is incorrect. Jackson is a current employee, since he is on the schedule. Choice **c** is incorrect. The manager would probably not describe Jackson as selfish. Choice **d** is the correct answer. Jackson appears to have respect for the manager's request. Jackson voices his concerns in a sensible and moderate tone and wants to collaborate on a resolution.
Section: Evaluate/Extend Meaning
Subsection: Style Techniques

43. c. Choice **a** is incorrect. Fred most likely would not respond with an agreeable attitude. Choice **b** is incorrect. Fred would most likely not be partial to the company. Choice **c** is the correct answer. If Fred were given a demand, it can most likely be assumed that Fred's feelings of anger would extend to feelings of resentment towards the manager and/or the company. Choice **d** is incorrect. Fred would most likely not be fearful.
Section: Evaluate/Extend Meaning
Subsection: Effect/Intention

44. a. Choice **a** is the correct answer. Fred did write that his plan was to have dinner with his family on Christmas Eve. Furthermore, a building supply store would not normally be open at 12:30 in the morning, especially not on Christmas Eve. Choice **b** is incorrect. The first part of this answer supports the idea that the flight is in the afternoon (especially when you consider the fact that Fred mentions in his email that he would be expected to work *before* the flight). But the second part of the answer is made up; it is not stated anywhere in the passage. Choice **c** is incorrect. The availability of refunds for the tickets has no relevance. Choice **d** is incorrect. The focus is not on Fred's fear.
Section: Construct Meaning
Subsection: Cause/Effect

45. a. Choice **a** is the correct answer. Jackson would most likely respond that his work environment was a pleasant one if he felt he was able to communicate openly and freely with his superiors and that they responded in kind. Choice **b** is incorrect. Jackson most likely would not feel burdened by his job. Choice **c** is incorrect. Jackson would probably feel as though he had been treated fairly. Choice **d** is incorrect. Jackson would not feel the situation was dramatic.
Section: Construct Meaning
Subsection: Cause/Effect

46. c. Choice **a** is incorrect. Cousins are not lineal descendants—they are related to each other through an aunt or an uncle, not in a direct "line," the way a parent and child are. Choice **b** is incorrect. Church members may or may not be directly related by blood. Choice **c** is the correct answer. The term *lineally descended from a man or woman* refers to the line of direct descendants that can be proven from generations past. Choice **d** is incorrect. Siblings are of the same generation; they are not descended from one another.
Section: Words in Context
Subsection: Same Meaning

47. b. Choice **a** is incorrect. Resignations are not initially submitted to the Chapter President. Choice **b** is the correct answer. Section 4 reads, "A member desiring to resign shall present her resignation in writing to the Chapter Registrar, who shall immediately report the resignation to the Office of the Organizing Secretary General." Choice **c** is incorrect. There is no reference in the passage to a Chapter Membership Chair. Choice **d** is incorrect. Resignations are not initially submitted to the Secretary General.
Section: Recalling Information
Subsection: Sequence

48. d. Choice **a** is incorrect. This is a requirement. Choice **b** is incorrect. This is a requirement. Choice **c** is incorrect. This is a requirement. Choice **d** is the correct answer. The bylaws state that discrimination based on race is not allowed.
Section: Construct Meaning
Subsection: Supporting Evidence

49. **b.** Choice **a** is incorrect. A member cannot resign if she is deceased. Choice **b** is the correct answer. The bylaws state that members with delinquent dues are not allowed to resign. Choice **c** is incorrect. There is no discussion in the passage about chapters voting on a person's resignation. Choice **d** is incorrect. While this choice has some truth to it—someone who doesn't pay her dues is breaking the rules of her chapter—answer **b** is the more specific, better option.
Section: Evaluate/Extend Meaning
Subsection: Fact/Opinion

50. **b.** Choice **a** is incorrect. This is the incorrect section of the bylaws. Choice **b** is the correct answer. Section 3 states that transfers must follow the same procedures as prospective new members. Choice **c** is incorrect. This is the incorrect section of the bylaws. Also, a National Member is not mentioned here. Choice **d** is incorrect. This is the incorrect section of the bylaws. Also, a National Member is not mentioned here.
Section: Construct Meaning
Subsection: Summary/Paraphrase

Language

1. **d.** Choice **a** is incorrect. There is no subjective pronoun in this sentence. Choice **b** is incorrect. There is no subjective pronoun in this sentence, and the sentence should read *My cousin and I.* . . . Choice **c** is incorrect. There is no subjective pronoun in this sentence. Choice **d** is the correct answer. The pronoun *She* is a subjective pronoun and is used correctly as the subject of the sentence; it performs the action of the verb.
Section: Usage
Subsection: Pronouns

2. **b.** Choice **a** is incorrect. *She* is a pronoun, but it's not an objective pronoun. It functions here as the subject of the sentence (with *Dana*), not the object. Choice **b** is the correct answer. The correct pronoun is *me*. An objective pronoun acts as the object of a sentence—it receives the action of the verb. The objective pronouns are *me, you, him, her, it, us,* and *them*. Choice **c** is incorrect. The pronoun *her* is incorrectly used as a subjective pronoun. There is no objective pronoun in the sentence. Choice **d** is incorrect. The objects in this sentence are *Dana* and *I*. The pronoun *I* is always a subjective pronoun and never an objective pronoun. The sentence should read: . . . *very kind to Dana and me.*
Section: Usage
Subsection: Pronouns

3. **c.** Choice **a** is incorrect. There is no possessive pronoun in this sentence. *Himself* is a reflexive pronoun. Choice **b** is incorrect. This sentence does not contain a possessive pronoun. Choice **c** is the correct answer. The word *her* is a possessive pronoun. Choice **d** is incorrect. This sentence does not contain a possessive pronoun.
Section: Usage
Subsection: Pronouns

4. b. Choice **a** is incorrect. The relative pronoun *whoever* is incorrectly used as the object of the preposition *to*. The sentence should read *to whomever wants it*. Choice **b** is the correct answer. The relative pronoun *whom* relates back to the noun *person* and is the object of the verbs *love* and *hate*. A relative pronoun is a pronoun that introduces a relative clause. It is called a "relative" pronoun because it "relates" to the word that it modifies. There are five relative pronouns: *who*, *whom*, *whose*, *which*, and *that*. Choice **c** is incorrect. The word *that* does not function as a relative pronoun in this sentence. Choice **d** is incorrect. The relative pronoun *which* is normally used for things or ideas, not for people.
Section: Usage
Subsection: Pronouns

5. b. Choice **a** is incorrect. Reflexive pronouns reflect back on the subject, like a mirror. There are only eight reflexive pronouns. The correct reflexive pronoun for this sentence is *myself*, not *me*, which is an objective pronoun. Choice **b** is the correct answer. *Yourself* is a reflexive pronoun. Choice **c** is incorrect. *Hisself* is not a word. The correct reflexive pronoun is *himself*. Choice **d** is incorrect. *Theirselves* is a common misuse of the reflexive pronoun *themselves*.
Section: Usage
Subsection: Pronouns

6. c. Choice **a** is incorrect. *These* is a plural form of a demonstrative pronoun, and therefore the noun that follows it should be plural. Choice **b** is incorrect. The correct form is *these*, not *this*. Choice **c** is the correct answer. The demonstrative pronoun *this* refers to the singular *one*. Choice **d** is incorrect. The demonstrative pronoun *those* measures far distance. *These* measures near distance. It's an incorrect choice because the pictures are *over there*.
Section: Usage
Subsection: Pronouns

7. b. Choice **a** is incorrect. *A person* is singular (third person). The pronoun *you* is second person. There is no person agreement. Choice **b** is the correct answer. An antecedent is the word, phrase, or clause to which a pronoun refers, understood by context. A pronoun must agree with its antecedent in person, number, or gender. The word *students* is neutral plural and agrees with the pronoun *their*. Choice **c** is incorrect. *They* is third person neutral plural. *He* is third person masculine singular. There is no agreement. Choice **d** is incorrect. Because *anybody* is third person singular, and *they* is third person plural, there is no number agreement.
Section: Usage
Subsection: Antecedent Agreement

8. d. Choice **a** is incorrect. The verb *studied* is past tense, which doesn't fit with the adverb *tomorrow*. Choice **b** is incorrect. It should be *We take*. Choice **c** is incorrect. Because *will eat* is the future tense of the verb *eat*, it cannot be used with the word *yesterday*. Choice **d** is the correct answer. The subject of this sentence is understood to be *you*. *Bring* is the proper verb form for a second person singular/plural subject.
Section: Usage
Subsection: Tense

9. c. Choice **a** is incorrect. The past tense form of the verb *get* is *got*. Choice **b** is incorrect. The verb *practices* is present tense. It does not agree with the adverb *yesterday*. Choice **c** is the correct answer. The past tense form of the verb *swim* is *swam*. Choice **d** is incorrect. *Will be* is the future tense form of the verb *be*.
Section: Usage
Subsection: Tense

10. a. Choice **a** is the correct answer. *Will take* is the correct future form of the verb *take*. Choice **b** is incorrect. *Will go*, not *will goes*, is the future form of the verb *go*. Choice **c** is incorrect. *Went* is the past form of the verb *go*. Choice **d** is incorrect. The future form of the verb *be* is *will be*, not *are*.
Section: Usage
Subsection: Tense

11. d. Choice **a** is incorrect. The present perfect is used when the action is not yet finished: He *still lives there*. Choice **b** is incorrect. *Saw* is the past tense form of the verb *see*. Choice **c** is incorrect. The present participle cannot be used with a past action. Choice **d** is the correct answer. Present perfect is a tense of verbs used to describe action that has been completed. The present perfect *have seen* is used when the time is not specific.
Section: Usage
Subsection: Perfect Tense

12. a. Choice **a** is the correct answer. The present progressive tense indicates continuing action, which is something going on now. This tense is formed with the helping verb *to be* in the present tense, plus the present participle of the verb (with an *-ing* ending). This sentence contains all of these elements. Choice **b** is incorrect. There is no *be* verb used as a helping verb with the word *finding*. *Finding* is used as a gerund and the subject of the sentence. Choice **c** is incorrect. This sentence has no progressive tense verb. The word *barking* is a gerund used as a direct object. Choice **d** is incorrect. There is no progressive verb in this sentence. *Have run* is the present perfect form of the verb *run*.
Section: Usage
Subsection: Tense

13. c. Choice **a** is incorrect. The subject of the sentence is *group*, a singular noun. The verb *are* is plural, so the verb should be changed to *is*. Choice **b** is incorrect. Because *sister* is closer to the verb and is singular, the verb should also be singular. Choice **c** is the correct answer. *Chorus* is singular and agrees with the verb *consists*. Choice **d** is incorrect. The verb *were* does not agree with the subject *group*, which is a singular noun. Change the verb to *was*.
Section: Usage
Subsection: Subject/Verb Agreement

14. b. Choice **a** is incorrect. The verb *infer* means *to form an opinion or reach conclusion based on evidence*. That doesn't fit with the meaning of this sentence. A better choice would be *indicated* or *implied*. Choice **b** is the correct answer. *May* is a verb used for polite requests, to suggest that the speaker is asking permission. Many people use *can* in sentences like this, but it is an incorrect choice. "Can I take your coat?" really means "Am I physically able to take your coat?" which is probably not what the speaker means to say. Choice **c** is incorrect. The word *adapt* means *to change or get used to*. The proper word is *adopt*, meaning *to stake or claim as one's own*. Choice **d** is incorrect. The word *immigrate* means *to move to*. *Emigrate* means *to leave from*.
Section: Usage
Subsection: Easily Confused Verbs

15. c. Choice **a** is incorrect. Since three people are being compared in this sentence, *funnier* (a word used when two people or things are being compared) is not correct. It should be *funniest*. Choice **b** is incorrect. The sentence should read, *Of the two dishes, this one is worse.* The term *the worst* should be used when several people or things are being compared, not just two. Choice **c** is the correct answer. *Farther* is the comparative form of the adjective *far*. Choice **d** is incorrect. *The sweetest* is not correct because the speaker is considering two drinks, not several. The sentence should read, *Of the two drinks, which one do you think is sweeter?*
Section: Usage
Subsection: Adjective

16. b. Choice **a** is incorrect. In forming superlative modifiers, you either add an *-est* ending or add the helper *most*. You never use both. Choice **b** is the correct answer. The superlative *best* is correctly used to compare more than two people or things. Choice **c** is incorrect. The superlative *most* should have been used to compare all the statues, not the comparative *more*. Choice **d** is incorrect. This sentence contains two superlatives modifying the same adjective. It can be *most happy* or *happiest*, but not both.
Section: Usage
Subsection: Adjective

17. **c.** Choice **a** is incorrect. *Fast* can be used as an adverb, but it is not a comparative adverb. The correct choice for this sentence is *faster*. Choice **b** is incorrect. *More carefully* is correct when two people or things are being compared, but in this sentence, four assistants are being considered. The sentence should read, *Of the four assistants, Josh works the most carefully*. Choice **c** is the correct answer. *More seriously* functions as a comparative adverb and is used correctly in this sentence. It modifies the verb *took*. Choice **d** is incorrect. *Hardest than* is not correct; it should be *harder than*.
Section: Usage
Subsection: Adverb

18. **a.** Choice **a** is the correct answer. The superlative adverb *best* is proper, as she is being compared to *all the students*. Choice **b** is incorrect. In this sentence, he is compared to himself. The comparative adverb should be *better*. Choice **c** is incorrect. This sentence is grammatically correct, *but more brightly* is a comparative adverb, not a superlative adverb. Here, it's comparing how brightly the sun shines with how brightly the moon shines. Choice **d** is incorrect. The term *the most soonest* is not grammatically correct. The sentence should read, *I wanted to tell you that next Friday is the soonest we can arrive*.
Section: Usage
Subsection: Adverb

19. **c.** Choice **a** is incorrect. *We played good* is grammatically incorrect because *played* is a verb, which means it should be modified by an adverb, not an adjective (*good*). It should read, *We played well*. Choice **b** is incorrect. *She walked slow . . .* is grammatically incorrect because *walked* is a verb, which means it should be modified by an adverb, not an adjective (*slow*). The beginning of the sentence should read, *She walked slowly . . .* Choice **c** is the correct answer. *Beautifully* is an adverb and it correctly modifies the verb *sings*. Choice **d** is incorrect. *Beautiful* is an adjective, which means it should modify a noun, not the verb *sings*.
Section: Usage
Subsection: Choose between Adjective/Adverb

20. **d.** Choice **a** is incorrect. Words such as *barely, hardly,* and *scarcely* have a negative meaning built into them and therefore should not be used with another negative. Choice **b** is incorrect. There are two negatives in this sentence. The sentence should be changed to *I do not want any second helpings*. Choice **c** is incorrect. This sentence also contains a double negative (*will not* and *no one*). It should be reworded to eliminate one of the negatives. Choice **d** is the correct answer. This sentence contains only one negative.
Section: Usage
Subsection: Use Negatives

21. d. Choice **a** is incorrect. This is a run-on sentence that can be corrected in a number of ways. One way is to make two sentences: put a period after the word *smart* and capitalize the pronoun *he*. Another way is to change the sentence to a complex sentence by placing a subordinate conjunction, such as *although*, before one of the clauses. Choice **b** is incorrect. It is a dependent clause fragment without a main independent clause. It can be fixed by replacing the period with a comma and adding an independent clause at the end, such as *she felt sleepy*. Choice **c** is incorrect. This is a sentence fragment. To correct this example, replace the period with a comma after the word *class* and add an independent clause, such as *all the students went out to the field*. Choice **d** is the correct answer. This example contains an independent clause connected to the subordinate clause by the conjunction *as*.
Section: Sentence Formation
Subsection: Sentence Recognition

22. d. Choice **a** is incorrect. This sentence could be better written as, *Because the waves were almost 15 feet tall, we decided not to surf.* Choice **b** is incorrect. This sentence is choppy and could be better written as *The first ever comic book convention lasted all day and featured several costumed super heroes.* Choice **c** is incorrect. The sentence does not flow logically or smoothly and could be better written as *Our Latin teacher in high school was birdlike, unfriendly woman, but she had sparkling eyes.* Choice **d** is the correct answer. This is the most correct, readable sentence.
Section: Sentence Formation
Subsection: Sentence Combining

23. d. Choice **a** is incorrect. The two independent clauses have been joined by a comma, creating a comma splice. To fix this sentence, add the word *and* before *the clerk*. Compound sentences may also be made by placing a semicolon after the first independent clause. Choice **b** is incorrect. The two independent clauses are joined without any sort of connector, creating a fused sentence. Choice **c** is incorrect. The two independent clauses are joined without the appropriate punctuation, creating a run-on sentence. Choice **d** is the correct answer. A compound sentence is a sentence that contains at least two independent clauses. The two independent clauses in this sentence are joined by a comma and the word *and* after the word *costume*.
Section: Sentence Formation
Subsection: Sentence Combining

24. b. Choice **a** is incorrect. To combine these two clauses, use a comma after the word *trouble*. Choice **b** is the correct answer. Two complete sentences have been joined with a comma and a coordinating conjunction (*and*). Coordination combines two ideas that are equally important. Choice **c** is incorrect. *During holidays* is not a clause. Choice **d** is incorrect. There is only one independent clause here, not two. Furthermore, the sentence is not worded correctly; *visiting* should be *to visit* so that it is parallel with *to eat*.
Section: Sentence Formation
Subsection: Sentence Combining

25. c. Choice **a** is incorrect. *Who is 10 years old* should be followed by a comma. Choice **b** is incorrect. The subordinate clause, starting with the phrase *even though*, requires a comma after the word *popcorn*. Choice **c** is the correct answer. The phrase *which was shaded by a large tree* is not essential to the meaning or grammar of the sentence—it's a side point. Therefore, it is correctly offset from the body of the sentence with a comma. It's O.K. that there are no commas around the word *Trevor*. It indicates that the speaker has more than one brother. If Trevor is the speaker's only brother, the sentence should read, *My brother, Trevor, loved to . . .* Choice **d** is incorrect. A comma should separate the subordinate clause (ending with the word *sidewalk*) and the main clause (starting with the word *Rhonda*).
Section: Sentence Formation
Subsection: Sentence Combining

26. d. Choice **a** is incorrect. This sentence is unclear, has multiple negatives, and is in the passive voice. The better sentence would be: *People pay more attention to commercials with human interest stories than to other kinds of commercials.* Choice **b** is incorrect. A better sentence would be: *Tanya worked in a medical lab last summer; medical research may be her career choice.* Choice **c** is incorrect. An unintentional shift in person takes place. *Students* is third person, while *you* is a second person pronoun. Change the sentence to: *Freshman college students must make many new choices, and sometimes they get confused.* Choice **d** is the correct answer. It is more direct and clearer than the other sentences.
Section: Sentence Formation
Subsection: Sentence Clarity

27. c. Choice **a** is incorrect. This sentence is not parallel. The first two verbs are infinitives (*to hike, to swim*), and the third verb is a gerund (*riding*). Verb forms should not be mixed. Choice **b** is incorrect. *Looking up irregular verbs* does not match the nouns in the list. Choice **c** is the correct answer. This sentence shows parallel structure by using the same pattern of words to show that the two ideas have the same level of importance. The conjunctions *not only* and *but also* connect the two verbs in the sentence (*dislikes, refuses*). Choice **d** is incorrect. The first two modifiers (*quickly, accurately*) are adverbs, but the third modifier (*in a detailed manner*) is not.
Section: Sentence Formation
Subsection: Sentence Clarity

28. a. Choice **a** is the correct answer. The sentence is concise and to the point. Choice **b** is incorrect. The sentence is much too wordy. It would have been better written as *We know your tax return filing policy and intend to comply fully.* Choice **c** is incorrect. The word *annual* means *every year*. Choice **d** is incorrect. The word *postpone* means *delay*. This makes the word *later* repetitive and unnecessary.
Section: Sentence Formation
Subsection: Sentence Clarity

29. a. Choice **a** is the correct answer. A good topic sentence must advance the point of a limited subject. Choice **b** is incorrect. This sentence has no specific purpose or point to advance. Choice **c** is incorrect. This sentence is too general, and the word *could* makes the idea seem incomplete (*when* could he be an angel?). Choice **d** is incorrect. This sentence is too narrow, and it starts with the word *And*, which doesn't make sense for a topic sentence.
Section: Paragraph Development
Subsection: Topic Sentence

30. b. Choice **a** is incorrect. The sentence *Wanda likes to travel* does not support the topic sentence *Wanda loves cars*. The sentences are too unrelated, and the second sentence does not expand on the idea presented in the first. Choice **b** is the correct answer. The fact that Sam loves to play tennis in particular supports the more general idea that he likes certain sports. Choice **c** is incorrect. The second sentence is too broad. In fact, it's broader than the topic sentence. It does not offer any supporting details. Choice **d** is incorrect. It would make more sense if the order of these two sentences were reversed. *The library is a great place to study* supports the broader claim that *the school has a variety of places where students can study*.
Section: Paragraph Development
Subsection: Supporting Sentences

31. d. Choice **a** is incorrect. The correct order is 1, 4, 2, 3. Choice **b** is incorrect. The correct order is 2, 3, 1. Choice **c** is incorrect. The order is 2, 3, 1. Choice **d** is the correct answer. The correct order is 1, 2, 3, 4.
Section: Paragraph Development
Subsection: Sequence

32. c. Choice **a** is incorrect. This sentence is related to the main topic of the paragraph, the lighting in hospital rooms. Choice **b** is incorrect. This sentence is related to the main topic of the paragraph, the lighting in hospital rooms. Choice **c** is the correct answer. The fact that hospital sheets are white doesn't have a direct connection to the topic of the paragraph. Choice **d** is incorrect. This sentence is related to the main topic of the paragraph, lighting in hospital rooms.
Section: Paragraph Development
Subsection: Unrelated Sentence

33. b. Choice **a** is incorrect. *However* does not establish the correct relationship between the two sentences. *Therefore* would be a better word. Choice **b** is the correct answer. The phrase *In addition* establishes the correct relationship between the two sentences. Choice **c** is incorrect. The phrase *In spite of* does not establish the correct relationship between the two sentences. Flooding is the result of too much rain. A better choice would be *As a consequence*. Choice **d** is incorrect. The connector *Furthermore* does not establish the correct relationship between the two sentences. A better phrase would be *Despite his intelligence*.
Section: Paragraph Development
Subsection: Connective/
Transitional Devices

34. **c.** Choice **a** is incorrect. The interjection *oh* is never capitalized unless it is the first word of a sentence. Choice **b** is incorrect. The word *I* is always capitalized, no matter its position. The rule also pertains to contractions using the word *I* (*I'm, I've*). Choice **c** is the correct answer. Both *Oh* and *I've* should be capitalized, since they start their respective sentences. Furthermore, the *I* in *I've* should always be uppercase. Choice **d** is incorrect. There is no reason for *Him* to be capitalized here.
Section: Capitalization
Subsection: First Word

35. **c.** Choice **a** is incorrect. The word *poet* is not a proper noun and should not be capitalized. Choice **b** is incorrect. *King Abboud* is correctly capitalized (*King* is a title, and *Abboud* is a proper name), but there is no reason for *Princess* or *Queen* to be capitalized. In this sentence, they function as common nouns, like *apple* or *tree*. Choice **c** is the correct answer. *Athena* is correctly capitalized as a proper name, and *Greek* is correctly capitalized as a proper adjective. All adjectives formed from the name of a country are capitalized (*Greece, Greek; China, Chinese; America, American*). Choice **d** is incorrect. The word *Russian* is a proper adjective and needs to be capitalized.
Section: Capitalization
Subsection: Proper Nouns

36. **d.** Choice **a** is incorrect. *Thursday* should be capitalized, because days of the week are always capitalized. *Spring* should be lowercase, because it is a common noun. Choice **b** is incorrect. *Friday* should be capitalized, because days of the week are always capitalized. Choice **c** is incorrect. *Saturday* should be capitalized, because days of the week are always capitalized. Choice **d** is the correct answer. *Sundays* is capitalized, as it should be. Days of the week, even in their plural form, should always be capitalized.
Section: Capitalization
Subsection: Proper Nouns

37. **c.** Choice **a** is incorrect. Months are always capitalized (*June*). Choice **b** is incorrect. Months are always capitalized, and so are specific holidays (*the 4th of July/the Fourth of July*). Choice **c** is the correct answer. Months are always capitalized (*May*). Choice **d** is incorrect. Months are always capitalized (*December*).
Section: Capitalization
Subsection: Proper Nouns

38. **b.** Choice **a** is incorrect. *West* should be lowercase. Directions are lowercase, unless they are a part of a proper name, at the beginning of a sentence, or in another standard situation that calls for capitalization. Choice **b** is the correct answer. *New York* and *Route* 95 should be capitalized because they are both proper nouns. Choice **c** is incorrect. *South* should be lowercase. Directions are lowercase, unless they are a part of a proper name, at the beginning of a sentence, or in another standard situation that calls for capitalization. Choice **d** is incorrect. *Middle East* should be capitalized because it is not a direction; it is a proper name for a geographical area.
Section: Capitalization
Subsection: Proper Nouns

39. c. Choice **a** is incorrect. *Doctor* should be lowercase because it is a common noun in this sentence, not a title. There are times when words like *doctor*, *president*, and *senator* should be capitalized, however. It is when they are used as a professional title, in the same way that you use *Ms.*, *Mrs.*, and *Mr.* before a person's name. Here is an example of that usage: *At the golf club we call her Jane, but at the hospital she is known as Doctor Cormack.* Choice **b** is incorrect. The term *vice president* should be lowercase because it is a common noun in this sentence, not a title. Choice **c** is the correct answer. *General* should be capitalized because it appears right before the name and serves as a title, like *Mr.* or *Ms.* Choice **d** is incorrect. *Uncle* should not be capitalized. It's just a common noun.
Section: Capitalization
Subsection: Proper Nouns

40. d. Choice **a** is incorrect. Indirect questions end with a period. Choice **b** is incorrect. This is an interrogative sentence and has to end with a question mark. Choice **c** is incorrect. When an acronym, such as *NATO*, is pronounced as a word, you don't normally add periods. Choice **d** is the correct answer. Gentle commands (*hand in*) end in a period.
Section: Punctuation
Subsection: End Marks

41. a. Choice **a** is the correct answer. The wording of the sentence indicates that it is a question, so it needs a question mark at the end. Choice **b** is incorrect. Even if the speaker is using the phrase *are you not* more as a conversational tool than as a direct question, it is still grammatically a question and therefore needs a question mark. Choice **c** is incorrect. The second half of this sentence is a description of what the waiter said, not a direct quote. While what the waiter actually said may have been a question (and would need a question mark if we wrote it down), this sentence is a declarative sentence. Therefore it needs a standard period. Choice **d** is incorrect. While it is correct that the sentence ends in a period (not a question mark), there is no need for the comma.
Section: Punctuation
Subsection: End Marks

42. a. Choice **a** is the correct answer. Because it concerns a demand, this sentence could reasonably end with either an exclamation point or a period. It depends on how much emphasis the speaker or writer wants to add. Choice **b** is incorrect. *What are you doing?* is a direct quote, so it needs quotation marks. Furthermore, there should be no comma after a question mark in this construction. The correct sentence is: *"What are you doing?" he shouted excitedly.* Choice **c** is incorrect. It is improper usage to add an exclamation point or *(!)* in the middle of a sentence. Choice **d** is incorrect. The sentence should read: *"Good heavens," he said. "I did not know that."*
Section: Punctuation
Subsection: End Marks

43. a. Choice **a** is the correct answer. This example shows two independent clauses separated by a comma and the word *but*. Choice **b** is incorrect. This sentence needs a comma before the word *yet* (*, yet*) to separate the two independent clauses. Choice **c** is incorrect. Because this sentence contains an independent clause followed by a dependent clause, no comma is required. Choice **d** is incorrect. Commas should surround *who likes animals* because that is a nonessential phrase. The sentence could stand on its own as a grammatically correct sentence without it.
Section: Punctuation
Subsection: Commas

44. b. Choice **a** is incorrect. When writing a series of three or more items, separate each item with punctuation, usually commas. Generally, a conjunction (*and*, *or*, *but*) will follow the last comma in the list. This example is a simple series. Choice **b** is the correct answer. All commas are correctly placed in this sentence. When writing a series of three or more items, separate each item with punctuation, usually commas. Generally, a conjunction (*and*, *or*, *but*) will follow the last comma in the list. Choice **c** is incorrect. Without a comma after the word *spectators*, the meaning is unclear. Were the police shouting? Choice **d** is incorrect. There is not a series in this sentence, because only two items are mentioned: *spaghetti and meatballs* (which is one dish) and *pizza*. A series has three or more items. The sentence should read: *This Italian restaurant serves the best spaghetti and meatballs and pizza in town.* If you wanted to treat *spaghetti* and *meatballs* as two separate items, then you could create a series. The sentence could be re-written as: *This Italian restaurant serves the best spaghetti, meatballs, and pizza in town.*
Section: Punctuation
Subsection: Commas

45. c. Choice **a** is incorrect. The word *boys* should be offset by a comma (right after *bed*) because the speaker is talking directly to the boys. Choice **b** is incorrect. The phrase *Liv and John* should be surrounded by commas because the speaker is talking directly to Liv and John. Choice **c** is the correct answer. The speaker is talking about his or her father, not talking directly to him. It is correct that there are no commas around the word *Dad*. Choice **d** is incorrect. The speaker is directly addressing a man and politely referring to him as *Sir*. There should be a comma after *you* to offset *Sir*.
Section: Punctuation
Subsection: Commas

46. c. Choice **a** is incorrect. Interjections, such as *well*, should be followed by a comma. Choice **b** is incorrect. *Yes* should be followed by a comma. Choice **c** is the correct answer. *Well* is correctly offset by a comma. Choice **d** is incorrect. The comma here is correct, but there should be another comma after *no*.
Section: Punctuation
Subsection: Commas

47. b. Choice **a** is incorrect. *A man of integrity* is an appositive that describes *Mr. Smith*, so a comma should come at the end of it. An appositive is a noun or noun phrase that describes something that appears right next to it in a sentence. If the appositive is not essential to the meaning or grammar of the sentence, then it is offset by comma(s). Choice **b** is the correct answer. The appositive *a star student* is correctly offset by commas. Choice **c** is incorrect. *CEO* should be surrounded by commas. Choice **d** is incorrect. This is a correctly punctuated sentence, but there is no appositive. The phrase *who received a scholarship* is not a noun or a noun phrase.
Section: Punctuation
Subsection: Commas

48. d. Choice **a** is incorrect. A comma is usually used after long introductory phrases. Here, a comma should be added after *station*. Choice **b** is incorrect. When there is an infinitive verb at the start of a sentence, place *in order* before it. If the resulting sentence makes sense, then it needs a comma at the end of the introductory phrase. Here, it would be after *vehicle*. Choice **c** is incorrect. There should be no comma in this sentence. If the two parts of the sentence were flipped around, it would require a comma: *When he reached the stop sign, Adams turned left*. Choice **d** is the correct answer. *Her head hanging on her chest* is an absolute phrase, a phrase that modifies the rest of the sentence. It is correctly offset by a comma.
Section: Punctuation
Subsection: Commas

49. c. Choice **a** is incorrect. The phrase *not the dance* should be surrounded by commas to offset it from the positive statement made by the rest of the sentence. Choice **b** is incorrect. In this usage, the word *however* should be surrounded by commas. Choice **c** is the correct answer. *For example* is correctly surrounded by commas. Choice **d** is incorrect. The phrase *as far as we know* should be offset from the rest of the sentence by commas. Here, the comma before *as* begins to offset it, but there should be a closing comma after *know*, too.
Section: Punctuation
Subsection: Commas

50. d. Choice **a** is incorrect. This sentence contains two independent clauses—clauses that would be grammatically correct if they stood on their own. To connect two independent clauses, you can use a semicolon or use a comma and a conjunction like *and*, *or*, or *but*. *However* is not one of these words. To make this sentence correct, add a semicolon: *Danica did as she was told; however, she grumbled constantly.* Another option is to simply swap *however,* with the conjunction *but*: *Danica did as she was told, but she grumbled constantly.* Choice **b** is incorrect. This sentence contains a simple series; there is no reason for semicolons. It should read, *. . .Eva Tyler, Jamal White, and Sam Stark.* Choice **c** is incorrect. Semicolons are unnecessary here. Semicolons should be used in a series when one or more of the items itself contains a comma(s). The point is to avoid confusion. Here, there are commas built into the individual items, but there are only two items—this is not a series. (Series have at least three items.) There is no confusion if you just use commas: *The test will be given on Wednesday, June 6, and Thursday, June 7.* Choice **d** is the correct answer. The sentence contains a series (three city/state pairs), and each item contains a comma within it, so the series needs semicolons.
Section: Punctuation
Subsection: Semicolons

51. b. Choice **a** is incorrect. The clause *she was going to Trenton on Saturday* is a description of something that Zelda said, not a word-for-word quote of what she said. (Zelda did not tell someone, "She was going to Trenton on Saturday," when referring to herself.) There should not be quotation marks. Choice **b** is the correct answer. The names of songs are always enclosed by quotation marks. Choice **c** is incorrect. There is no reason for the pair of quotation marks after *hurry*. Both sentences are a part of the same quote. It should read, *Jody said,* "We should hurry. The last feature has started." Choice **d** is incorrect. The sentence should have closing quotation marks after *coach*.
Section: Writing Conventions
Subsection: Quotation Marks

52. d. Choice **a** is incorrect. When a direct quote is introduced by *said* or a similar word, there should be a comma after *said*, and the first word of the quote should be capitalized (here, *Imagination*). Choice **b** is incorrect. This sentence has a comma in the right spot, but again the word *imagination* should be capitalized. Choice **c** is incorrect. For the same reason, *the* should be capitalized: *"The alien spaceship . . ."* Choice **d** is the correct answer. Here, *not a crook* is integrated into the grammar of the sentence; it's not offset by *said* or a similar word. There is no reason for a comma or quotation marks.
Section: Writing Conventions
Subsection: Quotation Marks

53. a. Choice **a** is the correct answer. Kevin said one sentence: *I love the beach, especially when it's not too windy*. Because of this, there is correctly a comma, not a period, after *Kevin said*. Choice **b** is incorrect. There should be a comma after *said*. Choice **c** is incorrect. There should not be a comma after *that*. The quote is integrated into the grammar of the sentence; it is not offset by a phrase like *He said*. Choice **d** is incorrect. Two commas should be added: *"Have it your way,"* Alberta added, *"if that's how you feel."*
Section: Punctuation
Subsection: Commas

54. a. Choice **a** is the correct answer. If the question mark governs the sentence as a whole but not the material being quoted, it is placed outside the quotation marks. Choice **b** is incorrect. Because the name of the song is also a question, the end mark should be *". . . Gone?"* Choice **c** is incorrect. There should be no comma after *that* because the quote is integrated into the grammar of the sentence. (If the quote were introduced by *Mr. Smith announced*, then a comma would be correct.) Choice **d** is incorrect. American usage places commas and periods inside the quotation marks. The correction should read: *". . . for a little while."*
Section: Writing Conventions
Subsection: Quotation Marks

55. c. Choice **a** is incorrect. The contraction for *who is* is not *whose* but *who's*. Choice **b** is incorrect. The contraction for *let us* is not *lets* but *let's*. Choice **c** is the correct answer. The correct contraction for *you are* is *you're*. Choice **d** is incorrect. In the contraction of *was not*, the apostrophe should go where the missing letter (*o*) was originally: *wasn't*.
Section: Writing Conventions
Subsection: Apostrophes

Language Mechanics

1. b. Choice **a** is incorrect. There is no infinitive phrase in this sentence. Choice **b** is the correct answer. The infinitive phrase is correctly used as a modifier. Choice **c** is incorrect. There is no subject in this sentence. Choice **d** is incorrect. There is no subject in this sentence.
Section: Sentences, Phrases, Clauses
Subsection: Phrases

2. d. Choice **a** is incorrect. This example is a fragment and not a sentence. Choice **b** is incorrect. This example is a fragment. Choice **c** is incorrect. There is no infinitive phrase in this sentence. Choice **d** is the correct answer. The infinitive phrase is the subject of the sentence.
Section: Sentences, Phrases, Clauses
Subsection: Phrases

3. c. Choice **a** is incorrect. There is no infinitive phrase in this sentence. Choice **b** is incorrect. This is a sentence fragment and not a complete sentence. Choice **c** is the correct answer. The infinitive phrase is correctly used as a direct object. Choice **d** is incorrect. This is not a sentence but an infinitive phrase.
Section: Sentences, Phrases, Clauses
Subsection: Phrases

4. c. Choice **a** is incorrect. There is no appositive in this sentence. Choice **b** is incorrect. There is no appositive in this sentence. Choice **c** is the correct answer. The appositive phrase *the largest city in the world* is correctly punctuated. Choice **d** is incorrect. This is not a complete sentence and contains no appositive.
Section: Sentences, Phrases, Clauses
Subsection: Commas

5. c. Choice **a** is incorrect. A comma is required after *player*. Choice **b** is incorrect. A comma is required after *appositive*. Choice **c** is the correct answer. The appositive phrase *a professional guide* is correctly punctuated. Choice **d** is incorrect. This sentence does not have an appositive.
Section: Sentences, Phrases, Clauses
Subsection: Commas

6. a. Choice **a** is the correct answer. The appositive *the manager of the Red Sox* is correctly punctuated. Choice **b** is incorrect. This sentence does not have an appositive. Furthermore, it should read: *My cousin, who lives at home, . . .* Choice **c** is incorrect. This sentence does not have an appositive. Choice **d** is incorrect. This sentence does not have an appositive.
Section: Sentences, Phrases, Clauses
Subsection: Commas

7. d. Choice **a** is incorrect. The modifier is misplaced in this sentence. The watch, not the man, was gold. Choice **b** is incorrect. The child did not eat a *cold bowl*. He ate *oatmeal* that was cold. Choice **c** is incorrect. The modifier is misplaced. The *buyer* did not have leather seats. The Chevrolet did. Choice **d** is the correct answer. There are no misplaced or dangling modifiers in this sentence.
Section: Sentences, Phrases, Clauses
Subsection: Phrases

8. b. Choice **a** is incorrect. What or who was tiring? The independent clause should be changed to *I/she/he was extremely tiring.* Choice **b** is the correct answer. The sentence is modified properly and correctly punctuated. Choice **c** is incorrect. The independent clause should be changed to *he did not fit into his pants.* This is a dangling modifier. Choice **d** is incorrect. The modifier is misplaced. The *house* was not made of barbed wire; the *fence* was.
Section: Sentences, Phrases, Clauses
Subsection: Clauses

9. c. Choice **a** is incorrect. It contains a dangling modifier. *Dana* was not fixed; the *car* was. Choice **b** is incorrect. This sentence contains a dangling modifier. The *sudden storm* is not walking to the movies; the *group* is. Choice **c** is the correct answer. The sentence has neither misplaced nor dangling modifiers and is correctly punctuated. Choice **d** is incorrect. The dangling modifier implies that the *sun* reached the station instead of the implied narrator.
Section: Sentences, Phrases, Clauses
Subsection: Commas

10. d. Choice **a** is incorrect. The sentence does not contain a prepositional phrase. *Held up* is a verb meaning *to rob.* Choice **b** is incorrect. The object of the prepositional phrase should be *me*, as in *with Tom and me.* Choice **c** is incorrect. The preposition *at* unnecessarily ends the sentence and lacks an object. Choice **d** is the correct answer. The two prepositional phrases *in the ocean* and *at high tide* are correctly used as part of the gerund.
Section: Sentences, Phrases, Clauses
Subsection: Phrases

11. d. Choice **a** is incorrect. There is no prepositional phrase in the sentence. *Practicing the piano daily* is a gerund phrase. Choice **b** is incorrect. There is no prepositional phrase in this sentence. Choice **c** is incorrect. It should read: *To whom did you send the memo?* Choice **d** is the correct answer. The prepositional phrase *on the kitchen table* is used correctly in this sentence.
Section: Sentences, Phrases, Clauses
Subsection: Phrases

12. c. Choice **a** is incorrect. There is no prepositional phrase in this sentence. *Take-out* is a noun. Choice **b** is incorrect. The term *ran up* is a verb and not a preposition. Choice **c** is the correct answer. The prepositional phrase *with the new television* is used correctly in the sentence. Choice **d** is incorrect. *Pull through* is a verb. There is no prepositional phrase in this sentence.
Section: Sentences, Phrases, Clauses
Subsection: Phrases/Clauses

13. a. Choice **a** is the correct answer. The subordinate clause *because I had an accident* is used before the independent clause *I got sent to the supervisor's office*. Choice **b** is incorrect. The independent clause *I did not get the prize* precedes the subordinate clause. Choice **c** is incorrect. The independent clause *The music was extremely loud* precedes the subordinate clause. Choice **d** is incorrect. The independent clause *My neighbors will be evicted* precedes the subordinate clause.
Section: Sentences, Phrases, Clauses
Subsection: Clauses

14. c. Choice **a** is incorrect. The independent clause *I will show you the book* comes before the subordinate clause. Choice **b** is incorrect. The independent clause encloses the subordinate phrase *that I bought last week*. Choice **c** is the correct answer. The subordinate clause *While waiters served beers in cups* precedes the independent clause *a band of musicians entertained the crowd of tourists*. Choice **d** is incorrect. The independent clause *I know the person* precedes the subordinate clause.
Section: Sentences, Phrases, Clauses
Subsection: Clauses

15. b. Choice **a** is incorrect. The subordinate clause *If you need me* is followed by the independent clause. Choice **b** is the correct answer. The independent clause *The friend who is visiting Jeremy makes terrific lasagna* is followed by the subordinate clause *although it contains too much spinach for my taste*. Choice **c** is incorrect. The subordinate clause *When you reach the end of the hallway* is followed by the independent clause. Choice **d** is incorrect. The subordinate clause *Whenever you dust the furniture* comes before the independent clause.
Section: Sentences, Phrases, Clauses
Subsection: Clauses

16. c. Choice **a** is incorrect. There is no subordinate clause in this sentence. Choice **b** is incorrect. This sentence contains two independent clauses joined by a semicolon. Choice **c** is the correct answer. The sentence starts with a subordinate clause that is correctly punctuated before the independent clause. Choice **d** is incorrect. There is no subordinate clause in this sentence.
Section: Sentences, Phrases, Clauses
Subsection: Clauses

17. c. Choice **a** is incorrect. In this sentence, the subordinate clause comes first. Choice **b** is incorrect. There is no subordinate clause in this sentence. Choice **c** is the correct answer. The independent clause comes first in this sentence. Choice **d** is incorrect. This sentence contains two independent clauses.
Section: Sentences, Phrases, Clauses
Subsection: Clauses

18. b. Choice **a** is incorrect. There is no prepositional phrase in this sentence. *Abroad* is an adverb modifying the verb *went*. Choice **b** is the correct answer. The prepositional phrase *behind the couch* contains a preposition and an object of the preposition. Choice **c** is incorrect. There is no prepositional phrase in this sentence. *You* (understood) is the subject, and *sit down* and *enjoy* are the predicates. Choice **d** is incorrect. There is no prepositional phrase in this sentence. *Put down* is a verb.
Section: Sentences, Phrases, Clauses
Subsection: Phrases

19. d. Choice **a** is incorrect. The sentence contains a misplaced modifier. The lunch was *eaten* slowly, not brought slowly. Choice **b** is incorrect. The sentence is unclear because it contains a dangling modifier. The *speaker* was eight years old, not the father. Choice **c** is incorrect. The sentence contains a misplaced modifier. The *book* was torn, not the student. Choice **d** is the correct answer. This sentence makes it clear that it was the *students* who read the novel.
Section: Sentences, Phrases, Clauses
Subsection: Phrases/Clauses

20. d. Choice **a** is incorrect. There should be a comma after *Patricia* and after *student*. Choice **b** is incorrect. There should be a comma after *roommate*. Choice **c** is incorrect. There should be a comma after *heirloom*. Choice **d** is the correct answer. The commas are placed correctly in this sentence to set off the appositive *Dolly*.
Section: Sentences, Phrases, Clauses
Subsection: Commas

Vocabulary

1. a. Choice **a** is the correct answer. The word *repudiated* means *refused to accept* or *rejected*. Choice **b** is incorrect. The word *controversial* is an adjective meaning *questionable*. Choice **c** is incorrect. The word *unknown* means *not known*. Choice **d** is incorrect. The word *popularity* is a noun meaning *the state of being well liked or a favorite*.
Section: Vocabulary
Subsection: Word Meaning

2. c. Choice **a** is incorrect. The word *random* is an adjective meaning *haphazardly* or *by chance*. Choice **b** is incorrect. The word *complimentary* is an adjective meaning *given without charge*. Choice **c** is the correct answer. The word *acerbic* means *expressing harsh criticism in a clever way*. Choice **d** is incorrect. The word *ethical* is an adjective meaning *righteous*.
Section: Vocabulary
Subsection: Word Meaning

3. a. Choice **a** is the correct answer. The word *defunct* is an adjective meaning *inactive*. Choice **b** is incorrect. The word *competitive* is an adjective meaning *determined by rivalry*. Choice **c** is incorrect. *Defunct* does not mean *small*. Choice **d** is incorrect. The word *undesirable* is an adjective meaning *not attractive* or *not pleasant*.
Section: Vocabulary
Subsection: Word Meaning

4. d. Choice **a** is incorrect. The word *uncouth* is an adjective meaning *having bad manners*. Choice **b** is incorrect. The word *engrained* means *deeply instilled*. Choice **c** is incorrect. The word *passive* is an adjective meaning *without participation*. Choice **d** is the correct answer. One definition of *refined* is *genteel*.
Section: Vocabulary
Subsection: Word Meaning

5. c. Choice **a** is incorrect. The word *loose* is an adjective meaning *free of attachment*. Choice **b** is incorrect. The word *expensive* is an adjective meaning *high-priced*. Choice **c** is the correct answer. The word *tight* is an adjective meaning *taut*. Choice **d** is incorrect. The word *cheap* is an adjective meaning *of low quality* or *at a low price*.
Section: Vocabulary
Subsection: Word Meaning

6. c. Choice **a** is incorrect. The word *questionable* is an adjective meaning *worthy of doubt*. Choice **b** is incorrect. The word *evasive* is an adjective meaning *able to avoid or escape*. Choice **c** is the correct answer. The word *praiseworthy* is an adjective meaning *laudable*. Choice **d** is incorrect. The word *uncouth* is an adjective meaning *strange and ungraceful in appearance or form*.
Section: Vocabulary
Subsection: Word Meaning

7. a. Choice **a** is the correct answer. The word *obscure* is an adjective meaning *unclear* or *not well-known*. Choice **b** is incorrect. The word *blatant* is an adjective meaning *extremely obvious*. Choice **c** is incorrect. The word *parallel* is an adjective meaning *at the same distance apart*. Choice **d** is incorrect. The word *corrosive* is an adjective meaning *harmful* or *destructive*.
Section: Vocabulary
Subsection: Word Meaning

8. b. Choice **a** is incorrect. The word *tasteful* is an adjective meaning *in good taste*. Choice **b** is correct. The word *uncivilized* is an adjective meaning *barbaric*. Choice **c** is incorrect. The word *confused* means *unable to think clearly*. Choice **d** is incorrect. The word *agreeable* is an adjective meaning *pleasing or consenting*.
Section: Vocabulary
Subsection: Word Meaning

9. c. Choice **a** is incorrect. The word *advertise* works in the first sentence but not the second. Choice **b** is incorrect. The word *present* works in the first sentence but not the second. Choice **c** is the correct answer. The word *tape* is a verb meaning *to electronically record* or *to stick with adhesive*. It works in both sentences. Choice **d** is incorrect. The word *staple* works in the second sentence but not the first.
Section: Vocabulary
Subsection: Multimeaning Words

10. d. Choice **a** is incorrect. *Public* works in the second sentence but not the first. Choice **b** is incorrect. *Focus* does not work well in either sentence. Choice **c** is incorrect. *Romance* works in the first sentence but not the second. Choice **d** is the correct answer. *Court* works in the first sentence as a verb meaning *to date*. It also works in the second sentence as a noun meaning *court of law*.
Section: Vocabulary
Subsection: Multimeaning Words

11. c. Choice **a** is incorrect. *Geometrical* works in the second sentence but doesn't make sense in the first. Choice **b** is incorrect. *Popular* could work in the second sentence, but it doesn't fit well in the first. Choice **c** is the correct answer. *Checkered* works in the first sentence as an adjective meaning *having problems or failures*. It also works in the second sentence as an adjective meaning *having a pattern of different squares of different colors*. Choice **d** is incorrect. *Troubled* works in the first sentence but not the second.
Section: Vocabulary
Subsection: Multimeaning Words

12. b. Choice **a** is incorrect. *Control* could work in the second sentence, but it doesn't make sense in the first. Choice **b** is the correct answer. *Station* works in the first sentence as a noun meaning a *TV channel's offices*. It also makes sense in the second sentence as a verb meaning *to put in a specific place*. Choice **c** is incorrect. *Antenna* doesn't work well in either sentence. Choice **d** is incorrect. *Anchor* works in the second sentence (as a verb meaning *to attach or connect something to a solid base*), but it wouldn't be logical in the first.
Section: Vocabulary
Subsection: Multimeaning Words

13. a. Choice **a** is the correct answer. The word *Convicted* means *found guilty of a crime*. Choice **b** is incorrect. The word *Emancipated* means *liberated*. Choice **c** is incorrect. The word *Curtailed* means *limited*. Choice **d** is incorrect. The word *Independent* is an adjective meaning *self-governing*.
Section: Vocabulary
Subsection: Words in Context

14. a. Choice **a** is the correct answer. The word *heinous* is an adjective meaning *terrible or shockingly evil*. Choice **b** is incorrect. The word *harassed* means *bothered*. Choice **c** is incorrect. The word *trivial* is an adjective meaning *of little importance*. Choice **d** is incorrect. The word *irrelevant* is an adjective meaning *not pertaining* or *not applicable*.
Section: Vocabulary
Subsection: Words in Context

15. c. Choice **a** is incorrect. The word *faculties* means *a group of teachers or professors* or *powers of the body or mind*. Choice **b** is incorrect. The word *bunk* is a noun meaning *a built-in bed* or *a sleeping place*. Choice **c** is the correct answer. The word *facilities* is a noun meaning *places to house groups of people for a particular purpose*. Choice **d** is incorrect. Prisoners do not sleep in hotels.
Section: Vocabulary
Subsection: Words in Context

16. d. Choice **a** is incorrect. The word *implemented* means *put into use.* Choice **b** is incorrect. The word *inundated* means *overwhelmed by*. Choice **c** is incorrect. The word *irritable* is an adjective meaning *easily annoyed*. Choice **d** is the correct answer. The word *incarcerated* means *under the court's jurisdiction in a correctional facility*.
Section: Vocabulary
Subsection: Words in Context

17. d. Choice **a** is incorrect. The word *symbol* is a noun meaning *a letter, character, or figure representing something else*. Choice **b** is incorrect. The word *issue* does not fit. Choice **c** is incorrect. The word *catechism* is a noun meaning *a test or an overview, often of a religious nature, in the form of questions and specific answers*. Choice **d** is the correct answer. The word *genre* is a noun meaning *a certain type of literature or art*.
Section: Vocabulary
Subsection: Words in Context

18. **a.** Choice **a** is the correct answer. The verb *compose* means *write music*. Choice **b** is incorrect. The word *attribute* is a verb meaning *explain by indicating a cause or origin*. Choice **c** is incorrect. *Retorted* means *responded*. *Recorded* would have been a better choice. Choice **d** is incorrect. The word *discover* is a verb meaning *find*.
Section: Vocabulary
Subsection: Words in Context

19. **b.** Choice **a** is incorrect. The word *deduct* is a verb meaning *take away*. Choice **b** is the correct answer. The word *credit* is a verb meaning *give appropriate recognition or honor*. Choice **c** is incorrect. The word *charge* does not fit. Choice **d** is incorrect. The word *arrange* is a verb meaning *put in order*.
Section: Vocabulary
Subsection: Words in Context

20. **b.** Choice **a** is incorrect. The word *rescinded* means *taken back*. Choice **b** is the correct answer. The word *recalls* means *remind one of* or *revive*. Choice **c** is incorrect. The word *appoints* means *puts into place*. Choice **d** is incorrect. The word *create* is a verb meaning *cause to come into being*.
Section: Vocabulary
Subsection: Words in Context

Spelling

1. **a.** Choice **a** is the correct answer. Choice **b** is not a correct spelling. Choice **c** is not a correct spelling. Choice **d** is not a correct spelling.
Section: Spelling
Subsection: Consonants

2. **d.** Choice **a** is not a correct spelling. Choice **b** is not a correct spelling. Choice **c** is not a correct spelling. Choice **d** is the correct answer.
Section: Spelling
Subsection: Vowels

3. **c.** Choice **a** is not a correct spelling. Choice **b** is not a correct spelling. Choice **c** is the correct answer. Choice **d** is not a correct spelling.
Section: Spelling
Subsection: Vowels

4. **d.** Choice **a** is not a correct spelling. Choice **b** is not a correct spelling. Choice **c** is not a correct spelling. Choice **d** is the correct answer.
Section: Spelling
Subsection: Consonants

5. **b.** Choice **a** is not a correct spelling. Choice **b** is the correct answer. Choice **c** is not a correct spelling. Choice **d** is not a correct spelling.
Section: Spelling
Subsection: Vowels

6. **a.** Choice **a** is the correct answer. Choice **b** is not a correct spelling. Choice **c** is not a correct spelling. Choice **d** is not a correct spelling.
Section: Spelling
Subsection: Vowels

7. **c.** Choice **a** is not a correct spelling. Choice **b** is not a correct spelling. Choice **c** is the correct answer. Choice **d** is not a correct spelling.
Section: Spelling
Subsection: Consonants

8. **a.** Choice **a** is the correct answer. Choice **b** is not a correct spelling. Choice **c** is not a correct spelling. Choice **d** is not a correct spelling.
Section: Spelling
Subsection: Vowels

9. d. Choice **a** is not a correct spelling. Choice **b** is not a correct spelling. Choice **c** is not a correct spelling. Choice **d** is the correct answer.
Section: Spelling
Subsection: Structural Unit

10. d. Choice **a** is not a correct spelling. Choice **b** is not a correct spelling. Choice **c** is not a correct spelling. Choice **d** is the correct answer.
Section: Spelling
Subsection: Vowels

11. c. Choice **a** is a correct spelling. Choice **b** is a correct spelling. Choice **c** is the correct answer. This is NOT a correct spelling. The word should be spelled *knife*; the *k* is silent. Choice **d** is a correct spelling.
Section: Spelling
Subsection: Consonants

12. a. Choice **a** is the correct answer. This is NOT a correct spelling in the context of this sentence. A better word would be *residents*, which means *people who live in a particular place. Residence* means *a place where people live*. Choice **b** is a correct spelling. Choice **c** is a correct spelling. Choice **d** is a correct spelling.
Section: Spelling
Subsection: Structural Unit

13. c. Choice **a** is a correct spelling. Choice **b** is a correct spelling. Choice **c** is the correct answer. This is NOT a correct spelling. The correct spelling is *hurriedly*. Choice **d** is a correct spelling.
Section: Spelling
Subsection: Structural Unit

14. b. Choice **a** is a correct spelling. Choice **b** is the correct answer. This is NOT a correct spelling. To create the *–ing* form of *benefit*, just add *–ing*; don't double the *t*. That is because there is no accent on the last syllable of *benefit*. Choice **c** is a correct spelling. Choice **d** is a correct spelling.
Section: Spelling
Subsection: Structural Unit

15. c. Choice **a** is a correct spelling. Choice **b** is a correct spelling. Choice **c** is the correct answer. This is NOT a correct spelling. The word *surround* contains two *r*'s, not one. Choice **d** is a correct spelling.
Section: Spelling
Subsection: Consonants

16. a. Choice **a** is the correct answer. This is NOT a correct spelling. The word *participants* contains an *a*, not an *e*, as the last vowel. Choice **b** is a correct spelling. Choice **c** is a correct spelling. Choice **d** is a correct spelling.
Section: Spelling
Subsection: Structural Unit

17. b. Choice **a** is a correct spelling. Choice **b** is the correct answer. This is NOT a correct spelling in the context of this sentence. A better choice would be *leased*, which means *contracted a rental agreement. Least* has several meanings; one correct usage is in the following sentence: *At least he tried his best.* Choice **c** is a correct spelling. Choice **d** is a correct spelling.
Section: Spelling
Subsection: Structural Unit

18. d. Choice **a** is a correct spelling. Choice **b** is a correct spelling. Choice **c** is a correct spelling. Choice **d** is the correct answer. This is NOT a correct spelling. The word should be spelled *cautious.*
Section: Spelling
Subsection: Consonants

19. **a.** Choice **a** is the correct answer. This is NOT a correct spelling. The prefix *non-* that is connected to the root word *interested* should be replaced with the prefix *un-* to make *uninterested*. Choice **b** is a correct spelling. Choice **c** is a correct spelling. Choice **d** is a correct spelling.
Section: Spelling
Subsection: Structural Unit

20. **b.** Choice **a** is a correct spelling. Choice **b** is the correct answer. This is NOT a correct spelling. The vowel beginning the word should be an *e*: *embarrassed*. Choice **c** is a correct spelling. Choice **d** is a correct spelling.
Section: Spelling
Subsection: Vowels

Mathematics Computation

1. **a.** Choice **a** is the correct answer. To multiply signed integers, count the number of negatives. If there is an even number of negatives, the sign of the final answer will be positive. If there is an odd number of negatives, the sign of the final answer will be negative: $(-3)(7)(-4) = 84$. Choice **b** is incorrect. There are an even number of negatives, so $(-3)(7)(-4) = 84$. Choice **c** is incorrect. $(-3)(7)(-4) = 84$. Choice **d** is incorrect. $(-3)(7)(-4) = 84$.
Section: Integers
Subsection: Multiplication

2. **b.** Choice **a** is incorrect. $135 - 201 = -66$. Imagine the number line. Reading the expression from left to right, 135 is on the positive side. Because the operation is subtraction, move left along the number line 201 units. The result puts the final value on the negative side. Choice **b** is the correct answer. To subtract integers, subtract the smaller absolute value from the larger absolute value. The sign of the answer is the sign of the larger absolute value. $|-201| - |135| = 66$. Because -201 is the larger absolute value and its sign is negative, the sign of the final answer is also negative. $135 - 201 = -66$. Choice **c** is incorrect. $135 - 201 = -66$. Choice **d** is incorrect. $135 - 201 = -66$.
Section: Integers
Subsection: Subtraction

3. **d.** Choice **a** is incorrect. $-48 + (-110) + 27 = -131$. Choice **b** is incorrect. $-48 + (-110) + 27 = -131$. Choice **c** is incorrect. $-48 + (-110) + 27 = -159 + 27 = -131$. Negative 159 represents a deficit. The addition of 27 is not enough to overcome the deficit, so the final answer is given the negative sign. Choice **d** is the correct answer. Add terms with the same sign and keep their sign: $-48 + (-110) + 27 = -159 + 27$. Then, subtract the smaller absolute value from the larger absolute value. The sign of the answer is the sign of the number with the larger absolute value: $-159 + 27 = -131$.
Section: Integers
Subsection: Addition

4. c. Choice **a** is incorrect. $69,496 \div (-1,022) = -68$. Choice **b** is incorrect. $69,496 \div (-1,022) = -68$. The negative is missing in this choice. Choice **c** is the correct answer. Dividing two integers with different signs results in a negative answer. Divide the integers as usual, and assign the final answer the negative sign. Choice **d** is incorrect. $69,496 \div (-1,022) = -68$.
Section: Integers
Subsection: Division

5. c. Choice **a** is incorrect. $68° + 25° = 93°$. Choice **b** is incorrect. $68° + 25° = 93°$. Choice **c** is the correct answer. The temperature increased by 25°. This is addition: $68° + 25° = 93°$. Choice **d** is incorrect. $68° + 25° = 93°$.
Section: Integers
Subsection: Addition

6. c. Choice **a** is incorrect. $\$900 \div 12 = \$75$. Choice **b** is incorrect. $\$900 \div 12 = \$75$. Choice **c** is the correct answer. The total loan amount is $900, with payments spread out over one year. There are 12 months in a year. We must divide: $\$900 \div 12 = \$75$. Choice **d** is incorrect. $\$900 \div 12 = \$75$.
Section: Integers
Subsection: Division

7. b. Choice **a** is incorrect. $5,280 \times 13 = 68,640$. Choice **b** is the correct answer. For every mile, there are 5,280 feet. This is multiplication: $5,280 \times 13 = 68,640$. Choice **c** is incorrect. $5,280 \times 13 = 68,640$. Choice **d** is incorrect. $5,280 \times 13 = 68,640$.
Section: Integers
Subsection: Multiplication

8. c. Choice **a** is incorrect. $-37 - (-9) = -37 + 9 = -28$. Choice **b** is incorrect. $-37 - (-9) = -37 + 9 = -28$. Choice **c** is the correct answer. We are presented with a double negative, which converts to addition. Subtract the smaller absolute value from the greater absolute value. The sign of the answer is the sign of the larger absolute value: $-37 - (-9) = -37 + 9 = -28$. Choice **d** is incorrect. $-37 - (-9) = -37 + 9 = -28$. Negative 37 represents a deficit. Because the addition of 9 is not enough to overcome the deficit, the final result is given a negative sign.
Section: Integers
Subsection: Subtraction

9. d. Choice **a** is incorrect. $1\frac{3}{4} \times 3 = 5\frac{1}{4}$. Choice **b** is incorrect. $1\frac{3}{4} \times 3 = 5\frac{1}{4}$. Choice **c** is incorrect. $1\frac{3}{4} \times 3 = 5\frac{1}{4}$. Choice **d** is the correct answer. $1\frac{3}{4} \times 3 = 5\frac{1}{4}$. Convert the mixed number to an improper fraction, and multiply the numerators and denominators. Then, convert the answer back to a mixed number: $1\frac{3}{4} \times 3 = \frac{7}{4} \times \frac{3}{1} = \frac{21}{4} = 5\frac{1}{4}$.
Section: Fractions
Subsection: Multplication

10. d. Choice **a** is incorrect. $\frac{2}{3} + \frac{1}{4} = \frac{11}{12}$. Choice **b** is incorrect. $\frac{2}{3} + \frac{1}{4} = \frac{11}{12}$. Choice **c** is incorrect. $\frac{2}{3} + \frac{1}{4} = \frac{11}{12}$. Choice **d** is the correct answer. To add fractions, there must be a common denominator. The common denominator is 12. After converting each fraction to an equivalent fraction with denominator 12, add the numerators and keep the denominator: $\frac{2}{3} + \frac{1}{4} = \frac{8}{12} + \frac{3}{12} = \frac{11}{12}$.
Section: Fractions
Subsection: Addition

11. a. Choice **a** is the correct answer. To divide fractions, rewrite the expression as multiplication by keeping the first term and multiplying by the reciprocal of the second term. Then, multiply the numerators, and multiply the denominators: $\frac{4}{7} \div \frac{7}{8} = \frac{4}{7} \times \frac{8}{7} = \frac{32}{49}$. Choice **b** is incorrect. $\frac{4}{7} \div \frac{7}{8} = \frac{32}{49}$. Choice **c** is incorrect. $\frac{4}{7} \div \frac{7}{8} = \frac{32}{49}$. Choice **d** is incorrect. $\frac{4}{7} \div \frac{7}{8} = \frac{32}{49}$.

Section: Fractions

Subsection: Division

12. a. Choice **a** is the correct answer. The original piece of fabric measured $\frac{3}{4}$ yd. $\frac{1}{3}$ yd. is used, which indicates subtraction: $\frac{3}{4} - \frac{1}{3}$. To subtract fractions, find the least common denominator, LCD, and convert the original fractions to equivalent fractions with the LCD. Finally, subtract the numerators, and keep the LCD: $\frac{3}{4} - \frac{1}{3} = \frac{9}{12} - \frac{4}{12} = \frac{5}{12}$. Choice **b** is incorrect. $\frac{3}{4} - \frac{1}{3} = \frac{9}{12} - \frac{4}{12} = \frac{5}{12}$. Choice **c** is incorrect. $\frac{3}{4} - \frac{1}{3} = \frac{9}{12} - \frac{4}{12} = \frac{5}{12}$. Choice **d** is incorrect. $\frac{3}{4} - \frac{1}{3} = \frac{9}{12} - \frac{4}{12} = \frac{5}{12}$.

Section: Fractions

Subsection: Subtraction

13. c. Choice **a** is incorrect. $1\frac{3}{4} + \frac{5}{8} + 2\frac{1}{2} = 4\frac{7}{8}$. Choice **b** is incorrect. $1\frac{3}{4} + \frac{5}{8} + 2\frac{1}{2} = 4\frac{7}{8}$. Choice **c** is the correct answer. To find the total, we must add. Convert each mixed number to an improper fraction. Find the LCD, and convert the fractions to equivalent fractions with the LCD. Finally, add the numerators, keep the LCD, and convert the answer back to a mixed number: $1\frac{3}{4} + \frac{5}{8} + 2\frac{1}{2} = \frac{7}{4} + \frac{5}{8} + \frac{5}{2} = \frac{14}{8} + \frac{5}{8} + \frac{20}{8} = \frac{39}{8} = 4\frac{7}{8}$. Choice **d** is incorrect. $1\frac{3}{4} + \frac{5}{8} + 2\frac{1}{2} = 4\frac{7}{8}$.

Section: Fractions

Subsection: Addition

14. d. Choice **a** is incorrect. $2\frac{2}{9} \times 7\frac{1}{5} = 16$. Choice **b** is incorrect. $2\frac{2}{9} \times 7\frac{1}{5} = 16$. Choice **c** is incorrect. $2\frac{2}{9} \times 7\frac{1}{5} = 16$. Choice **d** is the correct answer. To multiply mixed numbers, first convert them to improper fractions: $2\frac{2}{9} \times 7\frac{1}{5} = \frac{20}{9} \times \frac{36}{5}$. Reduce before multiplying: $\frac{20}{9} \times \frac{36}{5} = \frac{4}{1} \times \frac{4}{1}$. Multiply the numerators and denominators: $\frac{4}{1} \times \frac{4}{1} = 16$.

Section: Fractions

Subsection: Multiplication

15. b. Choice **a** is incorrect. $1\frac{3}{5} \div 2\frac{2}{3} = \frac{3}{5}$. Choice **b** is the correct answer. To divide mixed numbers, first convert them to improper fractions: $1\frac{3}{5} \div 2\frac{2}{3} = \frac{8}{5} \div \frac{8}{3}$. Then, change the operation to multiplication. Keep the first term, and multiply by the reciprocal of the second term: $\frac{8}{5} \times \frac{3}{8}$. Reduce before multiplying: $\frac{1}{5} \times \frac{3}{1} = \frac{3}{5}$. Choice **c** is incorrect. $1\frac{3}{5} \div 2\frac{2}{3} = \frac{3}{5}$. Choice **d** is incorrect. $1\frac{3}{5} \div 2\frac{2}{3} = \frac{3}{5}$.

Section: Fractions

Subsection: Division

16. d. Choice **a** is incorrect. $3\frac{2}{3} - 1\frac{4}{5} = 1\frac{13}{15}$. Choice **b** is incorrect. $3\frac{2}{3} - 1\frac{4}{5} = 1\frac{13}{15}$. Choice **c** is incorrect. $3\frac{2}{3} - 1\frac{4}{5} = 1\frac{13}{15}$. Choice **d** is the correct answer. To subtract mixed numbers, convert them to improper fractions: $3\frac{2}{3} - 1\frac{4}{5} = \frac{11}{3} - \frac{9}{5}$. Find the LCD, and convert the fractions to equivalent fractions with the LCD: $\frac{11}{3} - \frac{9}{5} = \frac{55}{15} - \frac{27}{15}$. Finally, subtract the numerators, and keep the LCD. Convert the answer back to a mixed number: $\frac{55}{15} - \frac{27}{15} = \frac{28}{15} = 1\frac{13}{15}$.

Section: Fractions

Subsection: Subtraction

17. d. Choice **a** is incorrect. $9.02 × 16 hours (2 days at 8 hours/day) = $144.32. Choice **b** is incorrect. $9.02 × 16 hours (2 days at 8 hours/day) = $144.32. Choice **c** is incorrect. $9.02 × 16 hours (2 days at 8 hours/day) = $144.32. Choice **d** is the correct answer. $9.02 × 16 hours (2 days at 8 hours/day) = $144.32.
Section: Decimals
Subsection: Multiplication

18. b. Choice **a** is incorrect. 43.95 + 120.00 + 74.99 = 238.94. Choice **b** is the correct answer. To add decimals, write the numbers vertically with the decimal points lined up. You may insert zeros as necessary. Add as you would whole numbers, keeping the decimal point in your answer lined up with the decimal points in the problem: 43.95 + 120.00 + 74.99 = 238.94. Choice **c** is incorrect. 43.95 + 120.00 + 74.99 = 238.94. Choice **d** is incorrect. 43.95 + 120.00 + 74.99 = 238.94.
Section: Decimals
Subsection: Addition

19. b. Choice **a** is incorrect. 1,895.51 − 68.74 = 1,826.77. Choice **b** is the correct answer. To subtract decimals, write the numbers vertically with the decimal points lined up. Subtract as you would whole numbers, keeping the decimal point in your answer lined up with the decimal points in the problem: 1,895.51 − 68.74 = 1,826.77. Choice **c** is incorrect. 1,895.51 − 68.74 = 1,826.77. Choice **d** is incorrect. 1,895.51 − 68.74 = 1,826.77.
Section: Decimals
Subsection: Subtraction

20. a. Choice **a** is the correct answer. To add decimals, write the numbers vertically with the decimal points lined up. You may insert zeros as necessary at the end of a decimal so the same number of digits appear in each number. Add as you would whole numbers, keeping the decimal point in your answer lined up with the decimal points in the problem: 197.4 + 0.72 + 17.43 + 0.286 = 215.836. Choice **b** is incorrect. 197.4 + 0.72 + 17.43 + 0.286 = 215.836. Choice **c** is incorrect. 197.4 + 0.72 + 17.43 + 0.286 = 215.836. Choice **d** is incorrect. 197.4 + 0.72 + 17.43 + 0.286 = 215.836.
Section: Decimals
Subsection: Addition

21. d. Choice **a** is incorrect. 2.068 − (−38.7) = 40.768. Choice **b** is incorrect. 2.068 − (−38.7) = 40.768. The double negative that is present converts the operation to addition. Choice **c** is incorrect. 2.068 − (−38.7) = 40.768. Choice **d** is the correct answer. A double negative is present and converts the operation to addition: 2.068 + 38.7. Line up the decimal points, and add as you would whole numbers, keeping the decimal point in your answer lined up: 2.068 + 38.7 = 40.768.
Section: Decimals
Subsection: Subtraction

22. b. Choice **a** is incorrect. $1,381.93 ÷ 11 = $125.63. Choice **b** is the correct answer. Because Adam's total earnings are paid over 11 weeks, division is required to find the earnings for each week. To divide decimals, place a decimal point on the answer line that lines up with the dividend. Divide as you would whole numbers, keeping the decimal point in place. $11)\overline{1381.93}$ with quotient 125.63. Choice **c** is incorrect. $1,381.93 ÷ 11 = $125.63. Choice **d** is incorrect. $1,381.93 ÷ 11 = $125.63.
Section: Decimals
Substraction: Division

23. d. Choice **a** is incorrect. $0.00076 \times 0.009 = 0.00000684$. Choice **b** is incorrect. $0.00076 \times 0.009 = 0.00000684$. Choice **c** is incorrect. $0.00076 \times 0.009 = 0.00000684$. Choice **d** is the correct answer. To multiply decimals, multiply as you would whole numbers: $76 \times 9 = 684$. Count the number of decimal places from both terms. In this case, there are eight decimal places. Starting from the rightmost digit in your answer, count eight places to the left. Place the decimal point there, and fill in any blanks with zeros: $0.00076 \times 0.009 = 0.00000684$. This may also be expressed as 6.84×10^{-6}.
Section: Decimals
Substraction: Multiplication

24. c. Choice **a** is incorrect.
$\frac{6(2) - 12 \div 6}{2^3 + \sqrt{49}} = \frac{12 - 2}{8 + 7} = \frac{10}{15} = \frac{2}{3}$. Choice **b** is incorrect. $\frac{6(2) - 12 \div 6}{2^3 + \sqrt{49}} = \frac{12 - 2}{8 + 7} = \frac{10}{15} = \frac{2}{3}$.
Choice **c** is the correct answer. Following PEMDAS, any parentheses or other grouping are done first, followed by the exponents:
$\frac{6(2) - 12 \div 6}{2^3 + \sqrt{49}} = \frac{6(2) - 12 \div 6}{8 + 7}$. Next, all multiplications and divisions are done in the order in which numbers appear, left to right:
$\frac{6(2) - (12 \div 6)}{8 + 7} = \frac{12 - 2}{8 + 7}$. Finally, all additions and subtractions are done from left to right, and the resulting fraction is reduced:
$\frac{12-2}{8+7} = \frac{10}{15} = \frac{2}{3}$. Choice **d** is correct.
$\frac{6(2) - 12 \div 6}{2^3 + \sqrt{49}} = \frac{12 - 2}{8 + 7} = \frac{10}{15} = \frac{2}{3}$.
Section: Order of Operations
Subsection: Order of Operations

25. b. Choice **a** is incorrect. $7 + 3(5^2 + \sqrt{16}) - 49 = 45$. Choice **b** is the correct answer. By order of operations, PEMDAS, calculations are done inside the parenthesis first, then exponents, then multiplication and division, and lastly addition and subtraction.
$7 + 3(5^2 + \sqrt{16}) - 49 = 7 + 3(25 + 4) - 49 = 7 + 3(29) - 49 = 7 + 87 - 49 = 94 - 49 = 45$.
Choice **c** is incorrect. $7 + 3(5^2 + \sqrt{16}) - 49 = 45$. Choice **d** is incorrect. $7 + 3(5^2 + \sqrt{16}) - 49 = 45$.
Section: Order of Operations
Subsection: Order of Operations

26. c. Choice **a** is incorrect. $4 + 7(3 - 9) + 6(3^2) = 16$. Choice **b** is incorrect. $4 + 7(3 - 9) + 6(3^2) = 16$. Choice **c** is the correct answer. By order of operations, PEMDAS, work inside parentheses is done first, then multiplication and division from left to right, and finally addition and subtraction, in the order they appear, left to right: $4 + 7(3 - 9) + 6(3^2) = 4 + 7(-6) + 6(9) = 4 - 42 + 54 = -38 + 54 = 16$. Choice **d** is incorrect. $4 + 7(3 - 9) + 6(3^2) = 16$.
Section: Order of Operations
Subsection: Order of Operations

27. a. Choice **a** is the correct answer. To calculate the percent of a given number, multiply the number by the decimal equivalent of the percentage: $0.80 \times 125 = 100$. Choice **b** is incorrect. $0.80 \times 125 = 100$. Choice **c** is incorrect. $0.80 \times 125 = 100$. Choice **d** is incorrect. $0.80 \times 125 = 100$.
Section: Percents
Subsection: Percents

28. **b.** Choice **a** is incorrect. $72 \div 160 = 0.45 = 45\%$. Choice **b** is the correct answer. The statement can be translated into the following mathematical expression: $72 = 160x$, where x is the percent. Divide 72 by 160 to isolate x. The result is $x = 72 \div 160 = 0.45$. The decimal is then converted to a percentage: 45%. Choice **c** is incorrect. $72 \div 160 = 0.45 = 45\%$. Choice **d** is incorrect. $72 \div 160 = 0.45 = 45\%$.
Section: Percents
Subsection: Percents

29. **c.** Choice **a** is incorrect. $4.7 \div 0.01 = 470$. Choice **b** is incorrect. $4.7 \div 0.01 = 470$. Choice **c** is the correct answer. The statement can be translated into the following mathematical expression: $4.7 = 0.01x$, where x is the number being changed and 1% is converted to its decimal form. Divide 4.7 by 0.01 to isolate x. The result is $x = 4.7 \div 0.01 = 470$. Choice **d** is incorrect. $4.7 \div 0.01 = 470$.
Section: Percents
Subsection: Percents

30. **d.** Choice **a** is incorrect. $x = 6$ solves $4x - 4 = 20$. Choice **b** is incorrect. $x = 6$ solves $4x - 4 = 20$. Choice **c** is incorrect. $x = 6$ solves $4x - 4 = 20$. Choice **d** is the correct answer. To solve an equation, isolate the variable. Bring the constants to one side by adding 4 to both sides, and combine terms. Divide both sides by the coefficient on the variable:
$$4x - 4 + 4 = 20 + 4$$
$$4x = 24$$
$$x = 6$$
Section: Algebraic Operations
Subsection: Solve Equations

31. **c.** Choice **a** is incorrect. $x = 3$ solves $3x - 12 = 24 - 9x$. Choice **b** is incorrect. $x = 3$ solves $3x - 12 = 24 - 9x$. Choice **c** is the correct answer. To solve an equation, isolate the variable. Bring all x-variables to one side of the equal sign and all constants to the other side. Combine terms. Divide both sides by the coefficient on the variable:
$$3x + 9x - 12 = 24 - 9x + 9x$$
$$12x - 12 + 12 = 24 + 12$$
$$12x = 36$$
$$x = 3$$
Choice **d** is incorrect. $x = 3$ solves $3x - 12 = 24 - 9x$.
Section: Algebraic Operations
Subsection: Solve Equations

32. **c.** Choice **a** is incorrect. Only like terms can be added. Choice **b** is incorrect. Only like terms can be added. Choice **c** is the correct answer. Only the first two terms in the expression are like terms because they match both in variable and exponent. To combine, add the coefficients and keep the variable: $(4x^2 + 3x^2) + 2x = 7x^2 + 2x$. Choice **d** is incorrect. Only like terms can be added.
Section: Algebraic Operations
Subsection: Simplify Expressions

33. **b.** Choice **a** is incorrect. $\sqrt{36} + \sqrt{64} = 14$. Choice **b** is the correct answer. First, find the square root of each number. Then, add the results: $\sqrt{36} + \sqrt{64} = 6 + 8 = 14$. Choice **c** is incorrect. $\sqrt{36} + \sqrt{64} = 14$. Choice **d** is incorrect. $\sqrt{36} + \sqrt{64} = 14$.
Section: Algebraic Operations
Subsection: Computations with Roots

34. d. Choice **a** is incorrect. $4^3 + 3^4 = 145$. Choice **b** is incorrect. $4^3 + 3^4 = 145$. Choice **c** is incorrect. $4^3 + 3^4 = 145$. Choice **d** is the correct answer. Exponential notation is shorthand for repeated multiplication: $4^3 = (4)(4)(4) = 64$. The same is true for $3^4 = (3)(3)(3)(3) = 81$. So, $4^3 + 3^4 = 64 + 81 = 145$.
Section: Algebraic Operations
Subsection: Computations with Exponents

35. b. Choice **a** is incorrect. $-(4^2) + 2^3 + (-1)^4 = -7$. Choice **b** is the correct answer. Exponential notation is shorthand for repeated multiplication. However, the exponent applies only to what is directly in front of it. The negative on -4 is not squared, only the 4. The negative on -1 is taken to the fourth power because it is enclosed in the parentheses: $-(4^2) + 2^3 + (-1)^4 = -16 + 8 + 1 = -8 + 1 = -7$. Choice **c** is incorrect. $-(4^2) + 2^3 + (-1)^4 = -7$. Choice **d** is incorrect. $-(4^2) + 2^3 + (-1)^4 = -7$.
Section: Algebraic Operations
Subsection: Computations with Exponents

36. d. Choice **a** is incorrect. $\sqrt[3]{125} - \sqrt[5]{32} = 3$. Choice **b** is incorrect. $\sqrt[3]{125} - \sqrt[5]{32} = 3$. Choice **c** is incorrect. $\sqrt[3]{125} - \sqrt[5]{32} = 3$. Choice **d** is the correct answer. Roots $\sqrt[a]{y} = x$ can be rewritten as $x^a = y$. Find a value of x such that $x^3 = 125$ is satisfied, then again for $x^5 = 32$. $\sqrt[3]{125} - \sqrt[5]{32} = 5 - 2 = 3$.
Section: Algebraic Operations
Subsection: Computations with Roots

37. c. Choice **a** is incorrect. $3xy + 2x^2y + 5xy + 7x^2y = 8xy + 9x^2y$. Choice **b** is incorrect. $3xy + 2x^2y + 5xy + 7x^2y = 8xy + 9x^2y$. Choice **c** is the correct answer. To simplify an expression, combine like terms. Like terms must match in both variable and exponent. To combine like terms, add or subtract the coefficients, and keep the variable and exponent: $3xy + 2x^2y + 5xy + 7x^2y = (3xy + 5xy) + (2x^2y + 7x^2y) = 8xy + 9x^2y$. Choice **d** is incorrect. $3xy + 2x^2y + 5xy + 7x^2y = 8xy + 9x^2y$.
Section: Algebraic Operations
Subsection: Simplify Expression

38. b. Choice **a** is incorrect. $w = 3$ solves $6w + 2 = 5w - 4 + 9$. Choice **b** is the correct answer. To solve an equation, isolate the variable. Bring all w-variables to one side of the equal sign and all constants to the other, and combine terms. Divide both sides by the coefficient on the variable:
$$6w - 5w + 2 = 5w - 5w - 4 + 9$$
$$w + 2 - 2 = 5 - 2$$
$$w = 3$$
Choice **c** is incorrect. $w = 3$ solves $6w + 2 = 5w - 4 + 9$. Choice **d** is incorrect. $w = 3$ solves $6w + 2 = 5w - 4 + 9$.
Section: Algebraic Operations
Subsection: Solve Equations

39. a. Choice **a** is the correct answer. All terms of the expression inside the parentheses must be squared. To raise exponents to a power, multiply the exponents: $(4x^3y^5)^2 = 4^2(x^3)^2(y^5)^2 = 16x^6y^{10}$. Choice **b** is incorrect. $(4x^3y^5)^2 = 16x^6y^{10}$. Choice **c** is incorrect. $(4x^3y^5)^2 = 16x^6y^{10}$. Choice **d** is incorrect. $(4x^3y^5)^2 = 16x^6y^{10}$.
Section: Algebraic Operations
Subsection: Computations with Exponents

40. c. Choice **a** is incorrect. $-4(5y - 1) + 7y = -13y + 4$. Choice **b** is incorrect. $-4(5y - 1) + 7y = -13y + 4$. Choice **c** is the correct answer. Before combining like terms, distribute the -4. Then, combine the y-terms and the constants using the operation indicated: $-4(5y - 1) + 7y = -20y + 4 + 7y = (-20y + 7y) + 4 = -13y + 4$. Choice **d** is incorrect. $-4(5y - 1) + 7y = -13y + 4$.
Section: Algebraic Operations
Subsection: Simplify Expression

Applied Mathematics

1. b. Choice **a** is incorrect. $1,000 \times 200 = 200,000$. Choice **b** is the correct answer. In front-end rounding, the first digit is rounded and all other digits go to zero. Consider 987. To round 9, look to the digit directly right of it. Since 8 is larger than 5, 9 is rounded up to 10. Therefore, 987 rounds to 1,000. Now consider 215. To round 2, look to 1. Since it is less than 5, 2 remains 2, and 215 rounds to 200. Therefore, $1,000 \times 200 = 200,000$. Choice **c** is incorrect. $1,000 \times 200 = 200,000$. Choice **d** is incorrect. $1,000 \times 200 = 200,000$.
Section: Estimation
Subsection: Rounding

2. c. Choice **a** is incorrect. $300 - 700 = -400$. Choice **b** is incorrect. $300 - 700 = -400$. Choice **c** is the correct answer. In front-end rounding, the first digit is rounded and all other digits go to zero. Consider 311. To round 3, look to the digit directly right of it. Since 1 is less than 5, 3 remains 3. Therefore, 311 rounds to 300. Consider 658. To round 6, look to 5. Since it is five, 6 rounds to 7, and 658 rounds to 700. Therefore, $300 - 700 = -400$. Choice **d** is incorrect. $300 - 700 = -400$.
Section: Estimation
Subsection: Rounding

3. d. Choice **a** is incorrect. 13,715 rounds to 14,000. Choice **b** is incorrect. 13,715 rounds to 14,000. Choice **c** is incorrect. 13,715 rounds to 14,000. Choice **d** is the correct answer. For 13,715, the digit in the thousands place is 3. To round to the nearest thousand, look to the digit directly right of it. Since 7 is greater than 5, 3 is rounded up to 4, and all digits behind it go to zero. Therefore, 13,715 rounds to 14,000.
Section: Estimation
Subsection: Rounding

4. b. Choice **a** is incorrect. 427.5192 rounds to 427.52. Choice **b** is the correct answer. For 427.5192, the digit in the hundredths place is 1. To round to the nearest hundredths, look to the digit directly to the right of 1. Since 9 is greater than 5, 1 is rounded up to 2, and all digits behind it go to zero. Therefore, 427.5192 is rounded to 427.52. Choice **c** is incorrect. 427.5192 rounds to 427.52. Choice **d** is incorrect. 427.5192 rounds to 427.52.
Section: Estimation
Subsection: Rounding

5. b. Choice **a** is incorrect. $54,970 = 5.497 \times 104$. Choice **b** is the correct answer. To convert a number into scientific notation, move the decimal behind the leftmost non-zero digit, in this case behind 5. Multiply this number by a power of 10. The exponent on the power of 10 is the number of moves, in this case 4. If the original number was greater than 1, the exponent on 10 is positive. If the original number is a decimal less than 1, the exponent on 10 is negative. Thus, $54,970 = 5.497 \times 10^4$. Choice **c** is incorrect. $54,970 = 5.497 \times 10^4$. Choice **d** is incorrect. $54,970 = 5.497 \times 10^4$.
Section: Number and Number Operations
Subsection: Exponents, Scientific Notation

6. d. Choice **a** is incorrect. $x = 12$ solves the proportion $\frac{3}{950} = \frac{x}{3,800}$. Choice **b** is incorrect. $x = 12$ solves the proportion $\frac{3}{950} = \frac{x}{3,800}$. Choice **c** is incorrect. $x = 12$ solves the proportion $\frac{3}{950} = \frac{x}{3,800}$. Choice **d** is the correct answer. To solve, set up a proportion. The ratio of gallons of paint to surface covered is 3 to 950. The proportion is $\frac{3}{950} = \frac{x}{3,800}$. To solve the proportion, use cross multiplication: $3(3,800) = 950x$. Then solve for x: $x = \frac{11,400}{950} = 12$.
Section: Number and Number Operations
Subsection: Ratio, Proportion

7. d. Choice **a** is a ratio equivalent to $\frac{2}{3}$. $(2 \times 2):(2 \times 3) = 4:6$. Choice **b** is a decimal equivalent to $\frac{2}{3}$. $2 \div 3 = 0.\overline{6}$. Choice **c** is a percent equivalent to $\frac{2}{3}$. $(2 \div 3) \times 100\% = 67\frac{2}{3}\%$. Choice **d** is the correct answer. It is NOT equivalent to $\frac{2}{3}$.
Section: Number and Number Operations
Subsection: Equivalent Forms

8. c. Choice **a** is incorrect. $(4 \div 25) \times 100\% = 16\%$. Choice **b** is incorrect. $(4 \div 25) \times 100\% = 16\%$. Choice **c** is the correct answer. To convert a fraction into a percent, divide the numerator by the denominator then multiply the result by 100%: $(4 \div 25) \times 100\% = (0.16) \times 100\% = 16\%$. Choice **d** is incorrect. $(4 \div 25) \times 100\% = 16\%$.
Section: Number and Number Operations
Subsection: Percent

9. b. Choice **a** is incorrect. $0.33 \times 1,592 = 525.36$. Choice **b** is the correct answer. To find the percent of a given number, convert the percent to its decimal form, then multiply it by the number: $0.33 \times 1,592 = 525.36$. Choice **c** is incorrect. $0.33 \times 1,592 = 525.36$. Choice **d** is incorrect. $0.33 \times 1,592 = 525.36$.
Section: Number and Number Operations
Subsection: Percent

10. b. Choice **a** is incorrect. $1 + 5 + 2 + 1 + 1 + 3 = 13$ is not divisible by 3. Choice **b** is the correct answer. To determine if a given number is divisible by 3, add the digits of the number. If the sum is divisible by 3, then the original number is also divisible by 3. $1 + 5 + 4 + 3 + 2 + 0 = 15$, which is divisible by 3. Therefore, 154,320 is divisible by 3. Choice **c** is incorrect. $2 + 1 + 7 + 9 + 0 + 0 = 19$ is not divisible by 3. Choice **d** is incorrect. $3 + 2 + 1 + 8 + 0 + 6 = 20$ is not divisible by 3.
Section: Number and Number Operations
Subsection: Factors, Multiples, Divisibility

11. c. Choice **a** is incorrect. 2 is a factor, not a multiple, of the set. Choice **b** is incorrect. 14 is a factor, not a multiple, of the set. Choice **c** is the correct answer. To find the least common multiple, or LCM, for a set of values, first find the prime factorization of each value: $14 = 2 \times 7$; $28 = 2^2 \times 7$; $42 = 2 \times 3 \times 7$. Identify the prime numbers that appeared in each factorization, note the count of each prime, and choose the highest count. In this case, 2 has count two, 3 has count one, and 7 has count one. Multiply these primes with their counts to find the LCM: $2^2 \times 3 \times 7 = 84$. Choice **d** is incorrect. 168 is a multiple of the set, but it is not the least common multiple.
Section: Number and Number Operations
Subsection: Factors, Multiples, Divisibility

12. b. Choice **a** is incorrect. 2 is a factor, but it is not the greatest common factor. Choice **b** is the correct answer. To find the greatest common factor, or GCF, find the prime factorization of each value: $132 = 2^2 \times 3 \times 11$; $140 = 2^2 \times 5 \times 7$; $252 = 2^2 \times 3^2 \times 7$. Identify the factors that are common to all three numbers. In this case, the values only share $2^2 = 4$. Choice **c** is incorrect. 12 is not a factor of 140. Choice **d** is incorrect. 28 is not a factor of 132.
Section: Number and Number Operations
Subsection: Factors, Multiples, Divisibility

13. b. Choice **a** is incorrect. $4^3 + 7^2 + 3^0 = 64 + 49 + 1 = 114$. Choice **b** is the correct answer. Exponential notation is shorthand for repeated multiplication. However, when zero is in the exponent regardless of the base, the answer is one. $4^3 + 7^2 + 3^0 = (4 \times 4 \times 4) + (7 \times 7) + 1 = 64 + 49 + 1 = 114$. Choice **c** is incorrect. $4^3 + 7^2 + 3^0 = 64 + 49 + 1 = 114$. Choice **d** is incorrect. $4^3 + 7^2 + 3^0 = 64 + 49 + 1 = 114$.
Section: Number and Number Operations
Subsection: Exponents, Scientific Notation

14. d. Choice **a** is incorrect. $39 + 8 = 47$. Choice **b** is incorrect. $39 + 8 = 47$. Choice **c** is incorrect. $39 + 8 = 47$. Choice **d** is the correct answer. The pattern follows an arithmetic sequence. Each subsequent value is found by adding the same constant to the previous value. The constant for this sequence is 8. $7 + 8 = 15$; $15 + 8 = 23$; $23 + 8 = 31$; $31 + 8 = 39$; $39 + 8 = 47$.
Section: Patterns, Functions, Algebra
Subsection: Number Pattern

15. d. Choice **a** is incorrect. $3 + 5 = 8$. Choice **b** is incorrect. $3 + 5 = 8$. Choice **c** is incorrect. $3 + 5 = 8$. Choice **d** is the correct answer. The pattern is two-fold. The pattern for the shapes is circle, square, star. The mathematical pattern is found by adding the number of shapes from the previous two entries to determine the number of shapes for the next entry. The number of shapes from the last two entries is 3 and 5; therefore, $3 + 5 = 8$ stars.
Section: Patterns, Functions, Algebra
Subsection: Geometric Pattern

16. b. Choice **a** is incorrect. $2(2x + 5) - 3(x - 1) = 4x + 10 - 3x + 3 = x + 13$. Choice **b** is the correct answer. First clear the parentheses through distribution: $(2 \times 2x) + (2 \times 5) + (-3 \times x) + (-3 \times -1). = 4x + 10 - 3x + 3$. Then, combine like terms: $(4x - 3x) + (10 + 3) = x + 13$. Choice **c** is incorrect. $2(2x + 5) - 3(x - 1) = 4x + 10 - 3x + 3 = x + 13$. Choice **d** is incorrect. $2(2x + 5) - 3(x - 1) = 4x + 10 - 3x + 3 = x + 13$.
Section: Patterns, Functions, Algebra
Subsection: Variable, Expression, Equation

17. c. Choice **a** is incorrect. The inequality symbol is facing the wrong direction. Choice **b** is incorrect. The inequality symbol is facing the wrong direction, and the value must be negative. Choice **c** is the correct answer. To solve the inequality, isolate the variable. First, subtract 4 from both sides to obtain $-3x \geq -27$. Next, divide both sides by -3. Dividing an inequality by a negative value requires that the inequality symbol be flipped: $x \leq -9$. Choice **d** is incorrect. The value must be negative: $27 \div -3 = -9$.
Section: Patterns, Functions, Algebra
Subsection: Inequality

18. b. Choice **a** is incorrect. $y = 3(4) - 7 = 5$.
Choice **b** is the correct answer. Substitute
the value 4 for x in the given expression:
$y = 3(4) - 7 = 5$. Choice **c** is incorrect.
$y = 3(4) - 7 = 5$. Choice **d** is incorrect.
$y = 3(4) - 7 = 5$.
Section: Patterns, Functions, Algebra
Subsection: Linear Equation

19. c. Choice **a** is incorrect. $4 = (\frac{1}{2})(22) - 7$.
Choice **b** is incorrect. $4 = (\frac{1}{2})(22) - 7$.
Choice **c** is the correct answer. To find x,
first substitute $y = 4$ in the given equation:
$4 = \frac{1}{2}x - 7$. Then, isolate x by adding 7 to
both sides: $4 + 7 = \frac{1}{2}x - 7 + 7$. Finally,
multiply both sides by 2: $2(11) = (2)(\frac{1}{2})x$.
The answer is $x = 22$. Choice **d** is incorrect.
$4 = (\frac{1}{2})(22) - 7$.
Section: Patterns, Functions, Algebra
Subsection: Linear Equation

20. c. Choice **a** is incorrect. Perimeter $= 2L + 2W$
$= 2(6) + 2(8) = 28$ ft. Choice **b** is incorrect.
Perimeter $= 2L + 2W = 2(6) + 2(8) = 28$ ft.
Choice **c** is the correct answer. The fence
will run around the perimeter of the garden.
The formula for perimeter of a rectangle is
$2L + 2W$. $2(6) + 2(8) = 12 + 16 = 28$ ft.
Choice **d** is incorrect. Perimeter $= 2L + 2W$
$= 2(6) + 2(8) = 28$ ft.
Section: Measurement
Subsection: Perimeter

21. a. Choice **a** is the correct answer. Calculate the
area of the wall: 9 ft. × 12 ft. = 108 sq. ft.
Then, calculate the area of the door:
4 ft. × 7 ft. = 28 sq. ft. Since the door is not
being painted, subtract the area of the door
from the area of the wall: 108 − 28 = 80 sq.
ft. Choice **b** is incorrect. (9 ft. × 12 ft.) −
(4 ft. × 7 ft.) = 80 sq. ft. Choice **c** is
incorrect. (9 ft. × 12 ft.) − (4 ft. × 7 ft.) =
80 sq. ft. Choice **d** is incorrect. (9 ft. × 12 ft.)
− (4 ft. × 7 ft.) = 80 sq. ft.
Section: Measurement
Subsection: Area

22. c. Choice **a** is incorrect. The area of a circle =
$\pi r^2 = (3.14)(5^2) = 78.5$ sq. in. Choice **b** is
incorrect. The area of a circle $= \pi r^2 =$
$(3.14)(5^2) = 78.5$ sq. in. Choice **c** is the
correct answer. The area of a circle is πr^2,
which requires the radius. Because the
diameter was given, the radius is half that
value: $r = 5$. Thus $\pi r^2 = (3.14)(5^2) =$
$(3.14)(2^5) = 78.5$ sq. in. Choice **d** is
incorrect. The area of a circle $= \pi r^2 =$
$(3.14)(52) = 78.5$ sq. in.
Section: Measurement
Subsection: Area

23. b. Choice **a** is incorrect. The circumference of
a circle = $2\pi r = 2(3.14)(7) = 43.96$ in.
Choice **b** is the correct answer. The
circumference of a circle is $2\pi r$. So, $2\pi r =$
$2(3.14)(7) = 43.96$ in. Choice **c** is incorrect.
The circumference of a circle $= 2\pi r =$
$2(3.14)(7) = 43.96$ in. Choice **d** is incorrect.
The circumference of a circle $= 2\pi r =$
$2(3.14)(7) = 43.96$ in.
Section: Measurement
Subsection: Circumference

24. **c.** Choice **a** is incorrect. $75 \times 3 = 225$. Choice **b** is incorrect. $75 \times 3 = 225$. Choice **c** is the correct answer. Distance is found by multiplying rate and time: 75 miles per hour × 3 hours = 225 miles. Choice **d** is incorrect. $75 \times 3 = 225$.
Section: Measurement
Subsection: Length, Distance

25. **a.** Choice **a** is the correct answer. Distance = Rate × Time. Use this formula to find Rate. Isolate Rate by dividing both sides by Time: Rate = Distance ÷ Time. So, Rate = $6.5 \div 2$ = 3.25 mph. Choice **b** is incorrect. Rate = $6.5 \div 2 = 3.25$ mph. Choice **c** is incorrect. Rate = $6.5 \div 2 = 3.25$ mph. Choice **d** is incorrect. Rate = $6.5 \div 2 = 3.25$ mph.
Section: Measurement
Subsection: Rate

26. **d.** Choice **a** is incorrect. $(13)(8)(3) = 312$ cu. in. Choice **b** is incorrect. $(13)(8)(3) = 312$ cu. in. Choice **c** is incorrect. $(13)(8)(3) = 312$ cu. in. Choice **d** is the correct answer. The volume of a box is found by multiplying length, width, and depth. So, $(13)(8)(3) = 312$ cu. in.
Section: Measurement
Subsection: Volume

27. **c.** Choice **a** is incorrect. Substituting $(14,-2)$ in this equation yields a false statement. Choice **b** is incorrect. Substituting $(14,-2)$ in this equation yields a false statement. Choice **c** is the correct answer. Substitute $(14,-2)$ in the given equation. If it yields a true statement, then $(14,-2)$ is a solution.
$$-2 = (-\tfrac{1}{2})(14) + 5$$
$$-2 = -7 + 5$$
$$-2 = -2$$
Choice **d** is incorrect. Substituting $(14,-2)$ in this equation yields a false statement.
Section: Problem Solving and Reason
Subsection: Evaluate Solution

28. **c.** Choice **a** is incorrect. The correct equation is $(x + 13) + x = 145$. Choice **b** is incorrect. The correct equation is $(x + 13) + x = 145$. Choice **c** is the correct answer. Let x = Liliana's age. Marisa's age is defined by Liliana's age: $x + 13$. The sum of their ages is 145, so $(x + 13) + x = 145$. Choice **d** is incorrect. The correct equation is $(x + 13) + x = 145$.
Section: Problem Solving and Reason
Subsection: Model Problem Situation

29. **a.** Choice **a** is the correct answer. Let x = the amount in Zach's savings account. The amount in Alexandre's account is eight dollars less than three times the amount in Zach's, so $3x - 8$. We are also told that Alexandre's account has $427 in it. Set the two expressions equal to each other: $3x - 8 = 427$. Choice **b** is incorrect. The correct equation is $3x - 8 = 427$. Choice **c** is incorrect. The correct equation is $3x - 8 = 427$. Choice **d** is incorrect. The correct equation is $3x - 8 = 427$.
Section: Problem Solving and Reason
Subsection: Model Problem Situation

30. **b.** Choice **a** is incorrect. $x = 11$ solves $2(x + 10) = 42$. Choice **b** is the correct answer. To solve the problem, first create an equation that models the situation: $2(x + 10) = 42$. Then isolate the variable, x.
$$2x + 20 = 42$$
$$2x + 20 - 20 = 42 - 20$$
$$2x = 22$$
$$2x \div 2 = 22 \div 2$$
$$x = 11$$
Choice **c** is incorrect. $x = 11$ solves $2(x + 10) = 42$. Choice **d** is incorrect. $x = 11$ solves $2(x + 10) = 42$.
Section: Problem Solving and Reason
Subsection: Solve Problem

31. **d.** Choice **a** is incorrect. $x = 4$ solves $5x - 12 = 2x$. Choice **b** is incorrect. $x = 4$ solves $5x - 12 = 2x$. Choice **c** is incorrect. $x = 4$ solves $5x - 12 = 2x$. Choice **d** is the correct answer. To solve the problem, first create an equation that models the situation: $5x - 12 = 2x$. Then isolate the variable, x.

$$5x - 2x - 12 = 2x - 2x$$
$$3x - 12 + 12 = 0 + 12$$
$$3x = 12$$
$$x = 4$$

Section: Problem Solving and Reason
Subsection: Solving Problems

32. **a.** Choice **a** is the correct answer. Olivia's base salary is $250. Her commission is the amount she will receive in addition to her base salary: base + commission. Her commission is calculated on sales *over* $1,500. To find the commission, first subtract $1,500 from her sales of $3,500: $3,500 - $1,500 = $2,000. Olivia will receive 5% of this amount. To find her total earnings, add the calculated commission to her base salary: $250 + (0.05 \times \$2,000) = $250 + $100 = $350. Choice **b** is incorrect. $250 + (0.05 \times \$2,000) = $250 + $100 = $350. Choice **c** is incorrect. $250 + (0.05 \times \$2,000) = $250 + $100 = $350. Choice **d** is incorrect. $250 + (0.05 \times \$2,000) = $250 + $100 = $350.

Section: Computation in Context
Subsection: Percents

33. **a.** Choice **a** is the correct answer. To find the new price, first find the dollar amount of the discount. Multiply the regular price by the decimal form of 30%: $75 \times 0.30 = $22.50. Next, subtract the discount amount from the regular price: $75 - $22.50 = $52.50. Choice **b** is incorrect. $75 - $22.50 = $52.50. Choice **c** is incorrect. $75 - $22.50 = $52.50. Choice **d** is incorrect. $75 - $22.50 = $52.50.

Section: Computation in Context
Subsection: Percents

34. **b.** Choice **a** is incorrect. ($672 - $53.76) \div 2 = $309.12. Choice **b** is the correct answer. To solve, first find 8% of $672: $672 \times 0.08 = $53.76. Next, subtract this amount from the total earnings: $672 - $53.76 = $618.24. Finally, divide the adjusted amount by two: $618.24 \div 2 = $309.12. Choice **c** is incorrect. ($672 - $53.76) \div 2 = $309.12. Choice **d** is incorrect. ($672 - $53.76) \div 2 = $309.12.

Section: Computation in Context
Subsection: Percents

35. **b.** Choice **a** is incorrect. $36(\frac{4}{3}) = 48$. Choice **b** is the correct answer. To solve the problem, first create an equation that models the situation. Let $x = $ number of students trying out for soccer: $\frac{3}{4}x = 36$. Isolate the variable, x, by multiplying both sides by $\frac{4}{3}$: $(\frac{3}{4})(\frac{4}{3})x = 36(\frac{4}{3})$. Therefore, $x = 48$. Choice **c** is incorrect. $36(\frac{4}{3}) = 48$. Choice **d** is incorrect. $36(\frac{4}{3}) = 48$.

Section: Computation in Context
Subsection: Fractions

36. a. Choice **a** is the correct answer. To solve, first find $\frac{1}{3}$ of 75: $(\frac{1}{3})(75) = 25$. Then, find $\frac{2}{5}$ of the result: $(\frac{2}{5})(25) = 10$. Choice **b** is incorrect. $(\frac{1}{3})(75)(\frac{2}{5}) = 10$. Choice **c** is incorrect. $(\frac{1}{3})(75)(\frac{2}{5}) = 10$. Choice **d** is incorrect. $(\frac{1}{3})(75)(\frac{2}{5}) = 10$.

Section: Computation in Context

Subsection: Fractions

37. c. Choice **a** is incorrect. $(\frac{7}{10})(120) = 84$. Choice **b** is incorrect. $(\frac{7}{10})(120) = 84$. Choice **c** is the correct answer. If $\frac{3}{10}$ of dinner sales are menu orders, then $\frac{7}{10}$ of sales come from buffet orders. Therefore, find $\frac{7}{10}$ of 120: $(\frac{7}{10})(120) = 84$. Choice **d** is incorrect. $(\frac{7}{10})(120) = 84$.

Section: Computation in Context

Subsection: Fractions

38. b. Choice **a** is incorrect. Line graphs are best for displaying changes in data over time. Choice **b** is the correct answer. Bar graphs are best for displaying results in categories. Choice **c** is incorrect. Circle graphs are best for displaying data as percentages. Choice **d** is incorrect. Stem-and-leaf plots are best for displaying data as ordered lists.

Section: Data Analysis

Subsection: Appropriate Data Display

39. b. Choice **a** is incorrect. The lowest temperature was 64°, recorded on June 5. Choice **b** is the correct answer. Find the lowest point on the graph. It falls between 60° and 65° on June 5. Since it occurs closer to 65° but not on 65°, it is fair to estimate 64°. Choice **c** is incorrect. The lowest temperature was 64°, recorded on June 5. Choice **d** is incorrect. The lowest temperature was 64°, recorded on June 5.

Section: Data Analysis

Subsection: Bar, Line, Circle Graph

40. d. Choice **a** is incorrect. Chocolate received less votes than vanilla. Choice **b** is incorrect. Chocolate chip mint received less votes than vanilla. Choice **c** is incorrect. Strawberry received less votes than vanilla. Choice **d** is correct. Vanilla received 42% of the votes, more than any other category in the circle graph.

Section: Data Analysis

Subsection: Bar, Line, Circle Graph

41. a. Choice **a** is the correct answer. Find "Boots" in the first column, and identify the count in the corresponding column. Lydia owns four pair of boots. Choice **b** is incorrect. Lydia owns five pairs of heels. Choice **c** is incorrect. Lydia owns seven pairs of sandals. Choice **d** is incorrect. Lydia owns eight pairs of casual shoes.

Section: Data Analysis

Subsection: Table, Chart, Diagram

42. a. Choice **a** is the correct answer. Locate the column for Tacoma. To find the mean, add the wages listed in the column, then divide that sum by four: $\frac{\$13 + \$15 + \$15 + \$16}{4} = \frac{\$59}{4}$ $= \$14.75$. Choice **b** is incorrect. $\frac{\$13 + \$15 + \$15 + \$16}{4} = \frac{\$59}{4} = \$14.75$. Choice **c** is incorrect. $\frac{\$13 + \$15 + \$15 + \$16}{4} = \frac{\$59}{4} = \$14.75$. Choice **d** is incorrect. $\frac{\$13 + \$15 + \$15 + \$16}{4} = \frac{\$59}{4}$ $= \$14.75$.

Section: Data Analysis

Subsection: Conclusions from Data

43. a. Choice **a** is the correct answer. To calculate a probability, we find the number of possible outcomes for the desired event and divide it by the number of all possible outcomes. In this case, there are three possible outcomes of drawing a red marble and 15 total possible outcomes. Thus, $\frac{3}{15}$ is the resulting fraction. Once the fraction is simplified, the probability of drawing a red marble is $\frac{1}{5}$. Choice **b** is incorrect. There are 15 total possible outcomes, not 14. Choice **c** is incorrect. There are 15 total possible outcomes, not five. Choice **d** is incorrect. There are three red marbles and 15 total possible outcomes.
Section: Statistics and Probability
Subsection: Probability

44. b. Choice **a** is incorrect. The probability is $\frac{3}{8}$. Choice **b** is the correct answer. To calculate a probability, we find the number of possible outcomes for the desired event and divide it by the number of all possible outcomes. Consider all the possible outcomes of three tosses: HHH, HHT, HTH, HTT, THH, THT, TTH, TTT. There are three outcomes that have two heads and eight total outcomes. Thus, the probability that two tosses will come up heads is $\frac{3}{8}$. Choice **c** is incorrect. The probability is $\frac{3}{8}$. Choice **d** is incorrect. The probability is $\frac{3}{8}$.
Section: Statistics and Probability
Subsection: Probability

45. b. Choice **a** is incorrect. $(69 + 75 + 80 + 75 + 91) \div 5 = 390 \div 5 = 78$. Choice **b** is the correct answer. The mean is found by adding all the given values, then dividing the sum by the number of values: $(69 + 75 + 80 + 75 + 91) \div 5 = 390 \div 5 = 78$. Choice **c** is incorrect. $(69 + 75 + 80 + 75 + 91) \div 5 = 390 \div 5 = 78$. Choice **d** is incorrect. $(69 + 75 + 80 + 75 + 91) \div 5 = 390 \div 5 = 78$.
Section: Statistics and Probability
Subsection: Statistics

46. a. Choice **a** is the correct answer. The median is found by first ordering the values, then identifying the middle. If no true middle exists, as in this case, add the two most middle values, and divide by two. 15, 21, 27, 33, 46, 58. The two middle values are 27 and 33. So, $(27 + 33) \div 2 = 60 \div 2 = 30$. Choice **b** is incorrect. $(27 + 33) \div 2 = 60 \div 2 = 30$. Choice **c** is incorrect. $(27 + 33) \div 2 = 60 \div 2 = 30$. Choice **d** is incorrect. $(27 + 33) \div 2 = 60 \div 2 = 30$.
Section: Statistics and Probability
Subsection: Statistics

47. b. Choice **a** is incorrect. An angle is made up of two rays that share an endpoint. Choice **b** is the correct answer. This is the definition of a ray. Choice **c** is incorrect. A segment is part of a line that starts and stops at distinct points. Choice **d** is incorrect. A plane is a flat, smooth surface that extends indefinitely in all directions.
Section: Geometry and Spatial Sense
Subsection: Point, Ray, Line, Plane

48. d. Choice **a** is incorrect. $\frac{3-7}{-4-2} = \frac{-4}{-6} = \frac{2}{3}$. Choice **b** is incorrect. $\frac{3-7}{-4-2} = \frac{-4}{-6} = \frac{2}{3}$. Choice **c** is incorrect. $\frac{3-7}{-4-2} = \frac{-4}{-6} = \frac{2}{3}$. Choice **d** is the correct answer. Slope is found by dividing the difference of the y-values by the difference of the x-values. It's important to keep the order in which the values are listed. For this example, $(-4,3)$ will be the first values listed: $\frac{3-7}{-4-2} = \frac{-4}{-6} = \frac{2}{3}$.
Section: Geometry and Spatial Sense
Subsection: Coordinate Geometry

49. d. Choice **a** is incorrect. An arc refers to a section of the circle's circumference. Choice **b** is incorrect. The radius is a straight line segment that extends from the center of a circle to a point on the circle. It is half the diameter. Choice **c** is incorrect. The circumference is the perimeter of the circle. Choice **d** is the correct answer. The diameter is a straight line segment that extends from a point on the circle through the center to another point on the circle.
Section: Geometry and Spatial Sense
Subsection: Parts of a Circle

50. c. Choice **a** is incorrect. The coordinates of each vertex must be multiplied by two. Choice **b** is incorrect. The coordinates of each vertex must be multiplied by two. Choice **c** is the correct answer. To dilate any shape, multiply each coordinate of the vertices by the given factor: $P(0,3) = (0 \times 2, 3 \times 2) = (0,6)$; $Q(4,3) = (4 \times 2, 3 \times 2) = (8,6)$; $R(4,0) = (4 \times 2, 0 \times 2) = (8,0)$; $S(4,0) = (4 \times 2, 0 \times 2) = (8,0)$. Choice **d** is incorrect. The coordinates of each vertex must be multiplied by two.
Section: Geometry and Spatial Sense
Subsection: Transformations

CHAPTER 4

PRACTICE EXAM 2

This practice exam for TABE 9 & 10 for Level A is a paper-and-pencil version of the computer-based exam you will see on test day. It mirrors the actual TABE exam in testing level, content, and topics covered.

This practice test contains the complete battery of 255 questions and answers for the four main and three optional areas on the TABE: **Reading, Mathematics Computation, Applied Mathematics, Language, Language Mechanics, Vocabulary,** and **Spelling**.

The tests in this book will show you how much you know and what kinds of problems you still need to study. Mastering these practice tests will allow you to reach your highest potential on the real TABE.

Reading

1. a b c d
2. a b c d
3. a b c d
4. a b c d
5. a b c d
6. a b c d
7. a b c d
8. a b c d
9. a b c d
10. a b c d
11. a b c d
12. a b c d
13. a b c d
14. a b c d
15. a b c d
16. a b c d
17. a b c d
18. a b c d
19. a b c d
20. a b c d
21. a b c d
22. a b c d
23. a b c d
24. a b c d
25. a b c d
26. a b c d
27. a b c d
28. a b c d
29. a b c d
30. a b c d
31. a b c d
32. a b c d
33. a b c d
34. a b c d
35. a b c d
36. a b c d
37. a b c d
38. a b c d
39. a b c d
40. a b c d
41. a b c d
42. a b c d
43. a b c d
44. a b c d
45. a b c d
46. a b c d
47. a b c d
48. a b c d
49. a b c d
50. a b c d

Language

1. a b c d
2. a b c d
3. a b c d
4. a b c d
5. a b c d
6. a b c d
7. a b c d
8. a b c d
9. a b c d
10. a b c d
11. a b c d
12. a b c d
13. a b c d
14. a b c d
15. a b c d
16. a b c d
17. a b c d
18. a b c d
19. a b c d
20. a b c d
21. a b c d
22. a b c d
23. a b c d
24. a b c d
25. a b c d
26. a b c d
27. a b c d
28. a b c d
29. a b c d
30. a b c d
31. a b c d
32. a b c d
33. a b c d
34. a b c d
35. a b c d
36. a b c d
37. a b c d
38. a b c d
39. a b c d
40. a b c d
41. a b c d
42. a b c d
43. a b c d
44. a b c d
45. a b c d
46. a b c d
47. a b c d
48. a b c d
49. a b c d
50. a b c d
51. a b c d
52. a b c d
53. a b c d
54. a b c d
55. a b c d

Language Mechanics

1.	a	b	c	d
2.	a	b	c	d
3.	a	b	c	d
4.	a	b	c	d
5.	a	b	c	d
6.	a	b	c	d
7.	a	b	c	d

8.	a	b	c	d
9.	a	b	c	d
10.	a	b	c	d
11.	a	b	c	d
12.	a	b	c	d
13.	a	b	c	d
14.	a	b	c	d

15.	a	b	c	d
16.	a	b	c	d
17.	a	b	c	d
19.	a	b	c	d
20.	a	b	c	d

Vocabulary

1.	a	b	c	d
2.	a	b	c	d
3.	a	b	c	d
4.	a	b	c	d
5.	a	b	c	d
6.	a	b	c	d
7.	a	b	c	d

8.	a	b	c	d
9.	a	b	c	d
10.	a	b	c	d
11.	a	b	c	d
12.	a	b	c	d
13.	a	b	c	d
14.	a	b	c	d

15.	a	b	c	d
16.	a	b	c	d
17.	a	b	c	d
19.	a	b	c	d
20.	a	b	c	d

Spelling

1.	a	b	c	d
2.	a	b	c	d
3.	a	b	c	d
4.	a	b	c	d
5.	a	b	c	d
6.	a	b	c	d
7.	a	b	c	d

8.	a	b	c	d
9.	a	b	c	d
10.	a	b	c	d
11.	a	b	c	d
12.	a	b	c	d
13.	a	b	c	d
14.	a	b	c	d

15.	a	b	c	d
16.	a	b	c	d
17.	a	b	c	d
19.	a	b	c	d
20.	a	b	c	d

Mathematics Computation

1.	ⓐ	ⓑ	ⓒ	ⓓ	15.	ⓐ	ⓑ	ⓒ	ⓓ	29.	ⓐ	ⓑ	ⓒ	ⓓ
2.	ⓐ	ⓑ	ⓒ	ⓓ	16.	ⓐ	ⓑ	ⓒ	ⓓ	30.	ⓐ	ⓑ	ⓒ	ⓓ
3.	ⓐ	ⓑ	ⓒ	ⓓ	17.	ⓐ	ⓑ	ⓒ	ⓓ	31.	ⓐ	ⓑ	ⓒ	ⓓ
4.	ⓐ	ⓑ	ⓒ	ⓓ	18.	ⓐ	ⓑ	ⓒ	ⓓ	32.	ⓐ	ⓑ	ⓒ	ⓓ
5.	ⓐ	ⓑ	ⓒ	ⓓ	19.	ⓐ	ⓑ	ⓒ	ⓓ	33.	ⓐ	ⓑ	ⓒ	ⓓ
6.	ⓐ	ⓑ	ⓒ	ⓓ	20.	ⓐ	ⓑ	ⓒ	ⓓ	34.	ⓐ	ⓑ	ⓒ	ⓓ
7.	ⓐ	ⓑ	ⓒ	ⓓ	21.	ⓐ	ⓑ	ⓒ	ⓓ	35.	ⓐ	ⓑ	ⓒ	ⓓ
8.	ⓐ	ⓑ	ⓒ	ⓓ	22.	ⓐ	ⓑ	ⓒ	ⓓ	36.	ⓐ	ⓑ	ⓒ	ⓓ
9.	ⓐ	ⓑ	ⓒ	ⓓ	23.	ⓐ	ⓑ	ⓒ	ⓓ	37.	ⓐ	ⓑ	ⓒ	ⓓ
10.	ⓐ	ⓑ	ⓒ	ⓓ	24.	ⓐ	ⓑ	ⓒ	ⓓ	38.	ⓐ	ⓑ	ⓒ	ⓓ
11.	ⓐ	ⓑ	ⓒ	ⓓ	25.	ⓐ	ⓑ	ⓒ	ⓓ	39.	ⓐ	ⓑ	ⓒ	ⓓ
12.	ⓐ	ⓑ	ⓒ	ⓓ	26.	ⓐ	ⓑ	ⓒ	ⓓ	40.	ⓐ	ⓑ	ⓒ	ⓓ
13.	ⓐ	ⓑ	ⓒ	ⓓ	27.	ⓐ	ⓑ	ⓒ	ⓓ					
14.	ⓐ	ⓑ	ⓒ	ⓓ	28.	ⓐ	ⓑ	ⓒ	ⓓ					

Applied Mathematics

1.	ⓐ	ⓑ	ⓒ	ⓓ	18.	ⓐ	ⓑ	ⓒ	ⓓ	35.	ⓐ	ⓑ	ⓒ	ⓓ
2.	ⓐ	ⓑ	ⓒ	ⓓ	19.	ⓐ	ⓑ	ⓒ	ⓓ	36.	ⓐ	ⓑ	ⓒ	ⓓ
3.	ⓐ	ⓑ	ⓒ	ⓓ	20.	ⓐ	ⓑ	ⓒ	ⓓ	37.	ⓐ	ⓑ	ⓒ	ⓓ
4.	ⓐ	ⓑ	ⓒ	ⓓ	21.	ⓐ	ⓑ	ⓒ	ⓓ	38.	ⓐ	ⓑ	ⓒ	ⓓ
5.	ⓐ	ⓑ	ⓒ	ⓓ	22.	ⓐ	ⓑ	ⓒ	ⓓ	39.	ⓐ	ⓑ	ⓒ	ⓓ
6.	ⓐ	ⓑ	ⓒ	ⓓ	23.	ⓐ	ⓑ	ⓒ	ⓓ	40.	ⓐ	ⓑ	ⓒ	ⓓ
7.	ⓐ	ⓑ	ⓒ	ⓓ	24.	ⓐ	ⓑ	ⓒ	ⓓ	41.	ⓐ	ⓑ	ⓒ	ⓓ
8.	ⓐ	ⓑ	ⓒ	ⓓ	25.	ⓐ	ⓑ	ⓒ	ⓓ	42.	ⓐ	ⓑ	ⓒ	ⓓ
9.	ⓐ	ⓑ	ⓒ	ⓓ	26.	ⓐ	ⓑ	ⓒ	ⓓ	43.	ⓐ	ⓑ	ⓒ	ⓓ
10.	ⓐ	ⓑ	ⓒ	ⓓ	27.	ⓐ	ⓑ	ⓒ	ⓓ	44.	ⓐ	ⓑ	ⓒ	ⓓ
11.	ⓐ	ⓑ	ⓒ	ⓓ	28.	ⓐ	ⓑ	ⓒ	ⓓ	45.	ⓐ	ⓑ	ⓒ	ⓓ
12.	ⓐ	ⓑ	ⓒ	ⓓ	29.	ⓐ	ⓑ	ⓒ	ⓓ	46.	ⓐ	ⓑ	ⓒ	ⓓ
13.	ⓐ	ⓑ	ⓒ	ⓓ	30.	ⓐ	ⓑ	ⓒ	ⓓ	47.	ⓐ	ⓑ	ⓒ	ⓓ
14.	ⓐ	ⓑ	ⓒ	ⓓ	31.	ⓐ	ⓑ	ⓒ	ⓓ	48.	ⓐ	ⓑ	ⓒ	ⓓ
15.	ⓐ	ⓑ	ⓒ	ⓓ	32.	ⓐ	ⓑ	ⓒ	ⓓ	49.	ⓐ	ⓑ	ⓒ	ⓓ
16.	ⓐ	ⓑ	ⓒ	ⓓ	33.	ⓐ	ⓑ	ⓒ	ⓓ	50.	ⓐ	ⓑ	ⓒ	ⓓ
17.	ⓐ	ⓑ	ⓒ	ⓓ	34.	ⓐ	ⓑ	ⓒ	ⓓ					

Reading

Phil Harmeson, a professor with the University of North Dakota, was noted for saying the following in a 2004 essay. Read what Harmeson said and then complete questions 1–5.

"Education is essential in a Constitutional government, and it needs to be supported adequately. An adequate education includes developing an understanding of our government system, our economic system, basic skills in the 3Rs, completion of a high school education, and an educational foundation to successfully matriculate in post-secondary or higher education and/or achieve occupational proficiency."

1. Based on an understanding of the quote, the word *adequate* could also mean _____.
   a. extensive
   b. superior
   c. understandable
   d. satisfactory

2. The reference to the 3Rs would logically NOT include which of the following?
   a. Reading
   b. Writing
   c. Science
   d. Arithmetic

3. After reading this quote, one would conclude Phil Harmeson could best be considered as a(n) _____ of formal education in America.
   a. proponent
   b. opponent
   c. adversary
   d. martyr

4. The last line of the quote reads, "successfully matriculate in post-secondary or higher education. . . ." The word *matriculate* means
   a. study.
   b. establish.
   c. examine.
   d. join with.

5. This quote would most likely NOT appear in which of the following publications?
   a. school journal
   b. newspaper
   c. memorandum
   d. textbook for an English or education studies class

Read the following passage and answer the questions that follow.

For decades, many archaeologists have held that people first arrived in this hemisphere between 12,000 and 20,000 years ago. During this period, the Earth underwent one of its periodic ice ages. Vast amounts of water froze into glaciers, and as a result, the depths of the oceans dropped as much as 200 to 300 feet (about 60 to 90 meters). Underwater ridges were exposed and formed land bridges, linking some continents and islands. As the glaciers advanced southward, ice covered large areas of North America, Europe, and Asia. People and animals were then forced to migrate in search of food and warmer climates.

Experts who adhere to this theory believe that a land bridge perhaps 1,000 miles (1,600 kilometers) wide connected Asia and North America during this period. According to these experts, herds of animals moved eastward across the bridge, and Asian hunters followed, tracking them throughout North and South America. When the climate warmed again, the glaciers melted and the oceans rose. Water that today forms the Bering Strait then covered the land bridge, ending the migration. To prove this theory, scientists have traditionally used the carbon-14 test, a method for determining the age of plant and animal remains.

6. Why does the writer list numeric values in different formats (for example, feet/meters and miles/kilometers) throughout the passage?
   a. for political correctness
   b. for mathematically-inclined readers
   c. to sound more professional
   d. to appeal to a broader audience

7. According to the passage, compared to approximately 15,000 years ago, the oceans of the world today are _____.
   a. deeper
   b. shallower
   c. approximately the same depth
   d. immeasurable

8. What word given in the passage might lead the reader to come to the conclusion that some of the ideas in the passage are a mixture of facts and opinions?
   a. theory
   b. warmer
   c. periodic
   d. migrate

9. Based on the reading of this passage, one might predict that had the glaciers not moved south
   a. the continents of North America, Europe, and Asia would have been forever destroyed.
   b. weather climates would never have changed.
   c. many people would have stayed in North America, Europe, and Asia.
   d. weather studies would never have advanced.

10. The author's intention by using the phrase *vast amounts* was to indicate that
   a. the area affected by the glacial melting was overwhelmingly large.
   b. scientists could not really measure how much land was affected.
   c. this was only a theory.
   d. the area's temperature could not be measured.

Read the following passage and answer questions 11–15 that follow.

Surgeon General's Report on Smoking
Few government reports have had the drama or impact of the one that was delivered on January 11, 1964, in the auditorium of the Old State Department Building in Washington, D.C.

On that Saturday morning, a day carefully chosen to make headlines in all the big Sunday newspapers, Surgeon General Luther Terry told the nation that "cigarette smoking is a health hazard of sufficient importance … to warrant appropriate remedial action." In other words, it was time to do something about smoking.

Although the basic facts about smoking and health had been known for some time, the federal government kept shying away from this issue. Not until 1962 did President John F. Kennedy decide that the government should study the problem. Kennedy asked Terry, the nation's chief health officer, to select an expert committee that would decide, simply, "Is smoking bad?"

Terry and ten people chosen from leading universities worked like prairie dogs, burrowing into stacks of research files stored underground in the basement of the National Library of Medicine in Bethesda, Maryland. After 14 months of study, the committee issued a

150,000-word report that made the following points:

- Cigarette smoking "contributes substantially to mortality"; that is, smoking can kill you.
- Cigarette smokers have a death rate almost 11 times higher than nonsmokers. The sharpest risk from smoking is lung cancer.
- It helps to quit smoking.

As a result of Terry's report, the major TV networks decided to reexamine their advertising policies. Within a few years, smoking ads disappeared from the nation's television screens. Later, the government required cigarette makers to display warning messages on their ads and packages. The number of smokers in the United States began to decline. However, it would have been very difficult to change attitudes without the surgeon general's chilling announcement.

11. Based on the passage, the author's main reason for writing this article was to
   a. show the dangers of cigarette smoking.
   b. communicate the story of how the government addressed smoking in society.
   c. destroy the tobacco industry.
   d. show the falsehoods of government control.

12. The OPPOSITE meaning of the term *sharpest risk*, as used in the passage, is _____.
   a. dullest risk
   b. happiest risk
   c. most popular risk
   d. most unlikely risk

13. What is the best summary of Surgeon General Terry's research on smoking?
   a. Smoking is a multi-million dollar business.
   b. The effects of smoking are endless.
   c. Smoking is popular with young boys.
   d. Smoking can be a direct cause of disease and death.

14. Based on a general understanding of this passage, what is the ultimate and most important cause/effect of choosing to smoke?
   a. Smoking is no longer a socially acceptable behavior.
   b. Smoking was once not a danger, but now it is.
   c. The detriments to one's health greatly increase with smoking.
   d. The amount of research available on smoking has grown.

15. Which of the following might be a more appropriate substitute for the word *chilling* as it is used in the last line of the passage?
   a. controversial
   b. scary
   c. fantastical
   d. irrelevant

Read the following passage and answer questions 16–20.

I. INTRODUCTION

A. Attention-getter—a statistic such as how many people in America have to wait to get expensive medical procedures done, and how many of those never get the medical procedures they need. Include the average price of certain types of plastic surgery in the United States.

B. Social significance—estimates suggest medical tourism could be a $2 billion business in India by 2014. The significance to the audience is that they could get into an accident and need an organ that would either be too costly in the U.S. or have a waiting list that is too long.

C. Credibility—I was reading an article in *Jane* magazine about cheap plastic surgery in Mexico and wanted to know more about inexpensive medical procedures in foreign countries.

D. Thesis statement—many Americans are traveling to foreign countries for medical procedures because they are much cheaper and more readily available than in the United States.

E. Preview—where people are going to get these medical procedures, what medical procedures are being performed, and the pros and cons of going to foreign countries for medical procedures.

II. BODY

A. Where people are traveling to get these medical procedures (www.mdse.edu).

   1. Mexico

   2. Thailand

   3. India

B. What medical procedures are being performed (www.medpro.biz).

   1. Organ

   2. Dental

   3. Plastic surgery

C. Pros (www.medcons.com).

   1. Faster

   2. Cheaper

D. Cons.

   1. Not knowing where the parts are coming from

   2. Not knowing doctors' qualifications

III. CONCLUSION

A. Review of main points: where the medical procedures are being performed, what medical procedures are being performed, and the pros and cons of getting such a procedure.

B. End by telling the audience that I hope that my speech has informed them about my topic.

16. The document can BEST be described as a(n) _____.

   a. map

   b. outline

   c. syllabus

   d. blueprint

17. Which of the following is NOT a synonym of the term *conclusion*?

   a. ending

   b. closing

   c. finale

   d. simulacrum

18. The speech outline references which type of sources?

   a. Web-based

   b. book-based

   c. journal-based

   d. newspaper-based

19. If the speaker wished to explain in detail the points of his/her speech, where in the outline would that information appear?

   a. Introduction

   b. Body

   c. Conclusion

   d. Purpose

20. Based on the speech points, the speaker believes a negative aspect of having a medical procedure performed in another country is
   a. better intelligence.
   b. lack of knowledge about doctors' qualifications.
   c. better health.
   d. the development of a strong work ethic.

Read the following excerpt from William Faulkner's piece of short fiction entitled Barn Burning *and then answer questions 21–25.*

The store in which the Justice of the Peace's court was sitting smelled of cheese. The boy, crouched on his nail keg at the back of the crowded room, knew he smelled cheese, and more; from where he sat he could see the ranked shelves close-packed with the solid, squat, dynamic shapes of tin cans whose labels his stomach read, not from the lettering which meant nothing to his mind but from the scarlet devils and silver curve of fish—this, the cheese which he knew he smelled and the hermetic meat which his intestines believed he smelled coming in intermittent gusts momentary and brief between the other constant one, the smell and sense just a little of fear but mostly of despair and grief, the old fierce pull of blood. He could not see the table where the Justice sat and before which his father and his father's enemy (*our enemy* he thought in that despair; *ourn! Mine and hisn both! He's my father!*) stood, but he could hear them, the two of them that is, because his father had no words yet:

"But what proof have you, Mr. Harris?"

"I told you. The hog got into my corn. I caught it up and sent it back to him. He had not fence that would hold it. I told him no, warned him. The next time I put the hog in my pen. When he came to get it I gave him enough wire to patch up his pen. The next time I put the hog up and kept it. I rode down to his house and saw the wire I gave him still rolled on to the spool in his yard. I told him he could have the hog when he paid me a dollar pound fee. That evening . . . [he] came with the dollar and got the hog. He was a strange [man]. He said, 'He say to tell you wood and hay kin burn.' I said, 'What?' That whut he say to tell you,' the [man] said. 'Wood and hay kin burn.' That night my barn burned. I got the stock out but I lost the barn."

21. According to the passage, where is the court case taking place?
   a. a basement
   b. a courtroom
   c. a country store
   d. a police station

22. What did the author mean when he wrote, ". . . from where he sat he could see the ranked shelves close-packed with the solid, squat, dynamic shapes of tin cans whose labels his stomach read, . . ."
   a. He was surrounded by factory workers putting labels on tuna cans.
   b. He was hungry, and the pictures on the can labels were making him hungrier.
   c. He was on a boat in the middle of the ocean.
   d. He was dreaming of cans of tuna.

23. What was Mr. Harris implying when he told the judge that the man he was facing in court had said, "Wood and hay kin burn"?
- **a.** Mr. Harris believed his barn was burned out of retaliation.
- **b.** Mr. Harris believed the entire discussion to be unnecessary.
- **c.** Mr. Harris was scared of the other gentleman.
- **d.** Mr. Harris did not understand the accusations he was making toward the other man.

24. Faulkner's use of improper grammar with the character of Mr. Harris sets the tone that Mr. Harris was
- **a.** angry.
- **b.** undereducated.
- **c.** aristocratic.
- **d.** neighborly.

25. The word *stock*, as used in the last line of the excerpt, also means
- **a.** animals.
- **b.** papers.
- **c.** vehicles.
- **d.** neighbors.

The following excerpt comes from a textbook on public speaking. Read the passage and then answer questions 26–30.

It's hard to answer a question well if you don't listen carefully to it. Give the questioner your full attention. Look directly at her or him rather than glancing around the room, at the floor, or at the ceiling. If the audience member is having a difficult time stating the question, you might even nod in encouragement to help the person along.

When faced with an unclear or unwieldy question, try to rephrase it by saying something like, "If I understand your question, it seems to me that you are asking…." Another option is simply to ask the audience member to repeat the question. Most people will restate it more succinctly and clearly. If you still don't understand, ask the questioner to give an example of what he or she means.

26. Which of the following is NOT discussed in the passage?
- **a.** nodding at the speaker
- **b.** smiling at the speaker
- **c.** rephrasing the speaker's words
- **d.** providing examples

27. The term *succinctly*, as used in the passage, means
- **a.** positively.
- **b.** intellectually.
- **c.** wordy.
- **d.** briefly.

28. What would be the most appropriate title for this passage?
- **a.** Listen Carefully
- **b.** Know Your Audience
- **c.** Calm Nerves Effectively
- **d.** Repeat and Repeat Again

29. Why is it important that the listener not glance "around the room, at the floor, or at the ceiling"?
- **a.** The listener may fall asleep.
- **b.** The speaker will be tempted to do the same.
- **c.** This signals to the speaker that you are not listening.
- **d.** The audience may laugh at the speaker.

30. The OPPOSITE meaning of the term *unwieldy*, as used in the passage, is
   a. of questionable reason.
   b. not awkward.
   c. entertaining.
   d. powerful.

The following is the introduction from a speech entitled Dying to be Thin, given by Jennifer Breuer, a student at the University of Wisconsin. Read the excerpt and then answer questions 31–35.

I was Julie's best friend. I watched her grow from a little girl who was doted on by her parents into a tomboy who carried frogs in her pockets. I watched her become a young woman, fussing with her hair and trying on every outfit in her closet before her first date. I always wanted to be just like her.

But then something went terribly wrong. Julie's shiny hair became dull and brittle. Her eyes lost their sparkle, and she didn't smile that brilliant smile anymore. I watched now, as she stepped onto the scale seven times a day, wore baggy clothes to cover her shriveled frame, and kept muttering about losing those last stubborn pounds. Julie had become anorexic.

One in every 100 teenage families in America suffers from anorexia, and *The New York Times* says this number is rising by 5 percent every year. Although this disease does strike men, says the newspaper, 90 percent of its victims are women, and 44 percent of those victims are college-age females.

From my research and my personal experience with Julie, I have discovered that anorexia is an extremely serious disease that strikes a large number of Americans. Today I will tell what anorexia is, what causes it, and what methods are used to treat it. Let's start by examining what anorexia is.

31. The speaker incorporates the use of _____ in her speech to better gain the attention of the reader.
   a. characterization
   b. irony
   c. persuasion
   d. emotional appeal

32. Which of the following is NOT one of the three main points the speaker wishes to share?
   a. the definition of anorexia
   b. examples of celebrities with anorexia
   c. causes of anorexia
   d. treatment of anorexia

33. According to the passage, which of the following is a symptom of anorexia?
   a. dull hair
   b. outgoing personality
   c. uncaring parents
   d. bone spurs

34. By what means does the speaker suggest she is a creditable resource for the topic?
   a. personal experience
   b. conversation with parents
   c. weeks of research
   d. rational conclusion

35. Based on the information given, what could one conclude to be the time period in which Julie began showing the first signs of her illness?
   a. unknown
   b. post-college years
   c. teenage years
   d. toddler years

Read the poem by Emily Dickinson and then answer questions 36–40.

I'm Nobody! Who are you? (#260)
I'm Nobody! Who are you?
Are you—Nobody—too?
Then there's a pair of us!
Don't tell! they'd advertise—you know!

How dreary—to be—Somebody!
How public—like a Frog—
To tell one's name—the livelong June—
To an admiring Bog!

36. The speaker in the poem cautions the reader not to tell anyone that they are nobodies. What is the speaker's attitude toward being a person of note?
   a. It can be dangerous to be well known.
   b. It is unpleasant to be well known.
   c. Fame is a wonderful feeling when you have a fawning audience.
   d. Advertising one's private life just makes one's ordinariness worse.

37. What comparison does the poet make with the "admiring bog"?
   a. a boring classroom
   b. a pair of ghosts living in the bayou
   c. a mundane life
   d. an audience interested in celebrity

38. Dickinson's work is often instantly recognizable. What style techniques does she use to make this poem effective?
   a. complex and abstract multisyllabic vocabulary
   b. rigid rhyme patterns that end every line
   c. unconventional use of dashes, exclamation points, and capital letters
   d. numerous examples of symbolism

39. Given that a bog is like a swamp, muddy and wet, what tone does Dickinson achieve in referring to an "admiring bog"?
   a. serious
   b. ironic
   c. secretive
   d. regretful

40. Dickinson compares being "somebody" to being a frog. What might her choice symbolize?
   a. The speaker admired frogs greatly.
   b. The speaker finds the idea of being famous deeply unappealing.
   c. Being famous can make a person do ugly things to keep fame.
   d. Famous people can wind up in the swamp feeling dreary.

Read Moira's one-act monologue, entitled The Not So Perfect Child, *and then answer questions 41–45.*

(Quiet anger)
You hate me don't you? I am never good enough for you.

(Anger builds)
No matter what I do it's not as good as my sister. I always have to hear how she would have done it better. Or how she already did it better.

(Hurt)
Why does she want to ruin my life? She just wants to blot me out like I was some sort of mistake . . . I'm just a copy . . . A copy of a copy . . . Not as good as the original . . . Not as good as you.

(Sarcastic and bitter)
You are so perfect . . . Everyone around me is so perfect . . . And there was nothing left over for me . . . I am the leftover failures . . . I am the fatty waste you toss to the dogs.

(Fury)

Everyone hates me! Why does everyone think I am so horrible . . . (Shakes and tries to hold back the fury) Probably because I am. A horrible creature doomed to walk this earth and suffer . . . For you.

(Cries uncontrollably . . . Struggles to speak) I'm hurting . . . Hurting so bad inside. Cut off from everyone . . . Punished for some past life wrongs . . . What did I do in a past life to deserve this . . . Or am I paying for the sins of my father . . . And mother . . . Am I your sin? Or do I remind you of some sin you want to forget?

(Anger builds)

Or I am a disappointment that keeps disappointing. I even disappoint myself.

(Furious)

I will never be my sister. I don't want to be her. I hate everything about her!

(Cries . . . Sadness)

But I don't want to be me either. Sometimes I want to fade away . . . Become a shadow . . . Fading away . . . Forgotten . . . Maybe if you forget about me I won't make you so sad anymore.

(She hears a knock at her door. She tries to fix her up . . . Wipes away the tears) What's that mom? I was just watching a video . . . Was it too loud? I'm sorry. . . . I'm really sorry.

Used by permission by D.M. Larson and freedrama.net.

41. Where is this monologue taking place?
  a. a shopping mall
  b. a church sanctuary
  c. the speaker's bedroom
  d. a school classroom

42. What is the likely age of the speaker in the monologue?
  a. young child
  b. teenager
  c. older woman
  d. unknown

43. The term *blot me out* as used in the monologue means
  a. remove.
  b. congratulate.
  c. sympathize.
  d. encourage.

44. To whom is the character in the monologue speaking?
  a. her mother
  b. herself
  c. her father
  d. her sister

45. Which of the following is NOT true?
  a. The speaker felt she was a disappointment to her mother.
  b. The speaker felt she was a disappointment to her father.
  c. The speaker felt she was a disappointment to her sister.
  d. The speaker felt she was a disappointment to both her parents and herself.

Study the following chart and then answer questions 46–50.

CRITERIA FOR EVALUATING WEB PAGES

EVALUATION OF WEB DOCUMENTS	HOW TO INTERPRET THE BASICS
Accuracy of Web Documents – Who wrote the page and can you contact him or her? – What is the purpose of the document and why was it produced? – How qualified is this person to write this document?	**Accuracy** – Make sure the author provides an email address or a contact address/phone number. – Know the distinction between author and Webmaster.
Authority of Web Documents – Who published the document and is it separate from the Webmaster? – Check the domain of the document. What institution, entity, or company publishes this document? – Does the publisher list his or her qualifications?	**Authority** – What credentials are listed for the author(s)? – Where is the document published? Check the URL domain.
Objectivity of Web Documents – What goals/objectives does this page meet? – How detailed is this information? – What opinions (if any) are expressed by the author?	**Objectivity** – What credentials are listed for the author(s)? – Where is the document published? Check the URL domain (.gov, .edu, .com, .biz, etc.) because some commercial sites may be biased.
Currentness of Web Documents – When was it produced? – When was it updated? – How up-to-date are the links (if any)?	**Currentness** – How many dead links are on the page? – Are the links current or updated regularly? – Is the information on the page outdated?

46. Why would it be important to differentiate between the author and the Webmaster in terms of the accuracy of Web documents?
   a. The author may not know the Webmaster.
   b. The Webmaster is the publishing agent.
   c. The reader may become confused with more than one person.
   d. If they were the same, the opinions expressed on the Website could be biased.

47. Why would "dead links" be a sign that the information on the Web page is not current?
   a. The information may not be of professional quality.
   b. Current information should be able to link to other recent Web pages.
   c. "Dead links" automatically falsify a Web page's purpose.
   d. Current Web pages have "built in" technologies that assure accuracy and currentness.

48. Which of the following is NOT part of an objective view?
   a. Web page detail
   b. publication location
   c. author credentials
   d. author's opinions

49. Which of the following is NOT a criterion for evaluating Web pages?
a. popularity
b. accuracy
c. authority
d. objectivity

50. How might the information in the table be best summarized?
a. Only Web pages from educational institutions can be considered accurate.
b. Web pages cannot be trusted.
c. Readers should be aware that not all Web pages have accurate information.
d. All Web pages must note an author and Webmaster.

Language

For questions 1–3, choose the sentence that correctly uses adjectives.

1. a. She protested that after recovering from her sprain, she felt good enough to start playing sports again.
b. We felt badly about having caused the accident.
c. Once the test was over, Fredi walked slow out of the classroom.
d. Bill thought the people in Martian costumes were the real thing.

2. a. She argued successfully and won the case.
b. The cabby drove skillfully through the traffic.
c. Sal's dog Fido smells carefully.
d. I earned a high grade on the test we took today.

3. a. The new device was the more cleverly designed bird feeder that Pat had ever owned.
b. Glenda's essay was the best of the two submitted.
c. It was the hottest summer recorded in two years.
d. The sergeant asked them if this was the best plan they could devise.

For questions 4–6, choose the sentence that correctly uses adverbs.

4. a. The forest fire in Arizona was deadly.
b. They behaved nice toward the girl with the limp.
c. The lonely hermit lived in a tar paper shack.
d. It is indeed true that the choir sings well.

5. a. The cellist played careless throughout the afternoon.
b. She wanted me to tell him whether the meat smelled rotten.
c. She is a powerful singer who sings our national anthem beautifully.
d. Last week, we had a terrible hot afternoon on Tuesday.

6. a. Audrey's camera worked perfect.
b. Lon's answer sounded correctly.
c. The ending of the play was staged dramatically.
d. He speaks fluent English for a first year student.

For questions 7–9, choose the sentence that contains correct antecedent agreement.

7. a. The can of lima beans is losing their label.
   b. Each of the assistants does work around his or her office.
   c. Neither the director nor the actors did his job.
   d. Mumps are a very dangerous disease.

8. a. Somebody has left their bag on the floor.
   b. Sometimes an employee does not agree with their boss's decision.
   c. Joe didn't think they should have to retake the test.
   d. If anyone has an opinion about the test, he or she should state it.

9. a. John and Julie have decided to go his or her separate ways.
   b. Both Julio and Juan think he should be first to interview for the job.
   c. Everyone should go to their cabin soon.
   d. After a two-month absence, Ruben visited his mother.

For questions 10–12, choose either an adjective (#1) or an adverb (#2) for correct sentence usage.

10. a. *#1 Adjective* He delivers milk in a friendly manner.
    #2 Adverb He delivers milk in a friendly manner.
   b. *#1 Adjective* He is not a strong student in art, but he writes good.
    #2 Adverb He is not a strong student in art, but he writes well.
   c. *#1 Adjective* She went to bed quiet.
    #2 Adverb She went to bed quietly.
   d. *#1 Adjective* The children behaved bad.
    #2 Adverb The children behaved badly.

11. a. *#1 Adjective* She felt disappointed.
    #2 Adverb She felt disappointedly.
   b. *#1 Adjective* The child cried bitterly.
    #2 Adverb The child cried bitterly.
   c. *#1 Adjective* The miserly vagabond often stole small items.
    #2 Adverb The miserly vagabond often stole small items.
   d. *#1 Adjective* The child was annoyed.
    #2 Adverb The child was annoyed.

12. a. *#1 Adjective* Richard talks carelessly.
    #2 Adverb Richard talks carelessly.
   b. *#1 Adjective* Do you feel happy when it snows?
    #2 Adverb Do you feel happily when it snows?
   c. *#1 Adjective* These flowers smell wonderful.
    #2 Adverb These flowers smell wonderfully.
   d. *#1 Adjective* The laundry you put on the line looks dry now.
    #2 Adverb The laundry you put on the line looks dry now.

For questions 13–14, choose the sentence that uses pronouns correctly.

13. a. Between you and I, I would rather finish watching the movie today.
   b. That is him who broke the window of my cousin's house
   c. Dad's story really surprised Dana and I.
   d. I gave her a box of candy for the holiday.

14. a. In the past, and perhaps now, people are looking for a leader which can restore order.
   b. Documentarians who fulfill these requirements are rare.
   c. He is a politician who we can really trust.
   d. I hope there will be a topic next week which I will be able to say something about.

For questions 15–16, choose the sentence that contains correct subject-verb agreement.

15. **a.** The quiz, as well as all the workbook exercises, were collected.
  b. His jacket, not his shirt or his socks, always seem to match his slacks.
  c. The women who went to the meeting were bored.
  d. The group of protesters were blocking the sidewalk.

16. **a.** Nearly one in four people worldwide are Muslim.
  b. Fifty percent of the list have been accomplished.
  c. Our staff meets on Tuesday mornings to discuss customer complaints.
  d. The team are headed to the nationals since winning the state finals.

For questions 17–18, choose the sentence that uses the correct verb tense.

17. **a.** I have drank wine only once and did not like it.
  b. She will make more money at her new job.
  c. He is a student at this school for three years.
  d. I have swam that lake many times.

18. **a.** When my brother cried, he wins the argument.
  b. They are liking that play very much.
  c. He swims in the pool every day.
  d. I brung milk to school every day, including today.

For questions 19–20, choose the sentence that correctly uses a negative.

19. **a.** I scarcely have any money.
  b. I hardly have none of my friends coming over.
  c. I don't want no seconds of that meat.
  d. I do not have no eraser with me.

20. **a.** She claims she has not seen neither Paul nor John since May.
  b. I did not have neither her address nor her phone number.
  c. He did not mention neither the flooding nor the landslide.
  d. He did not find the key either on or under the mat.

For questions 21–23, choose the sentence that illustrates sentence clarity by using modifiers correctly.

21. **a.** On his way home from work, Rob found a gold man's watch.
  b. After reading the original study, the article remains unconvincing.
  c. Having seen Blackpool Tower, the Eiffel Tower is more impressive.
  d. We slowly ate the lunch we had brought.

22. **a.** The torn mechanic's manual lay on the tool bench.
  b. After reading your letter, my cat will stay in until the birds fly off.
  c. The dealer sold the Cadillac with leather seats to the buyer.
  d. The three bankers talked quietly in the corner wearing suits.

23. **a.** They saw a fence behind the shed made of barbed wire.
b. The waiter served a well-buttered dinner roll to the woman.
c. Sally piled all her clothes in the hamper that she had worn.
d. When nine years old, my mother returned to college to complete her degree.

For questions 24–26, choose the sentence that most effectively combines the sentences.

24. Mr. Jones is my coach. He taught me how to bunt a baseball. He taught me to throw a curve ball.
a. Mr. Jones is my coach. He taught me how to bunt a baseball. He taught me to throw a curve ball.
b. Mr. Jones was my coach, and he taught me how to play baseball and bunt a baseball and throw a curve ball.
c. Mr. Jones, my coach, taught me baseball techniques such as bunting and throwing a curve ball.
d. My college baseball coach was Mr. Jones. He taught me baseball techniques such as bunting and throwing a curve ball.

25. My sister went shopping for me. She bought me a shirt. Next, she bought me some shoes. She bought me pants.
a. My sister went shopping for me. She bought me a shirt. Next, she bought me some shoes. She bought me pants.
b. My sister went shopping for me and bought me a shirt and some shoes. She also bought me pants.
c. I needed a shirt, some shoes, and some pants, so my sister went shopping for me.
d. My sister went shopping for me and bought a shirt, some shoes, and pants.

26. I like bull fights. They are colorful and full of action. There are picadors. They lance on horseback. There are banderillos and matadors. They fight on foot.
a. I like bull fights. They are colorful and full of action. There are picadors. They lance on horseback. There are banderillos and matadors. They fight on foot.
b. I like bull fights: they are colorful and full of action. Men known as picadors lance the bulls from horseback, but the banderillos and matadors fight on foot.
c. I like bull fights. They are colorful and full of action with picadors who lance the bull from horseback, and there are banderillos and matadors, who are very brave and fight the bull from the floor of the stadium arena.
d. The reason I like bull fights is because they are colorful and full of action, with picadors who lance the bulls from horseback and the brave banderillos and matadors who fight the bulls on foot.

For questions 27–29, three of the four passages in each section use signal words or phrases that connect the sentences logically, add to the coherence of the section, and unify the section or paragraph. Select the one example that does not contain these transitional phrases.

27. **a.** Many bicycle groups are advocating the use of bicycles as one solution to the problem of too many automobiles and too little gas. These groups have published some interesting ideas to back up their idea. For example, a recent study shows that 62.4 percent of all car trips average less than five miles.

  b. This is a distance that, under reasonable conditions, can take about 20 minutes on a bike. The bicycle, unlike the car, does not pollute and does not cause traffic jams.

  c. A lone hiker who walks into quicksand is in an awkward position, but even his or her case is not without hope. Attempts to force a way will prove worse than useless. Standing still and yelling will be fatal unless help arrives soon.

  d. The trapped person's first move might be to drop his or her pole behind him or her and fall back upon it, meanwhile stretching the traveler's arms out at right angles to his or her body. In this position, the person could float in water.

28. **a.** Therefore, the traveler could float in water and certainly float on sand if all heavy items carried are discarded. The traveler may now call out for help.

  b. If there is no prospect of help, the victim might begin to rescue him or herself. The first step in this operation is to get the pole at right angles to the body beneath the shoulders, and then to work it down until it is supporting the hips.

  c. The individual is able to pull his or her legs out of the muck one at a time. Much effort is required. The person should take frequent rests and not rush the process.

  d. Once the feet are out, the trapped hiker begins rolling to safe ground. Rolling is the easiest, and indeed the only way, of getting off the soft ground. It can be done in short stages.

29. **a.** I have gotten out of the habit of making my bed except on Fridays. I have some sound reasons for breaking the bed-making habit. In the first place, no one but me ever ventures in there. If there is a surprise fire inspection, I can quickly throw a spread over the whole mess. Otherwise, I am not bothered.

  b. In addition, I find nothing uncomfortable about crawling into that tangled mess. On the contrary, I enjoy poking out a comfortable space.

  c. I think that a tightly made bed is uncomfortable. Entering one makes me feel like a wrapped loaf of bread. I like being a slob.

  d. Finally, and most importantly, I think bed-making is a waste of time. I would rather spend the time checking my emails.

For questions 30–32, read the four sentences given. Then, choose the sequence that shows the best order for the set of instructions, directions, or chronology.

30. 1 There was much unrest in Germany during the 1920s.
2 Many historians say that World War II in 1939 was a natural result of World War I (1914–1918).
3 The American Congress voted against the Peace Treaty in 1921.
4 Germany thought the Versailles Peace Treaty of 1919 to be unfair.
  a. 4-3-1-2
  b. 1-2-4-3
  c. 3-4-2-1
  d. 2-3-4-1

31. 1 Go about 10 miles on Route 4.
2 First, get off the Interstate at Exit 32.
3 Then, turn left off Route 4 onto Franklin Street, and you'll see our yellow house second from the corner on the right.
4 At the end of the exit ramp, turn right on Route 4.
  a. 2-4-1-3
  b. 2-3-4-1
  c. 3-2-1-4
  d. 4-2-3-1

32. 1 The Vietnam War
2 World War II
3 The election of President Barack Obama
4 World War I
  a. 1-3-2-4
  b. 4-2-1-3
  c. 2-1-4-3
  d. 3-4-1-2

For questions 33–35, choose the topic sentence that makes the best use of the supporting details.

33. Supporting Details:
About 95 percent of all adults use the left side of the brain for speaking and writing.
The left side of the brain is also superior at doing math.
The right side of the brain is best at expressive and creative tasks.
The right side, however, has talents of its own. It excels at recognizing patterns, faces, and melodies.
  a. The left side of the brain controls the right side of the body.
  b. The right side of the brain controls the left side of the body.
  c. Scientists are highly critical of educational programs that are focused on tasks that develop only right or the left brain activities.
  d. Different sides of the brain control different activities.

34. Supporting Details:
People interested in dating often ask their friends if they know anyone who is available.
Some people advertise for dates on the Internet.
Some people believe that online dating stifles romance.
Others prefer to use dating services that, for a fee, guarantee a perfect match.
  a. Today there are a number of ways for people to get a date.
  b. Some believe that Internet dating may promote unhealthy relationships.
  c. People can be real nuts about how they try to grab a guy or a gal.
  d. Today's teenagers do not date anymore; they just go out in big groups.

35. Supporting Details:

People with claustrophobia, or fear of closed spaces, get anxious on elevators.
Agoraphobia is the fear of open spaces; those suffering from it are unlikely to leave home.
People with zoophobia, or fear of animals, are unlikely to own pets.
People with antlophobia, or fear of floods, are unlikely to live near rivers.

   a. Phobias are irrational fears, and they take a variety of forms that affect people's lives in different ways.
   b. Phobias can persist for years, even when there is no real danger from the feared person or object.
   c. Social phobia is the fear of situations in which one might be observed, judged, or embarrassed.
   d. Phobias are not as common a disorder as some people think.

For questions 36–38, choose the sentence that best serves as a topic sentence of a paragraph.

36. a. Alice is a tall woman.
   b. Alice is a woman from Virginia.
   c. Alice learned a lot about animals during her years on the farm.
   d. Alice was born in 1943.

37. a. The king of Jordan helped bring peace and prosperity to his country.
   b. George Lucas is a filmmaker.
   c. Thomas Jefferson became president in 1801.
   d. I will tell you about the president of Bolivia.

38. a. Too many people treat animals badly in experiments.
   b. Plagiarism is a very complex idea.
   c. My grandparents are strong and confident people who have helped me become the person I am today.
   d. I have always thought that vacations are very nice.

For questions 39–41, read the four sentences in the paragraph and choose the sentence that does not belong.

39. 1 To control a nosebleed, sit down and lean forward.
   2 Put pressure on the lower part of the side that is bleeding for about five minutes.
   3 Consult a doctor if the bleeding does not stop within 15 minutes.
   4 It is sometimes difficult to see a doctor without an appointment.
   a. Sentence 1
   b. Sentence 2
   c. Sentence 3
   d. Sentence 4

40. 1 Your attitude about your job may affect your chances of becoming sick.
   2 A cold and a viral infection are common illnesses.
   3 A university study indicates that workers with good attitudes become sick less often than workers with negative attitudes.
   4 Many people become sick before a job interview, a big test, or any major activity that they are dreading.
   a. Sentence 1
   b. Sentence 2
   c. Sentence 3
   d. Sentence 4

41. 1 Carpentry is rewarding in many ways.
2 Working with wood can be relaxing and creative.
3 Many carpenters get satisfaction from working with their hands.
4 My father, a carpenter, opened a woodworking shop.
  a. Sentence 1
  b. Sentence 2
  c. Sentence 3
  d. Sentence 4

For questions 42–44, choose the sentence that contains correct capitalization.

42. **a.** "My boyfriend will pass the test," she said, "but Oh, how he frets about taking it."
  b. The home economics teacher once told us, "by doing a simple test, you can discover if coffee contains chicory."
  c. An elderly lady in the seat behind me was complaining quite sadly, "oh, dear!"
  d. "Exult O shores!" is a line from a Walt Whitman poem.

43. **a.** Matthew said, "i'm going out for a walk!"
  b. Although Mrs. Johnson has seen odd happenings before, she stated that the headless chicken "Certainly takes the cake" when it comes to inexplicable activity.
  c. Come to the meeting prepared with the following: a presentation of the latest plan, an explanation of the changes to the original blueprint, and an updated environmental impact statement.
  d. The first rule is of comma usage is, "when you are in doubt, leave it out."

44. **a.** He said, "between you and me, I think his truck is a gas guzzler."
  b. "april is the cruelest month . . ." is the first line of a poem.
  c. "march, march, march is all we ever do," said the soldier.
  d. Did you ever hear the song that begins, "Oh what a beautiful morning"?

For questions 45–47, choose the sentence that correctly uses proper nouns and adjectives.

45. **a.** Did you ever see the movie *Never on a Sunday*?
  b. Congress argues about whether we should fortify the mexican border.
  c. I once saw a movie about a famous australian outlaw.
  d. I believe that Walt Whitman is one of America's most famous Poets.

46. **a.** My Summer home is near an ocean and a big city.
  b. My friend loves to eat German food.
  c. The President of China will be traveling to America in the near future.
  d. When Winter comes, we all head to the mountains.

47. **a.** Elizabeth's test scores have been improving, especially in her Biology course.
  b. Her favorite type of novel was an Elizabethan drama.
  c. Did you know that there is an organization called the society to preserve barbershop quartets?
  d. A three-lane Highway can be very dangerous.

For questions 48–50, choose the sentence that uses commas correctly.

48. a. Children stop jumping on the furniture this very moment.
    b. What I said Carmen and Roberto was to call home before you go out this evening.
    c. Ladies and gentlemen, will you please look at the high-wire act in the center ring?
    d. I am sorry I had to say that to you Roger.

49. a. I went to see the movie, *Midnight in Paris* with my friend, Jessie.
    b. Steve Meyerson, a local merchant, gave the keynote address.
    c. My father, who gave new meaning to the expression "hard working" never took a vacation.
    d. The cat was tired, it curled up and went to sleep.

50. a. I like pastas, although I also like many meat dishes.
    b. On March 4, 1931, she traveled to Canada.
    c. It wasn't an easy thing to say, but I finally told my father "Stop giving me advice!"
    d. As an actor, Russell Brand is a comedian not a dramatist.

For questions 51–52, choose the sentence that correctly uses apostrophes.

51. a. My mother's and father's cabin is in the Cascade Mountains.
    b. Who's turn is it to go to the store?
    c. The man forgot to pick up his wife's jacket from the cleaners.
    d. Great taste deserves it's own reward.

52. a. The T-shirt said, "The Flying Monkey's stole My Homework."
    b. Boat owner's are responsible for ensuring that their boats are properly secured.
    c. They're in safe hands with our experienced travel experts.
    d. Three large male lion's approached the 4×4 while we were in the trading post.

For question 53, choose the sentence that makes a correct statement about business letters.

53. a. If a woman wishes to indicate her marital status, she may close with: (*Miss* or *Mrs.*) *Alice Wright.*
    b. In writing to a professional, the salutation should be: *Dear Doc Jones,*
    c. An accepted business letter closing would be: *I hope to hear from you soon,*
    d. The heading of a business letter starts with *Dear Mr. Jones,*

For questions 54–55, choose the sentence that uses quotation marks correctly.

54. a. "Please do not tell me, I said, how the movie ends."
    b. "Do not go out tonight, and that is an order."! Said the doctor to the patient.
    c. "I believe," she said, "that Fran is telling only part of the truth."
    d. "Did you hear me ask, "Where is the money?"" she inquired.

55. a. "Please try to close the door behind you."
    b. The loaf was labeled "Hot" French Bread.
    c. This is "NOT" a garbage disposal!
    d. *Please* <u>do</u> <u>NOT</u> <u>flush</u> the "paper towels" down the toilet.

Language Mechanics

For questions 1–2, choose the sentence that has the correct punctuation using colons.

1. **a.** My hobbies are: skiing and reading.
   b. Please wake me at 7-25 A.M.
   c. When I have the time, I want to travel to: Rome, Israel, and Egypt.
   d. That summer we traveled through the following states: Arkansas, Kentucky, Louisiana, and Tennessee.

2. **a.** The conference speakers who were chosen by the steering committee included: Sean Smith, Bruce Chen, and Alicia Vanelli.
   b. Send a check or money order to: 221 Ash Street in our town.
   c. John has a serious problem: he does not know how to relax.
   d. During the next seven months, the state will complete these projects the Smith Tunnel, the Marsh Bridge, and the Cape Cod Island Connector.

For questions 3–4, choose the sentence that uses commas correctly.

3. **a.** Edith Cohen who likes movies wants to be a film critic.
   b. Senator Higgins, hoping for a compromise, began a long, impassioned speech.
   c. Until we found the source of the smoke everyone was nervously searching all the wastebaskets.
   d. This is a rough dangerous road to drive on at night.

4. **a.** Mindy might have mentioned that, "she was going to Boston tomorrow."
   b. He yelled "I found the jacket over here."
   c. "I like to work in my garden in the springtime," Max told me, "In the summer I head to the beach."
   d. Does she still say, "Stay in the kitchen until the dishes are dry"?

For questions 5–7, choose the sentence with correct usage of direct and indirect quotations.

5. **a.** Alice Johnson, a local realtor, reported last night that she saw three people running out of that old house.
   b. According to some philosophers, "imagination is more important than knowledge."
   c. "I am very sorry, she replied, I cannot possibly get there before 11:00 A.M."
   d. Joan said sadly, "Then Alice said innocently, "I was only trying to help.""

6. **a.** Mr. Jones, who was walking in the meadow yesterday, said, The runaway bull streaked right by me.
   b. He announced, it was large, "brown, and looked dangerous."
   c. Although Mr. Jones had seen odd things before, he stated, This was the oddest.
   d. "I was very scared," Mr. Jones announced, "but everything worked out in the end."

7. **a.** Sofia was singing that old song On Top of Old Smoky.
   b. For the career center, Bob created flyers that read, "You're invited to a 'free' resume workshop!"
   c. My brother said that "he would miss the party."
   d. "Please do not tell me," I said, "how the movie ends."

For questions 8–10, choose the sentence that uses semi-colons correctly.

8. **a.** Samuel followed his father's instructions; however, he was not happy about doing so.
   b. There were two representatives from Boston; Massachusetts, four from Albany; New York, and three from Cleveland; Ohio.
   c. Although gaining and maintaining a high level of physical fitness takes time; the effort pays off in the long run.
   d. The ice cream truck driver drove by my house today: he was tall and thin and wore a white uniform.

9. **a.** My aunt has wavy hair, she loves to wash and comb it.
   b. I did not go to the park; instead, I worked on my project.
   c. My cousin's new car is beautiful; but I have no desire to drive it.
   d. There are many ways to approach the problem; logically, mathematically, and scientifically.

10. **a.** In the fifteenth century, there were just a select few in France, Italy, and Germany; who could read.
    b. The Boston Red Sox will play exhibition games on Wednesday, March 15, Thursday, March 16, and Friday, March 17.
    c. The clock was stopped with two seconds remaining in the game between the Celtics and the Hawks; the fans went crazy.
    d. Despite what he told me about the teacher; I have decided to register for the class.

For questions 11–13, select the one example that correctly uses apostrophes.

11. **a.** Both girl's behavior was not what we required for the camping trip.
    b. The six family's efforts to save the barn were heroic.
    c. To fill up a gas tank in the old days, you had to spend only five dollars' worth of your budget.
    d. Did you see the sale on womens' gloves at the department store?

12. **a.** My two friends' homes will be featured in a magazine next month.
    b. The big house over there is my mother's-in-law house.
    c. Edith and Gwen's shoes were both made in Italy.
    d. Your the boss of this whole benefit party.

13. **a.** Theirs no time like the present.
    b. Who's dog is this?
    c. Several student's desks were pushed into the corner.
    d. The word *Mississippi* has four *i*'s and two *p*'s.

For questions 14–15, choose the best guideline for writing a business letter.

14. **a.** The heading of a business letter should include your name and the date.
   b. When you write an inside address in a business letter, it should include the street (*295 Belmont Street*) and city, state, and ZIP code (*Brockton, MA 02789*). Also show the date (*October 3, 2013*).
   c. If you are writing to a specific group, division, or company, use the following salutation: *Dear Guys.*
   d. The salutation of a business letter should use the person's title and full name if you are writing to a professional man or woman (*Dear Dr. John Able:*).

15. **a.** To communicate congeniality in a business letter, use the same type of closing that you would in a friendly letter (*Your good friend,*).
   b. When writing your business letter, try to relate to the reader with a final phrase like, *Thanking you in advance, Hoping to hear from you soon,* etc.
   c. In a business letter, here are some of the traps to avoid: using informal language; sending your letter without proofreading it or running a spelling and grammar check; and padding the letter with unnecessary or flowery words that don't add anything to the point you are trying to make.
   d. Sign your letter with your full name and title, such as *Mr. Charles Evans* or *Dr. Alberta Fulbright.*

For question 16, choose the best guideline for using business titles.

16. **a.** Address your business letter properly. For example, *President Richard Smith.*
   b. Always use the full title of the person you are writing: *Mr. Richard Thorpe, Sr. Ed.*
   c. Include as much information as you know about the person to whom you are addressing your business letter: *Dr. David X. Liu, Ph.D.*
   d. When you do not know the gender of the person you are addressing, use the person's first and last name only, without a title. For example, *Dear Leslie Smith:*

For questions 17–20, choose the sentence that correctly uses proper nouns and adjectives.

17. **a.** The Chinese noodles are in the kitchen pantry, directly behind the box of cereal.
   b. When in Scotland, I love to go to the Country to visit my distant relatives.
   c. I enjoy many different types of food, but italian food is my favorite.
   d. This is a new band that plays only christian music.

18. **a.** The fighting started south of the turkish border.
   b. In the past, a very clever lawyer was called a Philadelphia Lawyer.
   c. This library has more books than both pleasantville Libraries put together.
   d. I read a book about bears who live deep in the Michigan woods.

19. **a.** Did you manage to get the *Billy Elliot* Tickets?
   b. The various European cultures have been intermingling for thousands of years.
   c. The chilean winters are very hot and dry.
   d. The dutch language is spoken in the Netherlands.

20. **a.** Can you name the british Prime Minister?
   b. That person's grandmother was a spanish countess.
   c. The russian king was called a tsar.
   d. He lived in a town close to the Mexican border.

Vocabulary

For questions 1–8, choose the word or term that means the same, or about the same, as the underlined word.

1. absurd answer
   a. understandable
   b. ridiculous
   c. agreeable
   d. debatable

2. lustrous diamond ring
   a. popular
   b. expensive
   c. tarnished
   d. shiny

3. languid vacation
   a. expensive
   b. toxic
   c. relaxing
   d. busy

4. issue a reprieve
   a. postponement
   b. guilty verdict
   c. opinion of innocence
   d. valid sentence

5. engrossing conversation
   a. uncomfortable
   b. energized
   c. confusing
   d. absorbing

6. succumb to the disease
   a. acknowledge
   b. yield to
   c. cure
   d. study

7. docile dog
   a. standoffish
   b. violent
   c. easygoing
   d. diseased

8. dispute the charge
   a. appreciate
   b. approve
   c. discover
   d. fight

For questions 9–12, read the sentences, and then choose the word that best completes BOTH sentences.

9. The truck will take the _____ to the county dump.

   At one point in the film, the character will _____ to drop the loaded gun.

   a. agree
   b. decide
   c. garbage
   d. refuse

10. A lonely _____ fell from the eye of the little girl as she realized her dog was gone.

Please do not _____ the poster we are placing on the telephone pole.

    a. tear
    b. raindrop
    c. destroy
    d. staple

11. Were you able to _____ up the garden hose?

The _____ was not strong enough for the kite to remain in the air.

    a. air
    b. wind
    c. fasten
    d. fabric

12. One should never _____ a child to a scary movie at such a young age.

The movie deals with a _____ that is inappropriate for children.

    a. introduce
    b. subject
    c. assumption
    d. matter

For questions 13–16, read the following passage, which has four missing words. Then fill in each empty spot by choosing the word that makes the most sense in terms of grammar and meaning.

Helen Keller was born on June 27, 1880, in Tuscumbia, Alabama. A healthy child at birth, Keller became ill at the age of nineteen months, and this illness resulted in Keller's **(13)** deaf, blind, and unable to speak. Until the age of six, Keller was considered a wild child who had uncontrollable fits. After much frustration and doubt that Keller would ever be able to communicate, Keller's parents allowed Anne Sullivan to come and live in Tuscumbia to **(14)** young Helen how to use Braille and sign language and how to speak. Helen Keller became an ambassador of the United States as a symbol of courage and triumph to people all over the world.

Today, visitors can tour Ivy Green, the birthplace of Helen Keller. The well pump at which Keller spoke her first word is **(15)** on the property. Each summer, *The Miracle Worker*, a theatrical production **(16)** the story of Keller's life as a young girl, is presented on the grounds of Ivy Green.

13.   **a.** experiencing
      b. facilitating
      c. diagnosing
      d. becoming

14.   **a.** teach
      b. rally
      c. inoculate
      d. propose

15.   **a.** located
      b. established
      c. justified
      d. tied

16.   **a.** eluding
      b. photographing
      c. dramatizing
      d. practicing

For questions 17–20, read the following passage, which has four missing words. Then fill in each empty spot by choosing the word that makes the most sense in terms of grammar and meaning.

Popcorn is a snack food **(17)** by people around the world. Many flavors of popcorn are available to consumers. Some of the most unusual flavors available in stores today are bacon, shrimp, vinegar, and ketchup. The **(18)** of these unique flavors makes for great conversation.

According to history books, popcorn has been eaten for hundreds of years. Groups that seemed to appreciate the **(19)** of popcorn include Native Americans. It was a common practice in some tribes to sit around the campfire and enjoy the delicious treat. Corn was easy to grow, and popcorn was digested well.

Popcorn is used not only for eating but for decorating and crafting projects. One popular way to use popcorn is to **(20)** it into a garland and hang the creation on a Christmas tree. Another way is to use the popped kernels as playing pieces on board games such as Bingo. After the game is over, players can eat the popcorn.

17. a. remedied
b. enjoyed
c. promoted
d. described

18. a. understanding
b. annual
c. variable
d. variety

19. a. farming
b. position
c. economics
d. taste

20. a. shred
b. string
c. divide
d. cut

Spelling

For questions 1–10, choose the word that is spelled correctly and that best completes the sentence.

1. Rhonda believes the _____ reason she is being targeted is because she was involved with the plaintiffs in the case.
a. principle
b. principal
c. principul
d. prinsiple

2. The _____ was eventually deposed from power, and a new election was held.
a. demigogue
b. demegogue
c. demagogue
d. demagog

3. Shamika wanted to _____ with her colleagues before making a final decision.
a. confur
b. confir
c. conferr
d. confer

4. When we go on a summer picnic, we like to bring along lots of _____.
a. edables
b. edebles
c. edibles
d. edibbles

5. The building was so badly damaged during the hurricane that the owner is planning to _____ it.
   a. raise
   b. raze
   c. rase
   d. rasie

6. The couple was charged with the fraudulent use of a credit card in _____.
   a. Conneticut
   b. Connecticut
   c. Conecticut
   d. Connecut

7. The revival of learning in the arts and literature is known as a _____.
   a. rennaissance
   b. renaissance
   c. renussance
   d. renaisance

8. Sensing a fight was about to break out, the teacher had the _____ idea to move the other students out of the room.
   a. bold
   b. bolld
   c. bould
   d. boldd

9. The weather service said that the tornado did not pose an _____ threat to our town.
   a. imminent
   b. iminent
   c. immunent
   d. eminent

10. Did the sales manager _____ the sale of the shirt at a lower price?
   a. authoriz
   b. autherize
   c. authourize
   d. authorize

For questions 11–20, read the phrases. Then find the phrase that includes an underlined word that is NOT spelled correctly in the context of the phrase.

11. **a.** <u>austere</u> look
   b. <u>candid</u> smile
   c. <u>automatic</u> dishwasher
   d. <u>magnifiscent</u> sweater

12. **a.** <u>arranged</u> marriage
   b. <u>odiferous</u> smell
   c. weather <u>vain</u>
   d. <u>earnest</u> plea

13. **a.** <u>pyhsical</u> ability
   b. detailed <u>dissertation</u>
   c. sudden <u>epiphany</u>
   d. annoying <u>noise</u>

14. **a.** <u>energetic</u> staff
   b. <u>personnel</u> manual
   c. funny <u>anecdote</u>
   d. arrogant <u>potentaiton</u>

15. **a.** quick <u>descent</u>
   b. sacred <u>icon</u>
   c. store <u>reseat</u>
   d. <u>immigration</u> issue

16. **a.** <u>parrish</u> office
   b. <u>counter</u> option
   c. <u>booby</u> hatch
   d. <u>ascorbic</u> acid

17. **a.** <u>gamma</u> rays
  b. <u>oppozitional</u> candidate
  c. <u>vindictive</u> boss
  d. <u>suffrage</u> movement

18. **a.** <u>nervous</u> breakdown
  b. <u>bellwether</u> state
  c. <u>factitious</u> tale
  d. <u>emmaculate</u> conception

19. **a.** <u>comedic</u> star
  b. <u>composite</u> study
  c. <u>persuasive</u> speech
  d. <u>conscientuous</u> student

20. **a.** generous <u>ration</u>
  b. <u>intermediery</u> spokesperson
  c. <u>lucid</u> decision
  d. serious <u>deterrence</u>

Mathematics Computation

1. Evaluate $2,653 + 1,007 + (-588)$.
  a. 2,065
  b. 3,072
  c. 3,660
  d. 4,248

2. Evaluate $-492 - (-371)$.
  a. −121
  b. 121
  c. −863
  d. 863

3. Evaluate $(10)(17)(-2)$.
  a. −150
  b. 150
  c. −340
  d. 340

4. Evaluate $-12,560 \div 8$.
  a. −157
  b. 157
  c. −1,570
  d. 1,570

5. A hiker has reached the top of Longs Peak in Colorado with an elevation of 14,255 feet. An experienced scuba diver is diving in the Gulf of Mexico, 110 feet below the surface. What is the distance between the hiker and diver?
  a. −14,145 feet
  b. 14,145 feet
  c. −14,365 feet
  d. 14,365 feet

6. Chuck sold 13 hand-crafted wood pens at a local craft fair. Each pen retailed at $25. What was the total value of the pens?
  a. $300
  b. $325
  c. $350
  d. $375

7. Enrollment at a local private school increased by 245 students over seven years. What was the average increase in enrollment per year?
  a. 35
  b. 39
  c. 47
  d. 49

8. Evaluate $\frac{7}{15} + \frac{7}{9}$.
  a. $\frac{14}{26}$
  b. $\frac{14}{45}$
  c. $1\frac{11}{45}$
  d. $11\frac{1}{45}$

9. Evaluate $\frac{1}{12} - \frac{5}{8}$.

　　a. 1

　　b. −1

　　c. $\frac{13}{24}$

　　d. $-\frac{13}{24}$

10. Evaluate $2\frac{4}{7} \times 5\frac{1}{9}$.

　　a. $13\frac{1}{7}$

　　b. 12

　　c. $10\frac{4}{63}$

　　d. $7\frac{43}{63}$

11. Evaluate $-\frac{35}{45} \div \frac{10}{15}$.

　　a. $-\frac{14}{27}$

　　b. $\frac{14}{27}$

　　c. $-\frac{7}{6}$

　　d. $\frac{7}{6}$

12. Elena went fishing and caught three trout. They weighed $1\frac{3}{4}$ lbs., $2\frac{1}{8}$ lbs., and $3\frac{1}{2}$ lbs. respectively. What was the total weight of Elena's catch?

　　a. $2\frac{11}{24}$ lbs.

　　b. $6\frac{3}{8}$ lbs.

　　c. $6\frac{5}{14}$ lbs.

　　d. $7\frac{3}{8}$ lbs.

13. Janice must divide $143\frac{1}{2}$ oz. of strawberry jelly into jars that hold $1\frac{3}{4}$ oz. each. How many jars will Janice fill?

　　a. 82

　　b. 92

　　c. 143

　　d. 163

14. Find the area of a rectangular neighborhood playground that measures $108\frac{1}{3}$ ft. by $90\frac{3}{5}$ ft.

　　a. $9,720\frac{1}{5}$ sq. ft.

　　b. 9,750 sq. ft.

　　c. 9,815 sq. ft.

　　d. $9,845\frac{1}{3}$ sq. ft.

15. Evaluate $142.07 + 0.023 + 5.8$.

　　a. 142.88

　　b. 147.893

　　c. 148.10

　　d. 223.07

16. Evaluate $50.009 - 1.0762$.

　　a. 39.247

　　b. 48.247

　　c. 48.9332

　　d. 48.9328

17. Evaluate $(81.2)(3.7504)$.

　　a. 304.53248

　　b. 304.8248

　　c. 3045.3248

　　d. 3048.248

18. Evaluate $6.254 \div 0.02$.

　　a. 0.3127

　　b. 3.127

　　c. 31.27

　　d. 312.7

19. Ashtyn purchased school supplies for her three children. The sale totaled $247.39 at the register. Ashtyn gave the cashier $250 in cash. How much change did the cashier give back?

　　a. $2.61

　　b. $2.71

　　c. $2.79

　　d. $3.61

20. Each day, Derek jogs around a 1.25-mile track 3.5 times. How many total miles does Derek jog in five days?
a. 4.375 miles
b. 9.75 miles
c. 21.875 miles
d. 23.75 miles

21. A 2 by 4 wooden stud has a linear length of 7.375 feet. The stud is to be cut into blocks measuring 1.125 feet each. How many blocks can be cut from the stud?
a. 5 blocks
b. 6 blocks
c. 7 blocks
d. 8 blocks

22. Evaluate $2 + 40 \div (-5) + 3$.
a. 3
b. -3
c. -18
d. -21

23. Evaluate $\frac{12}{5} - \frac{1}{6}\left(3 - \frac{3}{5}\right)$.
a. $\frac{134}{25}$
b. $\frac{11}{5}$
c. $\frac{5}{2}$
d. 2

24. Reduce to the lowest terms: $\frac{6 - 2(4 + 7^2)}{16 \div 2(8)}$.
a. -100
b. 212
c. $-\frac{25}{16}$
d. $\frac{53}{16}$

25. Consider the work below. On which line was an error made?
Given: $7 + 3(2 - 3 \times 4)$
First: $7 + 3(2 - 12)$
Second: $7 + 3(-10)$
Third: $10(-10)$
Fourth: -100
a. First
b. Second
c. Third
d. Fourth

26. Reduce to lowest terms: $\frac{-9 + 18 \div 3(6)}{32 - 4(12) \div 3(2)}$.
a. undefined
b. 0
c. $\frac{9}{8}$
d. $-\frac{1}{3}$

27. What is 120% of 53?
a. 6.36
b. 63.6
c. 636
d. 44.2

28. 44.38 is 14% of what number?
a. 6.21
b. 3.17
c. 31.7
d. 317

29. 126 is what percent of 140?
a. 0.9%
b. 9%
c. 90%
d. 111%

30. In Jimmy's Auto Shop, 70% of the employees work part-time. If the shop has 30 employees, how many are part-time?
a. 43
b. 21
c. 9
d. 2

31. Amelia purchased a $15 sweater for which she was charged $1.08 in sales tax. What is the sales tax rate?
a. 16.2%
b. 13.9%
c. 7.2%
d. .072%

32. After a few days of rain, the depth of a local pond rose 1.5 feet. This increase is 30% of the original depth. Find the original depth of the pond.
a. 5 feet
b. 4.5 feet
c. 3.5 feet
d. 3 feet

33. Evaluate $2^3 \times 3^2$.
a. 36
b. 48
c. 54
d. 72

34. Evaluate $5^3 - (-4)^2$.
a. 23
b. 109
c. 117
d. 141

35. Evaluate $\sqrt{16 + 9}$.
a. 25
b. 11
c. 7
d. 5

36. Evaluate $\dfrac{\sqrt{100}}{\sqrt{36}}$.
a. $\frac{5}{2}$
b. $\frac{5}{3}$
c. $\frac{5}{9}$
d. $\frac{25}{3}$

37. Simplify $5x^3 + x^3y^2 + x^3 + x^2y^3$.
a. $6x^3 + x^3y^2 + x^2y^3$
b. $6x^3 + 2x^3y^2$
c. $7x^3y^2 + x^2y^3$
d. $8x^3y^2$

38. Simplify $5(6x + 2) - 7x$.
a. $23x - 2$
b. $23x + 10$
c. $30x + 10$
d. $30x - 2$

39. Solve for k: $3(k + 17) = 51$.
a. undefined
b. 34
c. 3
d. 0

40. Solve for n: $9 + 5(n + 3) = 4 + n$.
a. −2
b. 4
c. −5
d. 5

Applied Mathematics

1. Use front-end rounding to estimate the sum $3,081 + 6,826$.
a. 10,000
b. 9,000
c. 7,000
d. 11,000

2. Emily has $1,957 in her checking account. She writes a check for $238. Use front-end rounding to estimate Emily's new account balance.
   a. $2,000
   b. $1,900
   c. $1,800
   d. $1,700

3. Round 906,854,250 to the nearest hundred-thousand.
   a. 907,000,000
   b. 906,900,000
   c. 906,854,000
   d. 906,854,300

4. Round 18.2739 to the nearest tenth.
   a. 20
   b. 18
   c. 18.27
   d. 18.3

5. Convert 0.004221 to scientific notation.
   a. 4.221×10^3
   b. 42.21×10^{-3}
   c. 4.221×10^{-3}
   d. 4221×10^6

6. Evaluate $(6.41 \times 10^5)(3.7 \times 10^{-3})$. Express your answer in scientific notation.
   a. 2.3717×10^8
   b. 2.3717×10^3
   c. 2.3717×10^2
   d. 23.717×10^{-2}

7. Which of the following is equivalent to 2.75?
   a. 2:75
   b. $2\frac{5}{9}$
   c. 27.5%
   d. $\frac{11}{4}$

8. Find 8% of 64.
   a. 512
   b. 51.2
   c. 5.12
   d. 0.512

9. 629 is 85% of what number?
   a. 786.25
   b. 740
   c. 714
   d. 534.25

10. Find the greatest common factor of 165, 315, and 585.
   a. 3
   b. 5
   c. 9
   d. 15

11. Find the least common multiple of 42, 63, and 75.
   a. 1,050
   b. 3,150
   c. 28,350
   d. 198,450

12. If 3 is to 7 as 18 is to 42, write a proportion that reflects this relationship.
   a. $\frac{3}{7} = \frac{18}{42}$
   b. $\frac{3}{18} = \frac{7}{42}$
   c. $\frac{18}{7} = \frac{3}{42}$
   d. $\frac{3}{42} = \frac{7}{18}$

13. A local grocery store is having a sale on tomato sauce: 12 cans for $9. How many cans can be purchased for $21?
   a. 16 cans
   b. 24 cans
   c. 28 cans
   d. 36 cans

14. Find the next number in the following sequence:

10, 6, 2, −2, −6, −10, …

a. −16
b. −14
c. −12
d. −8

15. Find the next entry in the following pictorial sequence:

•, O, ⊙, ••, OO, ⊙⊙, •••, OOO, ⊙⊙⊙, …

a. ••••
b. OOOO
c. ⊙⊙⊙⊙
d. ••OO⊙⊙

16. Simplify the following expression: $2 − 9(x − 4)$.
a. $−7x + 28$
b. $−9x − 2$
c. $−9x − 34$
d. $−9x + 38$

17. Solve the following inequality: $−3x + 8 > −7$.
a. $x < −5$
b. $x > 5$
c. $x < 5$
d. $x \leq 5$

18. Alexis runs a maid service for an apartment building. She has expenses of $310 per month. If she charges $85 for each apartment, how many apartments must Alexis clean to make a profit of at least $1,900 per month?
a. 19
b. 26
c. 4
d. 22

19. Find the slope of the line whose equation is: $3x + 2y = 5$.
a. 3
b. 2
c. $−\frac{3}{2}$
d. $\frac{5}{2}$

20. Luke wants to create a corral for his horses that measures 40 feet wide by 80 feet long. He also wishes to further divide the corral into two equal areas by putting an additional fence down the width of the area. How much fencing will Luke need?
a. 240 ft.
b. 280 ft.
c. 1,600 ft.
d. 3,200 ft.

21. Donna wishes to have wall-to-wall carpet in three bedrooms. The first room measures 6 feet by 8 feet, the second room measures 7 feet by 9 feet, and the last room measures 8 feet by 10 feet. How much carpet will Donna need?
a. 96 sq. ft.
b. 182 sq. ft.
c. 189 sq. ft.
d. 191 sq. ft.

22. Find the area of shaded region in the image below. The outside circle has a diameter of 14 cm, and the inside circle has a diameter of 8 cm. Use 3.14 for π.

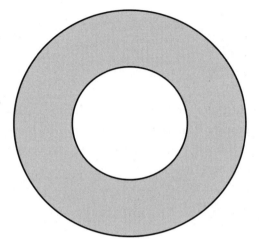

    a. 69.08 cm^2
    b. 103.62 cm^2
    c. 138.16 cm^2
    d. 414.48 cm^2

23. Find the circumference of a circle with a diameter of 1.5 meters. Use 3.14 for π.
    a. 9.42 meters
    b. 4.71 meters
    c. 3.53 meters
    d. 1.77 meters

24. Charles ran a total of 6.1 miles over three days. The first day he ran 1.7 miles, and the second day he ran 2.4 miles. How many miles did Charles run on the third day?
    a. 10.2 miles
    b. 4.1 miles
    c. 2.0 miles
    d. 3 miles

25. Walt Manufacturers can produce 27,630 widgets in 90 days. How many widgets can they produce per day?
    a. 307 widgets/day
    b. 279 widgets/day
    c. 170 widgets/day
    d. 37 widgets/day

26. Find the volume of a circular cylinder whose diameter is 5 inches and whose height is 4 inches. Use 3.14 for π.
    a. 62.8 cu. in.
    b. 78.5 cu. in.
    c. 100.0 cu. in.
    d. 125.6 cu. in.

27. Evaluate $x^2 + x + 2$ when $x = -3$.
    a. 5
    b. 8
    c. 14
    d. −10

28. Five times the sum of two consecutive even integers is 170. Create an equation that models this situation.
    a. $5x + (x + 1) = 170$
    b. $5x + (x + 2) = 170$
    c. $5[x + (x + 2)] = 170$
    d. $5[x + (x + 1)] = 170$

29. The length of a rectangle is seven more than twice its width. The perimeter of the rectangle is 122 inches. Create an equation that models this situation.
    a. $6w + 14 = 122$
    b. $6w + 7 = 122$
    c. $4w + 14 = 122$
    d. $4w + 7 = 122$

30. Four times the sum of three consecutive integers is 192. Find the three integers.
   a. 14, 16, 18
   b. 15, 16, 17
   c. 17, 18, 19
   d. 20, 21, 23

31. The sum of the interior angles of a triangle is 180°. If the measure of the second angle is five less than six times the measure of the first angle, and the measure of the third angle is nine more than the first, find the measure of the first angle.
   a. 127°
   b. 31°
   c. 25°
   d. 22°

32. Susan earned a 92% on her algebra test. She answered 46 problems correctly. How many problems were on the test?
   a. 44
   b. 50
   c. 54
   d. 56

33. Jeff is a car salesman. He earns 25% commission on all sales over $5,000. How much commission does Jeff earn on a car sold for $27,500?
   a. $1,250
   b. $5,625
   c. $6,750
   d. $6,875

34. Kenneth and his wife enjoyed dinner at a local restaurant. The bill came to $63.72 with tax included. To round off the final total, Kenneth left a $13.28 tip. What percent tip did Kenneth leave? Round to the nearest whole percent.
   a. 15%
   b. 20%
   c. 21%
   d. 22%

35. Heather saves $\frac{1}{4}$ of her take-home pay each month. If she earns $3,700 a month, how much will Heather have in her savings after five months?
   a. $4,625
   b. $4,500
   c. $4,375
   d. $925

36. In a local neighborhood, $\frac{4}{5}$ of the occupants own their homes. If there are 1,200 homes, how many occupants rent their homes?
   a. 960
   b. 240
   c. 600
   d. 800

37. Over a three-month period, 56 movies were released. Of those movies, $\frac{6}{7}$ of them were comedies. Of those comedies, $\frac{1}{3}$ of them were rated PG-13. How many PG-13 comedies were released during that three-month period?
   a. 16
   b. 24
   c. 40
   d. 48

38. A manager of a large clothing store is interested in how sales change over one year's time. She decides to track monthly net sales. Which type of data display should the manager choose?
  a. line graph
  b. bar graph
  c. circle graph
  d. stem-and-leaf plot

39. Rick and Diane decide to have a contest on who could collect the most aluminum cans in four weeks. How many cans did Diane collect in week three?

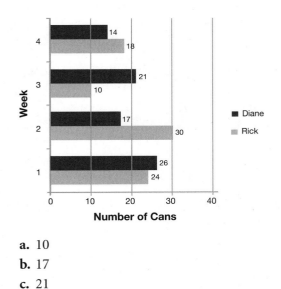

  a. 10
  b. 17
  c. 21
  d. 30

40. Consider the Venn diagram below. Which values do Group A and Group C share?

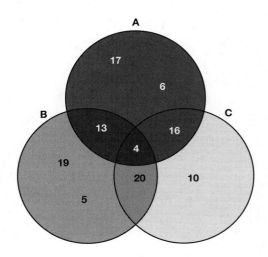

  a. 4 and 20
  b. 10 and 20
  c. 4 and 13
  d. 4 and 16

41. Claire's Café kept track of the dessert sales for the weekend. Which dessert had the second most sales for the entire weekend?

DESSERT	FRIDAY	SATURDAY
Apple Strudel	18	10
Carrot Cake	1	4
Chocolate Torte	21	24
Key Lime Pie	3	12
Peanut Butter Pie	16	17

  a. Apple Strudel
  b. Chocolate Torte
  c. Key Lime Pie
  d. Peanut Butter Pie

42. The percentages for Rico's monthly household budget are represented in the circle graph. If his monthly take-home pay is $5,800, how much does Rico spend on transportation each month?

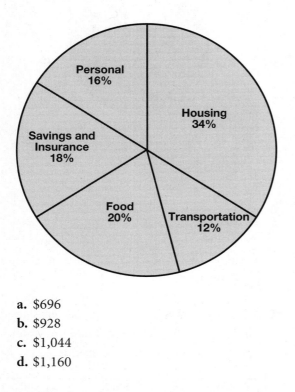

a. $696
b. $928
c. $1,044
d. $1,160

43. A single die has a value of 1 through 6 on each of its six sides. What is the probability of rolling a number less than 5 on a single roll?
a. $\frac{1}{3}$
b. $\frac{2}{3}$
c. $\frac{1}{2}$
d. $\frac{5}{6}$

44. Consider a family with three children. Assume that the probability of having a boy is equally likely as the probability of having a girl. What is the probability that at least two of the family's children are girls?
a. $\frac{1}{4}$
b. $\frac{1}{2}$
c. $\frac{3}{8}$
d. $\frac{5}{8}$

45. Find the mean of the following data set: 4.6, 5.2, 6.8, 7.4, 4.9, 6.5.
a. 7.1
b. 5.85
c. 5.9
d. 6.5

46. Find the range for the following data set: 85, 72, 64, 51, 83, 55, 83.
a. 32
b. 34
c. 72
d. 83

47. What are two lines with the same slope called?
a. adjacent
b. parallel
c. perpendicular
d. intersecting

48. Find the midpoint between the points (1,8) and (7,−6).
a. (1,4)
b. (4,0)
c. (4,1)
d. (4,7)

49. If the circumference of a given circle is 94.2 cm, what is its radius? Use 3.14 for π.
   a. 5.48 cm
   b. 15.0 cm
   c. 30.0 cm
   d. 47.1 cm

50. The vertices of a given triangle are located at the following points: (0,0) (3,5) (4,1). Find the coordinates of its translated image given the rule $T(x,y) = (x + 3, y + 5)$.
   a. (3,5) (6,10) (7,6)
   b. (5,3) (6,7) (10,6)
   c. (5,3) (8,8) (9,4)
   d. (3,5) (6,6) (7,10)

Answers and Explanations, Test 2

Reading

1. d. Choice **a** is incorrect. The term *extensive* refers to being more than adequate. Choice **b** is incorrect. The term *superior* refers to something higher in rank. Choice **c** is incorrect. The term *understandable* refers to something being comprehensible. Choice **d** is the correct answer. The term *satisfactory* refers to being *adequate*.
   Section: Words in Context
   Subsection: Same Meaning

2. c. Choice **a** is incorrect. The 3 Rs include reading. Choice **b** is incorrect. The 3 Rs include writing. Choice **c** is the correct answer. The 3 Rs do not include science. Choice **d** is incorrect. The 3 Rs include arithmetic.
   Section: Evaluate/Extend Meaning
   Subsection: Effect/Intention

3. a. Choice **a** is the correct answer. Harmeson was a *proponent*, or an *advocate*, of formal education in America. Choice **b** is incorrect. An *opponent* is not in support. Choice **c** is incorrect. An *adversary* is an enemy. Choice **d** is incorrect. A *martyr* is one who willingly endures persecution.
   Section: Construct Meaning
   Subsection: Main Idea

4. a. Choice **a** is the correct answer. The word *matriculate* means *study*. Choice **b** is incorrect. The word *establish* means *to set in a position*. Choice **c** is incorrect. The word *examine* means *to look closely*. Choice **d** is incorrect. *Join with* means *to combine*.
   Section: Words in Context
   Subsection: Same Meaning

5. c. Choice **a** is incorrect. A school journal could contain this passage. Choice **b** is incorrect. A newspaper could contain the passage. Choice **c** is the correct answer. A memorandum is traditionally used to disseminate brief information, not essays. Choice **d** is incorrect. A textbook in an English or education studies class might contain this passage.
Section: Evaluate/Extend Meaning
Subsection: Generalizations

6. d. Choice **a** is incorrect. It has no reference to politics. Choice **b** is incorrect. Someone who is "mathematically-inclined" would get no benefit from this. Choice **c** is incorrect. A professional tone is not achieved by this. Choice **d** is the correct answer. Depending on which country the reader lives, measurements are either in metric format or standard format.
Section: Recall Information
Subsection: Stated Concepts

7. a. Choice **a** is the correct answer. According to the passage, the melting of the glaciers formed deeper oceans. Choice **b** is incorrect. The melting of the glaciers did not make the oceans shallower. Choice **c** is incorrect. The melting of the glaciers did change the depth of oceans. Choice **d** is incorrect. Ocean depths can be measured.
Section: Construct Meaning
Subsection: Compare/Contrast

8. a. Choice **a** is the correct answer. A theory is based on facts but is ultimately an educated opinion. Choice **b** is incorrect. The word *warmer* is fact-based. Choice **c** is incorrect. The word *periodic* is fact-based. Choice **d** is incorrect. The word *migrate* is fact-based.
Section: Evaluate/Extend Meaning
Subsection: Fact/Opinion

9. c. Choice **a** is incorrect. There is no evidence to support this prediction. Choice **b** is incorrect. There is no evidence to support this prediction. Choice **c** is the correct answer. One could assume had the glaciers not moved, people and animals would not have moved from the areas they inhabited. Choice **d** is incorrect. There is no evidence to support this prediction.
Section: Evaluate/Extend Meaning
Subsection: Predict Outcomes

10. a. Choice **a** is the correct answer. Pointing out the large amount of land affected by the glacial melting was the intention of the writer. Choice **b** is incorrect. The author was not addressing the measurement of the land. Choice **c** is incorrect. The fact that this is a theory is not relevant. Choice **d** is incorrect. The author was not addressing the temperature.
Section: Evaluate/Extend Meaning
Subsection: Effect/Intention

11. b. Choice **a** is incorrect. The author's main purpose was not to show the dangers of cigarette smoking. Choice **b** is the correct answer. The passage was written as a report on the history of the government's involvement with smoking. Choice **c** is incorrect. The author was not out to destroy the tobacco industry. Choice **d** is incorrect. The author was not trying to show the falsehoods of government control.
Section: Construct Meaning
Subsection: Conclusion

12. d. Choice **a** is incorrect. The term *dullest risk* is not the opposite meaning in this context. Choice **b** is incorrect. The term *happiest risk* is not the opposite meaning in this context. Choice **c** is incorrect. The term *most popular risk* is not the opposite meaning in this context. Choice **d** is the correct answer. In terms of the passage, the opposite meaning would be a less restrictive, or a *more unlikely risk*.
Section: Words in Context
Subsection: Opposite Meaning

13. d. Choice **a** is incorrect. This is not a summary of Surgeon General Terry's research. Choice **b** is incorrect. This is not a summary of Surgeon General Terry's research. Choice **c** is incorrect. This is not a summary of Surgeon General Terry's research. Choice **d** is the correct answer. Surgeon General Terry spoke candidly about the results of cigarette smoking in terms of health.
Section: Construct Meaning
Subsection: Summary/Paraphrase

14. c. Choice **a** is incorrect. This is not the ultimate cause/effect. Choice **b** is incorrect. This is not the ultimate cause/effect. Choice **c** is the correct answer. Surgeon General Terry wanted everyone to know the dangers of cigarette smoking. Choice **d** is incorrect. This is not the ultimate cause/effect.
Section: Construct Meaning
Subsection: Cause/Effect

15. b. Choice **a** is incorrect. The purpose of the announcement was not to be *controversial*. Choice **b** is the correct answer. The main purpose was for the American public to *fear* the effects of smoking. Choice **c** is incorrect. The announcement was not *fantastical*. Choice **d** is incorrect. The announcement was extremely relevant.
Section: Words in Context
Subsection: Appropriate Word

16. b. Choice **a** is incorrect. The document is not a map. Choice **b** is the correct answer. The document is an outline. Choice **c** is incorrect. The document is not a syllabus. Choice **d** is incorrect. The document is not a blueprint.
Section: Evaluate/Extend Meaning
Subsection: Genre

17. d. Choice **a** is incorrect. The word *ending* is the same as a conclusion. Choice **b** is incorrect. The word *closing* is the same as a conclusion. Choice **c** is incorrect. The word *finale* is the same as a conclusion. Choice **d** is the correct answer. A *simulacrum* is not a conclusion, but rather an image of something.
Section: Words in Context
Subsection: Same Meaning

18. a. Choice **a** is the correct answer. The outline gives the webpage addresses for each source in the body of the speech. Choice **b** is incorrect. The outline does not reference a book. Choice **c** is incorrect. The outline does not reference a journal. Choice **d** is incorrect. The outline does not reference a newspaper.
Section: Interpret Graphic Information
Subsection: Reference Sources

19. b. Choice **a** is incorrect. The introduction of a speech does not go into detail about the points of the speech. Choice **b** is the correct answer. The body of a speech elaborates upon each main point. Choice **c** is incorrect. The conclusion of the speech does not go into detail about the points of the speech. Choice **d** is incorrect. The purpose of the speech provides more of a summary statement.
Section: Recall Information
Subsection: Sequence

20. b. Choice **a** is incorrect. The author does not mention *intelligence* as a negative aspect. Choice **b** is the correct answer. The outline lists now knowing doctors' qualifications as a con in the body of the document. Choice **c** is incorrect. The author does not mention *health* as a negative aspect. Choice **d** is incorrect. The author does not mention *work ethic* as a negative aspect.
Section: Construct Meaning
Subsection: Supporting Evidence

21. c. Choice **a** is incorrect. The passage does not reference a basement. Choice **b** is incorrect. The passage does not reference an official courtroom. Choice **c** is the correct answer. The passage references the surroundings of a country store. Choice **d** is incorrect. The passage does not reference a police station.
Section: Construct Meaning
Subsection: Supporting Evidence

22. b. Choice **a** is incorrect. There is no mention of or reference to factory workers. Choice **b** is the correct answer. The passage reads that his stomach read the labels, which implies that he was hungry. Choice **c** is incorrect. There is no mention of a boat or the ocean. Choice **d** is incorrect. There is no implication that this was a dream.
Section: Construct Meaning
Subsection: Main Idea

23. a. Choice **a** is the correct answer. Mr. Harris was implying that the fire was started intentionally, out of spite. Choice **b** is incorrect. Mr. Harris did think the discussion was necessary. Choice **c** is incorrect. Mr. Harris was not scared of the other gentleman. Choice **d** is incorrect. Mr. Harris did understand the accusations he was making.
Section: Evaluate/Extend Meaning
Subsection: Effect/Intention

24. b. Choice **a** is incorrect. Although Mr. Harris appeared angry, it was not the source of his bad grammar. Choice **b** is the correct answer. It appears that Mr. Harris was undereducated based on his use of improper grammar. Choice **c** is incorrect. Mr. Harris would not be considered an aristocrat. Choice **d** is incorrect. Mr. Harris would not be described as neighborly.
Section: Construct Meaning
Subsection: Character Aspects

25. a. Choice **a** is the correct answer. The term *stock* is a shortened version of the term *livestock*, which refers to *animals*. Choice **b** is incorrect. The term was referring to animals. Choice **c** is incorrect. The term was referring to animals. Choice **d** is incorrect. The term was referring to animals.
Section: Words in Context
Subsection: Same Meaning

26. b. Choice **a** is incorrect. The passage does address nodding. Choice **b** is the correct answer. The passage does not address smiling. Choice **c** is incorrect. The passage does address rephrasing. Choice **d** is incorrect. The passage does address providing examples.
Section: Construct Meaning
Subsection: Supporting Evidence

27. d. Choice **a** is incorrect. The term *positively* means *confident*. Choice **b** is incorrect. The term *intellectually* means *given to study and reflection*. Choice **c** is incorrect. The term *wordy* means *too much verbiage*. Choice **d** is the correct answer. The term *succinctly* means *briefly*.
Section: Words in Context
Subsection: Same Meaning

28. a. Choice **a** is the correct answer. This title states the central idea of the entire passage. Choice **b** is incorrect. While this is important, it is not the main focus of the passage. Choice **c** is incorrect. This title is not relevant to the overall meaning of the passage. Choice **d** is incorrect. This title is not the central idea of the entire passage.
Section: Construct Meaning
Subsection: Summary/Paraphrase

29. c. Choice **a** is incorrect. The listener falling asleep is not relevant to the passage. Choice **b** is incorrect. The speaker has no reason to be tempted to glance around. Choice **c** is the correct answer. Giving the speaker your full attention signifies that you are listening. Choice **d** is incorrect. The audience laughing is not a valid concern.
Section: Construct Meaning
Subsection: Conclusion

30. b. Choice **a** is incorrect. This is not an opposite meaning of *unwieldy*. Choice **b** is the correct answer. The word *unwieldy* means *awkward*. The opposite of *awkward* is *not awkward*. Choice **c** is incorrect. This is not an opposite meaning of *unwieldy*. Choice **d** is incorrect. This is not an opposite meaning of *unwieldy*.
Section: Words in Context
Subsection: Opposite Meaning

31. d. Choice **a** is incorrect. The speaker does not really use characterization, although she does use her friend as an example. Choice **b** is incorrect. Nothing ironic occurs in the passage; the author's tone is utterly serious. Choice **c** is incorrect. The speaker does not use the tool of persuasion. Choice **d** is the correct answer. The speaker uses an emotional appeal to convince the listener of the effect that anorexia can have on a person.
Section: Construct Meaning
Subsection: Supporting Evidence

32. b. Choice **a** is incorrect. The definition of anorexia is one of the three main points. Choice **b** is the correct answer. Examples of celebrities with anorexia are not discussed. Choice **c** is incorrect. The causes of anorexia are one of the three main points discussed. Choice **d** is incorrect. The treatment of anorexia is one of the three main points discussed.
Section: Recall Information
Subsection: Sequence

33. a. Choice **a** is the correct answer. According to the passage, dull hair is a symptom of anorexia. Choice **b** is incorrect. An outgoing personality is not mentioned as a symptom of anorexia. Choice **c** is incorrect. The description of uncaring parents is not discussed as a symptom of anorexia. Choice **d** is incorrect. Bone spurs are not discussed as a symptom of anorexia.
Section: Construct Meaning
Subsection: Supporting Evidence

34. a. Choice **a** is the correct answer. The speaker's credibility is based on her personal experience. Choice **b** is incorrect. The speaker's credibility is not based on conversations with parents. Choice **c** is incorrect. Even though the speaker has done research for her paper, her credibility is not based on that research; it is based on her personal experience with a friend. Choice **d** is incorrect. The speaker's credibility is not based on a rational conclusion.
Section: Construct Meaning
Subsection: Character Aspects

35. c. Choice **a** is incorrect. The reader can make an educated guess based on information given in the excerpt. Choice **b** is incorrect. The reader can assume that the onset of anorexia began before the post-college years. Choice **c** is the correct answer. Based on the passage, one can assume that the onset of anorexia really began in Julie's teenage years. Choice **d** is incorrect. The passage does not imply that signs of anorexia occurred in the toddler years.
Section: Construct Meaning
Subsection: Conclusion

36. b. Choice **a** is incorrect. There is no evidence presented in the poem that it is dangerous to be famous. Choice **b** is correct. By comparing celebrity to a frog living in a bog, the speaker makes it clear that she would find fame a dismal experience. Choice **c** is incorrect. This answer is the opposite of what the speaker implies in her poem; a fawning audience is compared to "an admiring bog." Choice **d** is incorrect. The speaker does not want the reader to share their private status with the world; instead, she wants them to remain unknown entities. She is not concerned about being viewed as ordinary.
Section: Construct Meaning
Subsection: Character Aspects

37. d. Choice **a** is incorrect. There are no references to classrooms, learning, teachers, or students. Choice **b** is incorrect. Although fame is compared to life in a swamp ("Bog"), the tone of this poem is not frightening and makes no mention of otherworldly spirits of any sort. Choice **c** is incorrect. The speaker implies that a mundane or seemingly boring life is preferable to one that is "public." Choice **d** is correct. The speaker compares an "admiring bog" to people who are attracted to famous people.
Section: Construct Meaning
Subsection: Compare/Contrast

38. c. Choice **a** is incorrect. The poem contains few multisyllabic or abstract words. Choice **b** is incorrect. Only two lines of the eight rhyme: frog/bog. Choice **c** is correct. The poet uses capital letters in unusual ways, as in "Nobody," "Somebody," and "Bog"; she also uses nine dashes and several exclamation points in an eight-line poem. Choice **d** is incorrect. Although Dickinson uses a simile by comparing a frog to being a public figure, the poem is not laden with symbolism.
Section: Evaluate/Extend Meaning
Subsection: Style Techniques

39. **b.** Choice **a** is incorrect. Rather than serious, the tone of the poem is flippant. Choice **b** is correct. The poem is highly ironic, with a humorous, tongue-in-cheek quality; while many people seek fame or imagine that it offers an amazing world of riches, Dickinson compares fame to the life of a frog in a swamp. Choice **c** is incorrect. Although the speaker seems, in a sense, to be whispering to the reader in the first stanza, she is not primarily interested in being secretive as much as keeping herself apart from a public life. Choice **d** is incorrect. Again, the tone here is playful, with no atmosphere of sorrow or regret for something out of reach; rather, the speaker wants to remain out of reach.
Section: Evaluate/Extend Meaning
Subsection: Effect/Intuition

40. **b.** Choice **a** is incorrect. There is no evidence that the speaker appreciates frogs. Choice **b** is correct. Comparing being a public figure to being a frog is a comparison few readers would find positive. Choice **c** is incorrect. There is no evidence in the poem for this answer and no allusion to famous people's actions. Choice **d** is incorrect. The poem focuses on how being a public figure would itself be a dreary thing, not how fame affects the famous.
Section: Evaluate/Extend Meaning
Subsection: Effect/Intention

41. **c.** Choice **a** is incorrect. There is no implication that the setting is in a shopping mall. Choice **b** is incorrect. There is no implication that the setting is in a church sanctuary. Choice **c** is the correct answer. The reader can assume from the details given that the setting is the speaker's bedroom. Choice **d** is incorrect. There is no implication that the setting is in a school classroom.
Section: Construct Meaning
Subsection: Supporting Evidence

42. **d.** Choice **a** is incorrect. The reader cannot accurately assume the age of the speaker. Choice **b** is incorrect. The reader cannot accurately assume the age of the speaker. Choice **c** is incorrect. The reader cannot accurately assume the age of the speaker. Choice **d** is the correct answer. The age of the speaker cannot be assumed.
Section: Evaluate/Extend Meaning
Subsection: Generalizations

43. **a.** Choice **a** is the correct answer. The speaker believed her mother wanted to remove her from existence in life. Choice **b** is incorrect. The speaker was not referring to her mother congratulating her. Choice **c** is incorrect. The speaker did not believe her mother sympathized with her. Choice **d** is incorrect. The speaker did not portray her mother as one who would encourage her.
Section: Words in Context
Subsection: Same Meaning

44. **b.** Choice **a** is incorrect. The speaker was not speaking directly to her mother. Choice **b** is the correct answer. The speaker was having a conversation with herself. Choice **c** is incorrect. The speaker was not talking to her father. Choice **d** is incorrect. The speaker was not talking to her sister.
Section: Evaluate/Extend Meaning
Subsection: Generalizations

45. c. Choice **a** is incorrect. The speaker *did* feel she was a disappointment to her mother. Choice **b** is incorrect. The speaker *did* feel she was a disappointment to her father. Choice **c** is the correct answer. The speaker did not mention that she felt she was a disappointment to her sister. Choice **d** is incorrect. The speaker *did* feel she was a disappointment to her parents and to herself.
Section: Evaluate/Extend Meaning
Subsection: Effect/Intention

46. d. Choice **a** is incorrect. There is no relevance as to whether or not the author knows the Webmaster. Choice **b** is incorrect. The reader does not know whether the Webmaster is the publishing agent. Choice **c** is incorrect. The reader is not likely to become confused. Choice **d** is the correct answer. Biased opinions are possible if the author and the Webmaster are the same person.
Section: Evaluate/Extend Meaning
Subsection: Author Purpose

47. b. Choice **a** is incorrect. The "professional quality" of a Web page's information has nothing to do with whether the information is current or not. Choice **b** is the correct answer. A professionally-produced Web page is usually updated frequently. Choice **c** is incorrect. One cannot assume a dead link falsifies a Web page's purpose. Choice **d** is incorrect. Current Web pages do not necessarily have "built in" technologies that assure accuracy and currentness.
Section: Evaluate/Extend Meaning
Subsection: Author Purpose

48. d. Choice **a** is incorrect. A person or group putting together a Web page may not be objective. Choice **b** is incorrect. A location does not ensure objectivity. Choice **c** is incorrect. An author's credentials do not ensure objectivity. Choice **d** is the correct answer. The author's opinions may or may not be objective.
Section: Recall Information
Subsection: Stated Concepts

49. a. Choice **a** is the correct answer. Web pages are not necessarily useful, helpful, or accurate based on their popularity. Choice **b** is incorrect. A Web page's evaluation should include accuracy. Choice **c** is incorrect. A Web page's evaluation should include authoritative authenticity. Choice **d** is incorrect. A Web page's evaluation should include objectivity.
Section: Recall Information
Subsection: Stated Concepts

50. c. Choice **a** is incorrect. Some Web pages from educational institutions do not give accurate information. Choice **b** is incorrect. Many Web pages are trustworthy. Choice **c** is the correct answer. Readers should be aware that some Web pages are accurate and some are not. Choice **d** is incorrect. Web pages are not required to have author and Webmaster information recorded.
Section: Evaluate/Extend Meaning
Subsection: Fact/Opinion

Language

1. d. Choice **a** is incorrect. *Well* should be used instead of *good* when referring to health or physical condition. Choice **b** is incorrect. A linking verb links its subject to a subject complement. A subject complement can be a modifier (which describes the subject). When it is a modifier, it must be an adjective because it describes the subject (which is always a noun or pronoun). It does not modify the linking verb itself and therefore should not be an adverb (*We felt bad . . .*). Choice **c** is incorrect. An adjective describes a noun or pronoun and answers these questions: how many, which one, what kind? In this example, the adverb *slowly* is correct. Choice **d** is the correct answer. *Real* is an adjective; it is only used to describe nouns and pronouns.
Sections: Usage
Subsections: Adjective

2. d. Choice **a** is incorrect. *Successfully* is an adverb modifying the verb *argued*. Choice **b** is incorrect. *Skillfully* is an adverb modifying the verb *drove*. Choice **c** is incorrect. *Carefully* is an adverb describing how the dog is smelling. It modifies the verb *smell*. Choice **d** is the correct answer. *High* is an adjective modifying the noun *grades*.
Section:Usage
Subsection: Adjective

3. d. Choice **a** is incorrect. The sentence requires the superlative adjective *most*. Choice **b** is incorrect. The word *better* is the correct adjective for this sentence. Choice **c** is incorrect. The sentence should read: *It was the hotter of the two summers.* Choice **d** is the correct answer. The adjective *best* correctly modifies the noun *plan*.
Section: Usage
Subsection: Adjective

4. d. Choice **a** is incorrect. Some words ending in *-ly* are adjectives and not normally adverbs. *Deadly* is one of them. Other common examples are *cowardly, miserly, lonely,* etc. The adjective *deadly* refers to the *kind* of forest fire. Choice **b** is incorrect. *Nice* is an adjective. The adverb *nicely* is needed because it describes how they behaved. Choice **c** is incorrect. This sentence does not contain any adverbs. Choice **d** is the correct answer. *Well* is an adverb that tells how the choir sings.
Section: Usage
Subsection: Adverb

5. c. Choice **a** is incorrect. *Carelessly* should be used instead of *careless*. *Carelessly* is an adverb that modifies *played*. It tells us how the cellist played. Choice **b** is incorrect. *Rotten* is an adjective that modifies the noun *meat*. Choice **c** is the correct answer. *Beautifully* is an adverb that modifies *sings*. Choice **d** is incorrect. *Hot* is an adjective that modifies the noun *afternoon*. *Terrible* is also an adjective that modifies the adjective *hot*. To tell just how hot it is, the correct adverb *terribly* is used.
Section: Usage
Subsection: Adverb

6. c. Choice **a** is incorrect. How did the camera work? It worked *perfectly*. Adverbs answer *how*. Choice **b** is incorrect. After linking verbs (*look, sound, taste, smell, feel, seem*), adjectives, not adverbs, are used. Choice **c** is the correct answer. Adverbs answer *how*. *Dramatically* tells how the ending was staged. Choice **d** is incorrect. This sentence does not contain any adverbs. *Fluent* is an adjective modifying the proper noun *English*.
Section: Usage
Subsection: Adverb

7. b. Choice **a** is incorrect. A prepositional phrase or a clause between the subject and verb does not change the number of the antecedent. *Can* is singular and thus requires the singular possessive pronoun *its*. Choice **b** is the correct answer. Here, . . . *his or her office* refers to its singular antecedent *Each*. An antecedent is the word, phrase, or clause to which a pronoun refers and with which the pronoun must agree. Choice **c** is incorrect. With compound subjects joined by the words *either . . . or* or *neither . . . nor*, the pronoun must agree with the antecedent closest to the pronoun. The sentence should read *Neither . . . nor the actors did their job.* Choice **d** is incorrect. There are some antecedents that may look plural but that are generally accepted as singular (*news, measles, mumps, physics*, etc.). The sentence should read *Mumps is. . . .*
Section: Usage
Subsection: Antecedent Agreement

8. d. Choice **a** is incorrect. Pronoun antecedent agreement is when the pronoun agrees in number (singular or plural) and person (first, second, or third person) with its antecedent. *Somebody* is singular and *their* is plural. Choice **b** is incorrect. This sentence can be corrected by making the pronoun *their* singular (*his* or *her*) to agree with the antecedent (*employee*). Choice **c** is incorrect. The antecedent *Joe* takes a third person singular verb (*he should* instead of *they should*). Choice **d** is the correct answer. *Anyone* is a singular antecedent that agrees with the third person singular verb (*he or she should*).
Section: Usage
Subsection: Antecedent Agreement

9. d. Choice **a** is incorrect. Subjects joined by *and* form a compound subject and require a plural pronoun (*they*). Choice **b** is incorrect. This sentence has a plural subject (*Both*). It requires the plural pronoun *they*. Also, the word *he* is an unclear referent; the reader cannot tell whether Juan thinks he or Julio should be interviewed first, and vice versa. Choice **c** is incorrect. The antecedent *Everyone* is singular and requires a singular pronoun (*his or her* cabin). Choice **d** is the correct answer. *His* refers to *Ruben* (the antecedent), not *mother*.
Section: Usage
Subsection: Antecedent Agreement

10. a. Choice #1 is correct. The adjective describes in what kind of manner he delivers milk.
  b. Choice #2 is correct. The adverb describes how he writes (*well*).
  c. Choice #2 is correct. The adverb describes how she went to bed (*quietly*).
  d. Choice #2 is correct. The adverb describes how they behaved (*badly*).
  Section: Usage
  Subsection: Choose Between Adjective/ Adverb

11. a. Choice #1 is correct. A predicate adjective always follows a *be* verb, and adjectives always follow verbs such as *feel, taste,* and *look*.
  b. Choice #2 is correct. The adverb *bitterly* describes how the child cried.
  c. Choice #1 is correct. *Miserly* is a *-ly* word that is an adjective, not an adverb. Some other words in this category are *elderly, friendly,* and *lovely*.
  d. Choice #1 is correct. Descriptive words following a *be* verb are always adjectives (. . . *was annoyed*).
  Section: Usage
  Subsection: Choose Between Adjective/ Adverb

12. **a.** Choice #2 is correct. Here, *carelessly* is an adverb that modifies the verb *talks*; it tells *how* Richard talks.
   b. Choice #1 is correct. After a sense word (*feel*), the simple rule to follow is: subject + sense verb + adjective.
   c. Choice #1 is correct. After a sense word (*smell*), the simple rule to follow is: subject + sense verb + adjective.
   d. Choice #1 is correct. After a sense word (*looks*), the simple rule to follow is: subject + sense verb + adjective.
   Section: Language/Usage
   Subsection: Choose Between Adjective/Adverb

13. **d.** Choice **a** is incorrect. The word *I* is a subject pronoun, not an objective pronoun, which is needed because *me* is the correct object of the preposition, not *I* (*between you and me*). Choice **b** is incorrect. A predicate nominative pronoun (*he*) is required following a *be* verb, not the objective pronoun *him*. Choice **c** is incorrect. *Dana* and *I* are the direct objects of the sentence. As *I* is never objective, the proper pronoun is *me*. Choice **d** is the correct answer. The pronoun *her* is an objective pronoun because it is the indirect object of *box of candy*.
   Section: Usage
   Subsection: Pronouns

14. **b.** Choice **a** is incorrect. The word *who* is used to refer to people, not *which*. Choice **b** is the correct answer. The relative pronoun *who* is used to refer to people. Choice **c** is incorrect. In formal grammar, *whom* is the correct relative pronoun, as it is the object of the verb *trust*. Choice **d** is incorrect. The relative pronoun *that* is used for essential phrases, not *which*.
   Subject: Usage
   Subsection: Pronouns

15. **c.** Choice **a** is incorrect. The plural verb *were* does not agree with the third person singular subject *quiz*. Change the verb to *was*. Choice **b** is incorrect. The plural verb *seem* does not agree with the third person singular subject *jacket*. Change the verb to *seems*. Choice **c** is the correct answer. The plural subject *women* agrees with the plural verb *were*. Choice **d** is incorrect. The plural verb *were* does not agree with the third person singular subject *group*. Change the verb to was.
   Section: Usage
   Subsection: Subject/Verb Agreement

16. **c.** Choice **a** is incorrect. *People* is not a collective noun like *team* or *staff*. It is a plural noun. However, the subject of this sentence is *one*, which is singular and requires the singular verb *is*. Choice **b** is incorrect. In this sentence, the object of the preposition is *list*, which is always singular. Therefore, the correct verb is *has*. Choice **c** is the correct answer. *Staff*, a collective noun, is acting as a single unit in this sentence and requires the singular verb *meets*. Choice **d** is incorrect. *Team* is being used in this sentence as a cohesive unit, so a singular verb is required (*is*).
   Subject: Usage
   Subsection: Subject/Verb Agreement

17. b. Choice **a** is incorrect. *Drank* is past tense of *drink*, which is an irregular verb, and drunk is always used with the participial (past perfect) form of the verb (verb + have). Choice **b** is the correct answer. The future tense verb *will make* is used to describe an action that will happen. Choice **c** is incorrect. The present perfect tense is used to talk about things that started in the past and continue into the present and/or the future (*has been*). It shows how long something has lasted (*three years*). Choice **d** is incorrect. The past perfect form of *swim* is *have swum*, not *have swam*.
Section: Usage
Subsection: Tense

18. c. Choice **a** is incorrect. The verb *cried* is past tense, but it should be present tense (*cries*). Or, make both verbs past tense (*cried, won*). Choice **b** is incorrect. The following verbs are usually used only in present tense: *be, have, hear, know, like, love, see, smell, think, want*, etc. Choice **c** is the correct answer. *Swims* is the present tense of the verb *to swim*. The present tense is used for actions that happen often, generally, or never. Choice **d** is incorrect. In this sentence, *. . . every day, including today* is an indication for a present-tense verb (*bring*).
Section: Usage
Subsection: Tense

19. a. Choice **a** is the correct answer. The following list contains words that are regarded as negative. If you use the words that follow in your sentences once, your statements will be negative: *no, not, none, nothing, nowhere, neither, nobody, no one, hardly, scarcely, barely*. If you have two negatives (*not, no*), the results will have the opposite meaning. Choice **b** is incorrect. There is a double negative in the sentence (*hardly, none*), which changes the meaning of the sentence. Choice **c** is incorrect. There is a double negative in the sentence (*not, no*), which changes the meaning of the sentence. Choice **d** is incorrect. There is a double negative in the sentence (*not, no*), which changes the meaning of the sentence.

20. d. Choice **a** is incorrect. The double negative is *not, neither/nor*. To make this sentence negative, eliminate the *not*. Choice **b** is incorrect. This sentence contains the double negative *not, neither/nor*. To make this sentence negative, eliminate the *not* and rewrite it as *I had neither. . . .* Choice **c** is incorrect. The double negative (*not, neither/nor*) makes this sentence positive. To make it negative, eliminate the *not* and rewrite it as *He mentioned neither. . . .* Choice **d** is the correct answer. There is only one negative in this sentence (*not*), making it negative.
Section: Language/Usage
Subsection: Use Negatives

21. d. Choice **a** is incorrect. The modifier is misplaced in this sentence. The man was not gold; the watch was. The sentence should read, *On his way home, Rob found a man's gold watch.* Choice **b** is incorrect. This sentence contains a dangling modifier. The article did not read the study; the speaker did. The sentence is much clearer this way: *After reading the original study, I found the article unconvincing.* Choice **c** is incorrect. This sentence has a dangling modifier that makes it sound like one tower saw the other. For clarity, the sentence should read, *Having seen Blackpool Tower, I was more impressed with the Eiffel Tower.* Choice **d** is the correct answer. The adverb slowly clearly modifies how the lunch was eaten, which makes for a clear sentence.

22. c. Choice **a** is incorrect. The mechanic was not torn, his manual was. The adjective is misplaced, modifying *mechanic*. The sentence should read, *The mechanic's torn manual. . . .* Choice **b** is incorrect. The cat cannot read. The sentence should read, *Having read your letter, I will ensure that the cat will. . . .* Choice **c** is the correct answer. A misplaced modifier would make it sound like the buyer has leather seats. This is not the case in this sentence. Choice **d** is incorrect. There is no corner that wears suits; this is a case of a misplaced modifier. The sentence should read, *The three bankers wearing suits talked quietly in the corner.*

23. b. Choice **a** is incorrect. The shed was not made of barbed wire, although the misplaced modifier makes it seem so. The sentence should read, *They saw a fence made of barbed wire behind the shed.* Choice **b** is the correct answer. The roll was well buttered, not the woman. Choice **c** is incorrect. Sally did not wear a hamper. This is a misplaced clause that modifies the wrong noun. The sentence should read, *Sally put all the clothes that she had worn in the hamper.* Choice **d** is incorrect. The speaker's mother did not return to college when she was nine. The sentence should read, *When I was nine years old, my mother. . . .*
Section: Language/Sentence Formation
Subsection: Sentence Clarity

24. c. Choice **a** is incorrect. These three short, choppy sentences are not the best way to express this information. Choice **b** is incorrect. This example combines the sentences but makes for a long and monotonous example with too many connecting *and*'s. Choice **c** is the correct answer. This is the best example of combining these sentences. Choice **d** is incorrect. This is a good example of combining sentences, but it is not the best out of the four choices.

25. d. Choice **a** is incorrect. These three short, choppy sentences are not the best way to express this information. Choice **b** is incorrect. This example contains two sentences. As they both refer to the shopping trip, it is better than the first example, but it isn't the best. Choice **c** is incorrect. This example combines the sentences, but changes their meaning. Choice **d** is the correct answer. This sentence is the best example of combining the original sentences. It combines all the information and limits the pronoun *me* to one usage.

26. b. Choice **a** is incorrect. These six short, choppy sentences are not the best way to express this information. Choice **b** is the correct answer. This example does the best job in giving out all the information using a colon and a conjunction. Choice **c** is incorrect. This example contains only two sentences, but the second sentence is extremely long and uninspiring. Choice **d** is incorrect. Although it is only one sentence in length, it does not flow as easily as choice **b**, which varies the lengths of the clauses.
Section: Language/Sentence Formation
Subsection: Sentence Combining

27. c. Choice **a** is incorrect. This selection includes a reference to words in the topic sentence (Many bicycle groups . . . *These groups* . . .) and a standard signal phrase that introduces a supporting sentence (*For example,*). Choice **b** is incorrect. This selection contains a pronoun reference (*This*) that refers back to the prior passage (*five miles*) and a contrasting phrase (*unlike the car*) that connects to the earlier topic (*bicycle*). Choice **c** is the correct answer. This selection contains no single connecting words or transitional phrases. Choice **d** is incorrect. It contains three transitional phrases that show the chronology of the action (*first move, meanwhile, In this position*).
Section: Language/Paragraph Development
Subsection: Connective/Transitional Devices

28. c. Choice **a** is incorrect. This selection contains two transitions. One indicates a result of the action of the last sentence in the prior passage (*therefore*) and one repeats a key phrase from it (*Therefore, could float in water, now*). The word *now* also adds coherence because it is a signal word indicating chronology. Choice **b** is incorrect. This selection has a reference to a preceding mention of help and chronological signal words (*first step, then*). Choice **c** is the correct answer. It contains no signal words or transitional phrases. Choice **d** is incorrect. This selection has a chronological signal word (*Once*), a reference to a preceding sentence (*Rolling*), and a pronoun referring back to rolling (*It*).
Section: Language/Paragraph Development
Subsection: Connective/Transitional Devices

29. c. Choice **a** is incorrect. This section has a signal phrase that indicates an example and a second that indicates a contrasting point (*In the first place, Otherwise*). Choice **b** is incorrect. This example includes standard signal phrases that indicate additional information and a contrasting point (*In addition, On the contrary*). Choice **c** is the correct answer. There are no signal words or transitional phrases in this selection. Choice **d** is incorrect. This example includes a standard closing signal word (*Finally,*) and a highly useful signal phrase that helps the reader to weigh the importance of the following point (*most importantly,*).
Section: Language/Paragraph Development
Subsection: Connective/Transitional Devices

30. a. Choice **a** is the correct answer. The Germans thought that the treaty was unfair. When the U.S. refused to ratify the treaty, it weakened the League of Nations and ultimately led to World War II. Choice **b** is incorrect. The unrest in Germany started after the treaty. Choice **c** is incorrect. The U.S. Senate voted against the treaty in 1921. The treaty itself was introduced in 1919. Choice **d** is incorrect. The sentences are not in chronological order.
Section: Language/Paragraph Development
Subsection: Sequence

31. a. Choice **a** is the correct answer. This is the proper order of steps to get you from the Interstate to the speaker's house on Franklin Street. Choice **b** is incorrect. This order of steps has the driver reaching the destination before the car leaves the exit ramp. Choice **c** is incorrect. These steps are out of order: the driver leaves Route 4 before the car gets off the Interstate. Choice **d** is incorrect. These steps are out of order. The car reaches Route 4 before it leaves the Interstate.
Section: Language/Paragraph Development
Subsection: Sequence

32. b. Choice **a** is incorrect. America entered the Vietnam War in 1959; World War II occurred in the 1940s. Choice **b** is the correct answer. The events are in the proper chronological order. Choice **c** is incorrect. The other events happened before Barack Obama was elected. Choice **d** is incorrect. The election of Barack Obama occurred last in the order of these events.
Section: Language/Paragraph Development
Subsection: Sequence

33. d. Choice **a** is incorrect. None of the supporting sentences make this claim. Choice **b** is incorrect. None of the supporting sentences make this claim. Choice **c** is incorrect. None of the supporting sentences make this claim. Choice **d** is the correct answer. All four supporting details support this topic sentence.
Structure: Language/Paragraph Development
Subsection: Supporting Sentence

34. a. Choice **a** is the correct answer. Three of the four details support this topic sentence. Choice **b** is incorrect. None of the supporting sentences make this claim. Choice **c** is incorrect. None of the supporting sentences make this claim. Choice **d** is incorrect. None of the supporting sentences make this claim.
Structure: Language/Paragraph Development
Subsection: Supporting Sentence

35. a. Choice **a** is the correct answer. All of the supporting sentences offer details that expand upon the two main ideas in this topic sentence. Choice **b** is incorrect. This sentence brings up a main idea that the details do not support. Choice **c** is incorrect. This sentence would work better as another supporting sentence, not a topic sentence. Choice **d** is incorrect. This sentence brings up a main idea that the details do not support.
Structure: Language/Paragraph Development
Subsection: Supporting Sentence

36. c. Choice **a** is incorrect. This sentence is very simple and doesn't offer much to expand upon. If the paragraph is going to be about Alice's height, what about her height is interesting? Choice **b** is incorrect. This sentence is very simple and doesn't offer much to expand upon. If the paragraph is going to be about the fact that Alice comes from Virginia, what about this fact is interesting? Choice **c** is the correct answer. This sentence provides a specific, solid idea for a paragraph and gives the reader a good sense of what it will be about: the things that Alice learned on the farm. Choice **d** is incorrect. This sentence is very simple and doesn't offer much to expand upon. The reader has no idea what the paragraph will be about.
Section: Language/Paragraph Development
Subsection: Topic Sentence

37. a. Choice **a** is the correct answer. This sentence is specific enough to tell the reader what to expect in the paragraph (the ways in which the king helped his country) but broad enough to serve as a main idea that supporting sentences can round out. Choice **b** is incorrect. This is not a good topic sentence because it gives no clue about what part of George Lucas's many film-related activities will be discussed. Also, this is much too broad of a topic to be covered in a single paragraph. Choice **c** is incorrect. This sentence is specific, but it doesn't offer a main idea for a paragraph to expand upon. Choice **d** is incorrect. This sentence is too broad and unclear. Specifically, what does the writer want to tell the reader?
Section: Language/Paragraph Development
Subsection: Topic Sentence

38. c. Choice **a** is incorrect. This topic is too broad and badly defined. What people? What kind of experiments? Choice **b** is incorrect. This sentence is too broad and doesn't give the reader a clear sense of what the paragraph will be about. How is plagiarism complex? Why is that important? Choice **c** is the correct answer. This is an excellent topic sentence. The reader can look forward to discovering the interaction between the grandparents and their grandchild. Choice **d** is incorrect. This sentence is too broad.
Section: Language/Paragraph Development
Subsection: Topic Sentence

39. d. Choice **a** is incorrect. This sentence offers one step to take if you have a nosebleed. It fits with the other sentences that do the same. Choice **b** is incorrect. This sentence offers one step to take if you have a nosebleed. It fits with the other sentences that do the same. Choice **c** is incorrect. This sentence offers one step to take if you have a nosebleed. It fits with the other sentences that do the same. Choice **d** is the correct answer. Read with the other sentences, this sentence seems like an out-of-the-blue comment about doctors. It doesn't have anything to do with nosebleeds.
Section: Language/Paragraph Development
Subsection: Unrelated Sentence

40. b. Choice **a** is incorrect. This sentence belongs because it is a topic-developing sentence and needs to be just where it is placed. Choice **b** is the correct answer. This sentence does not belong. It may be factually correct, but it does not relate to the other sentences. Choice **c** is incorrect. This sentence belongs because it supports Sentences 1 and 3. Choice **d** is incorrect. This sentence belongs because it supports the preceding sentence (Sentence 3).
Section: Language/Paragraph Development
Subsection: Unrelated Sentence

41. d. Choice **a** is incorrect. It works as a topic sentence for the two sentences that follow. Choice **b** is incorrect. Along with Sentence 3, it works as a supporting sentence for Sentence 1. Choice **c** is incorrect. Along with Sentence 2, it works as a supporting sentence for Sentence 1. Choice **d** is the correct answer. The other three sentences talk about the ways in which carpentry is rewarding in general. This sentence stands out because it doesn't talk about the ways in which carpentry is rewarding and because it talks about a specific man, the speaker's father.
Section: Language/Paragraph Development
Subsection: Unrelated Sentence

42. d. Choice **a** is incorrect. The interjection *Oh* should not be capitalized because it appears in the middle of the sentence. Choice **b** is incorrect. The first word of a complete sentence quotation is always capitalized. Choice **c** is incorrect. The first word of a quotation followed by a comma is always capitalized (*Oh*). Choice **d** is the correct answer. The interjection *O*, although rare in modern literature, is always capitalized.
Section: Language/Capitalization
Subsection: First Word

43. c. Choice **a** is incorrect. The first word of a complete sentence quotation is always capitalized. More important, the pronoun *I*, by itself or with a contraction (*I'm, I've*), is always capitalized. Choice **b** is incorrect. If the quote is integrated into the syntax of the sentence, don't capitalize the first word. Choice **c** is the correct answer. Lowercase the first word in a list if the items are not complete sentences. Choice **d** is incorrect. Capitalize the first word of a saying, a slogan, a motto, or dialogue when it appears within a sentence (*When*).
Section: Language/Capitalization
Subsection: First Word

44. d. Choice **a** is incorrect. The first word of a quote set off by a comma (*Between*) must be capitalized. Choice **b** is incorrect. The first word of a sentence requires capitalization. Choice **c** is incorrect. The first word of a sentence—and the first word of a quote set off by a comma—should be capitalized. Choice **d** is the correct answer. The interjection *Oh* is capitalized when it is the first word of a sentence or a quote.
Section: Language/Capitalization
Subsection: First Word

45. a. Choice **a** is the correct answer. Titles of movies, as well as books and other full works, are always capitalized. Choice **b** is incorrect. The word *Mexican* is a proper adjective and needs to be capitalized. Choice **c** is incorrect. The word *Australian* is a proper adjective and needs to be capitalized. Choice **d** is incorrect. The word *poet* is not a proper noun and should not be capitalized.
Section: Language/Capitalization
Subsection: Proper Nouns

46. b. Choice **a** is incorrect. *Summer* should not be capitalized in this sentence. It serves as an adjective describing the noun *home*. Choice **b** is the correct answer. *German,* in this sentence, is a proper adjective referring to the noun *food.* Choice **c** is incorrect. The word *President,* in this sentence, is a common noun and should not be capitalized. Choice **d** is incorrect. *Winter* is a common noun, so it should be lowercase.
Section: Language/Capitalization
Subsection: Proper Nouns

47. b. Choice **a** is incorrect. *Elizabeth* is correctly capitalized, since it is a proper name (and it is the first word of the sentence). *Biology* should be lowercase, however, because it serves as a common adjective for the noun *course.* Choice **b** is the correct answer. *Elizabethan,* as used in this sentence, is a proper adjective referring to Queen Elizabeth of Shakespeare's day. Choice **c** is incorrect. As obscure as this organization may be to some, the Society to Preserve Barbershop Quartets is the name of an organization and should be capitalized Choice **d** is incorrect. *Highway* is a common noun that should not be capitalized.
Section: Language/Capitalization
Subsection: Proper Nouns

48. c. Choice **a** is incorrect. A comma is needed after the word *Children* because the speaker is addressing them directly. Choice **b** is incorrect. Commas should surround *Carmen and Roberto* because the speaker is addressing them directly. Choice **c** is the correct answer. The speaker is talking to the ladies and gentlemen of the audience, so the phrase *Ladies and gentlemen* is offset from the body of the sentence by a comma. Choice **d** is incorrect.

49. b. Choice **a** is incorrect. The commas after *movie* and *friend* are unnecessary and incorrect unless *Midnight in Paris* is the only movie in the world and Jessie is the writer's only friend. The sentence should read, *I went to see the movie* Midnight in Paris *with my friend Jessie.* Choice **b** is the correct answer. If an identification comes after the noun, it should always be surrounded by commas. Choice **c** is incorrect. The phrase *who gave new meaning to the expression "hard working"* is a side point in the sentence; the sentence would be grammatical and make sense without it. Because of this, the phrase should be set off on both sides by commas. The sentence should read: *My father, who gave new meaning to the expression "hard working," never took a vacation.* Choice **d** is incorrect. This sentence contains a comma splice, which is a term used for the linking of two independent clauses with only a comma. A compound sentence with a comma also requires a coordinating conjunction, such as *and, but, or, nor,* etc.

50. b. Choice **a** is incorrect. The writer should not use commas in front of dependent clauses (with subordinating conjunctions like *although, because, when, etc.*) when they follow the independent clause (a complete sentence). Choice **b** is the correct answer. A comma is used to separate parts of dates and addresses (*March 4, 1931*). Choice **c** is incorrect. The first comma is correct, because it separates two clauses, but there should be a comma after *father* to set off the quote. Choice **d** is incorrect. A comma should be used to separate the contrasting elements (*comedian, not a dramatist*).
Section: Language/Punctuation
Subsection: Commas

51. c. Choice **a** is incorrect. Because they own the cabin jointly, only the last owner's name should have an apostrophe (*mother and father's*) to indicate that here *mother and father* is a unit. Choice **b** is incorrect. The possessive form of *who* is *whose*, not *who's* (which means *who is*). Choice **c** is the correct answer. This sentence uses the apostrophe (*wife's*) correctly. Choice **d** is incorrect. The writer has mistaken *it's* (*it is*) for the possessive pronoun *its*. Possessive personal pronouns do not require an apostrophe.
Section: Language/Writing Conventions
Subsection: Apostrophes

52. c. Choice **a** is incorrect. Do not use an apostrophe when making a word plural; the plural of *monkey* is *monkeys*. Choice **b** is incorrect. The term *boat owners* is plural, not possessive, and therefore does not require an apostrophe. Choice **c** is the correct answer. The apostrophe is correctly used because *They're* is a contraction meaning *They are*. Choice **d** is incorrect. *Lions* is a plural word and does not require an apostrophe.
Section: Language/Writing Conventions
Subsection: Apostrophes

53. a. Choice **a** is the correct answer. If a woman wishes to indicate her marital status, the title is enclosed in parentheses. Or she may simply choose to sign her name. If there is no specific title in the signature, the receiver would probably use *Ms.* in the reply. Choice **b** is incorrect. When writing to professionals, use their titles. A colon always follows the salutation (*Dear Professor Rodin:*), and the formal title is used. Choice **c** is incorrect. The body of a business letter should end with a period, not a comma. Then begin the closing. Choice **d** is incorrect. The heading of a business letter starts with the writer's address and date.
Section: Language/Writing Conventions
Subsection: Letter Parts

54. c. Choice **a** is incorrect. The phrase *I said* identifies the speaker and is not part of the quotation, so it should not be inside the quotation marks. Choice **b** is incorrect. Exclamation points are placed within the closing quotation marks if the quotation is an exclamation. Choice **c** is the correct answer. When a quoted expression is divided into two parts by an interrupting expression (*she said,*) the second part also starts with quotation marks. Choice **d** is incorrect. *Where is the money?* should be enclosed by a set of single quotation marks, because it is a quotation within a quotation.
Section: Writing Conventions
Subsection: Quotation Marks

55. a. Choice **a** is the correct answer. Assuming this is a direct quotation from an identifiable person, the quotation marks are placed correctly. Choice **b** is incorrect. The entire label should be in quotation marks (*"Hot French Bread"*). Choice **c** is incorrect. Although many people make this mistake, quotation marks should not be used to emphasize a word or phrase (here, the writer tried to emphasize the word *not*). Furthermore, in standard written English, you should not put words in all caps in order to emphasize them. You can either italicize or underline the words you want to call attention to, use an exclamation point at the end of the sentence, or simply let the words speak for themselves. Choice **d** is incorrect. As in the previous answer, *paper towels* should not be surrounded by quotation marks. In addition, asterisks and all caps are not ways to add emphasis in standard written English.
Section: Writing Conventions
Subsection: Quotation Marks

Language Mechanics

1. d. Choice **a** is incorrect. *My hobbies are skiing and reading* is a grammatically simple sentence that does not need a colon. Choice **b** is incorrect. A colon should be used between the hour and minutes when writing time (7:25 A.M.). Choice **c** is incorrect. There is no reason for a colon here. If the series (*Rome, Israel, and Egypt*) were offset somehow, then you would use a colon. Consider this example: *When I have the time, I want to travel to these places: Rome, Israel, and Egypt.* Choice **d** is the correct answer. The phrase *the following states* sets the series apart from the body of the sentence, so it is correct to use a colon.
Section: Sentences, Phrases, Clauses
Subsection: Colon

2. c. Choice **a** is incorrect. The colon is preceded by a group of words that is not logically complete. In other words, the colon is used where a period would never be logical (*The conference speakers . . . included Sean Smith . . .*). Choice **b** is incorrect. This sentence does not require a colon. Choice **c** is the correct answer. This sentence has two independent clauses. The second clause fills in the information that is hinted at in the first—it explains what John's problem is. Choice **d** is incorrect. The phrase *these projects* sets off the words that follow from the body of the sentence. A colon should come after *these projects*.
Section: Sentences, Phrases, Clauses
Subsection: Colon

3. b. Choice **a** is incorrect. Commas (or dashes) should be used to set off nonessential clauses (*who likes movies*). Choice **b** is the correct answer. Commas are used to set off the nonessential phrase *hoping for a compromise*. Choice **c** is incorrect. A comma should be used after an introductory adverb clause (*Until we . . . of the smoke*). Choice **d** is incorrect. In most cases, a comma should separate two or more adjectives preceding a noun (*rough, dangerous*).
Section: Sentences, Phrases, Clauses
Subsection: Commas

4. d. Choice **a** is incorrect. This is an indirect quotation and does not require quotation marks or a comma after *that*. Choice **b** is incorrect. Preceding the quote, there should be a comma after *yelled*. Choice **c** is incorrect. There should be a period after the phrase *Max told me*, not a comma, because each of the two quotes is a complete sentence. If the two quotes formed one sentence, the comma would be correct. Note this correct example: *"I like to work in my garden in the springtime," Max told me, "but in the summer I head to the beach."* Choice **d** is the correct answer. The quoted material should be preceded by a comma.
Section: Sentences, Phrases, Clauses
Subsection: Commas

5. a. Choice **a** is the correct answer. *Three people running out of that old house* is an indirect quote and does not require quotation marks. Choice **b** is incorrect. A direct quote should begin with a capital letter. Choice **c** is incorrect. When quoted material is divided into two parts by an interrupting expression such as *she replied*, only the actual quote should be contained in quotation marks, not the entire sentence. Choice **d** is incorrect. Single quotation marks are used to enclose a quotation within a quotation. The sentence should be: *Joan said sadly, "Then Alicia said innocently, 'I was only trying to help.'"*.
Section: Sentences, Phrases, Clauses
Subsection: Quotation Marks

6. d. Choice **a** is incorrect. This sentence contains a direct quotation, so it needs an opening quotation mark before *The* and a closing quotation mark after *me*. Choice **b** is incorrect. The opening quotation mark has to be placed before the word *it*. *It* is the beginning word of the quotation and should also be capitalized. Choice **c** is incorrect. This sentence contains a direct quote, so it requires quotation marks before the word *This* and after the word *oddest*. Choice **d** is the correct answer. The direct quotation is correctly punctuated.
Section: Sentences, Phrases, Clauses
Subsection: Quotation Marks

7. d. Choice **a** is incorrect. Use quotation marks to enclose titles of songs (*"On Top of Old Smoky"*). Choice **b** is incorrect. On the flyer, no quotation marks should be used around the word *free*. Sometimes people use quotation marks to emphasize an important word or phrase, but that is an incorrect use of quotation marks. Choice **c** is incorrect. This sentence contains an indirect quotation and does not require quotation marks. Choice **d** is the correct answer. When a quoted sentence is divided into two parts by an interrupting expression such as *I said*, the second part of the quotation begins with quotation marks and a lowercase letter (*"how the movie ends."*).
Section: Sentences, Phrases, Clauses
Subsection: Quotation Marks

8. a. Choice **a** is the correct answer. A semicolon can be used between independent clauses joined by such words as *for instance, that is*, and *however*. Choice **b** is incorrect. Commas normally separate items in a series, but when one (or more) of the items already has a comma built into it, you should use semicolons for the series. This sentence gets that wrong. The sentence should read, *There were two representatives from Boston, Massachusetts; four from Albany, New York; and three from Cleveland, Ohio.* That is because the items should each be formatted as *city, state* (note the comma). As a result, when they are combined together in the series, the items should be separated with semicolons, not commas, to avoid confusion with the commas that are already "baked in." Choice **c** is incorrect. Do not use a semicolon to link a dependent clause or a phrase to an independent clause (*time; the effort*). Choice **d** is incorrect. The two statements are independent clauses. Use a semicolon to link them, not a colon.
Section: Sentences, Phrases, Clauses
Subsection: Semicolon

9. b. Choice **a** is incorrect. The two statements are independent clauses. Use a semicolon to link them, not a comma. Choice **b** is the correct answer. A semicolon can be used between independent clauses joined by such words as *for instance, that is*, and *instead*. Choice **c** is incorrect. The word *but* is a conjunction that connects two independent clauses to create one sentence; you don't need a semicolon to do the job. Instead, add a comma (here, after *beautiful*) to provide some separation between the two clauses. Choice **d** is incorrect. A colon, not a semicolon, should be used to set off a list.
Section: Sentences, Phrases, Clauses
Subsection: Semicolon

10. c. Choice **a** is incorrect. A comma, not a semicolon, should be used in this series. Choice **b** is incorrect. A semicolon should be used between items in a series if the items themselves contain commas. Choice **c** is the correct answer. When the thoughts of two independent clauses are closely related, a semicolon can be used instead of a period. Choice **d** is incorrect. Semicolons connect independent clauses—clauses that would work as grammatical sentences if they stood by themselves. *Despite what he told me about the teacher* is not a self-sufficient sentence— it's a side point to the independent clause *I have decided to register for the class.* As a result, a comma, not a semicolon, should be used here.
Section: Sentences, Phrases, Clauses
Subsection: Semicolons

11. c. Choice **a** is incorrect. The word *both* implies that we are talking about two girls, not one. Therefore *girl's* (the possessive form of the singular noun) is wrong. It should be *girls'* (possessive plural). Choice **b** is incorrect. Since there are six families, not one family, the possessive word should be spelled *families'*. Choice **c** is the correct answer. *Dollars* is a plural word and it's correct to add just an apostrophe at the end to make it possessive. (A possessive is necessary when the word *worth* is used in this way. Here's another example: *two months' worth of work.*) Choice **d** is incorrect. *Women, men, children,* and certain other plural words are treated like singular words when it comes to possessives. You just add *'s*. That is because they are already plural—adding an *s'* would be redundant (a plural *s* on top of an already plural word).
Section: Writing Conventions
Subsection: Apostrophes

12. a. Choice **a** is the correct answer. To form the possessive of a plural noun ending in -*s*, add only the apostrophe (*friends'*). Choice **b** is incorrect. In compound words, only the last word is possessive in form (*mother-in-law's*). Choice **c** is incorrect. When two or more people possess something individually (in this example, it's shoes), each of their names is possessive (*Edith's and Gwen's*). Choice **d** is incorrect. In this sentence, what is needed is a contraction (*You're*) and not a possessive adjective (*Your*).
Section: Writing Conventions
Subsection: Apostrophes

13. d. Choice **a** is incorrect. *Theirs* is a possessive pronoun. What's needed is the contraction *There's*, which is a shortened form of the phrase *There is*. Choice **b** is incorrect. *Who's* is a contraction that means *Who is*. What's needed is *Whose*. Choice **c** is incorrect. The word *several* is a signal that we're talking about a group of students, not just one. The sentence should be phrased, *Several students' desks . . .* Choice **d** is the correct answer. Sometimes it's necessary to treat letters, numbers, and symbols as words. To make them plural, add an *'s* or an *s*. (Here is another example: *the 1970s.*)
Section: Writing Conventions
Subsection: Apostrophes

14. b. Choice **a** is incorrect. The heading of a business letter should include your address and the current date. Choice **b** is the correct answer. As business letters are formal, include the company name on the first line, the number and name of the street on the second line, and the city, state, and ZIP code on the third line. Choice **c** is incorrect. A salutation is never informal in a business letter. Choice **d** is incorrect. When using a title for a salutation, a full name is not necessary unless the last name is similar to another person of the same title. A colon always follows the salutation (*Dear Dr. Able:*).
Section: Writing Conventions
Subsection: Business Letter-Parts

15. c. Choice **a** is incorrect. The closing of a business letter should be formal (especially if you do not have a close relationship with the reader). Choice **b** is incorrect. The body of a letter should always end with a proper sentence and a period. Choice **c** is the correct answer. These three guides (and there are several more) should be followed when writing a business letter. Choice **d** is incorrect. The signature should consist of your first and last names (and your middle name if you choose). Do not use *Mr.* if you are a man, as it is unnecessary. If a woman wishes to indicate her marital status, she may place it in parentheses before her name like this: (*Mrs.*) *Jane A. Doe.*
Subject: Writing Conventions
Subsection: Business Letter-Parts

16. d. Choice **a** is incorrect. Do not substitute a business title for a courtesy title. Address your letter to *Mr. Richard Lambert, President, Alpha Company*, not *President Richard Lambert*. Choice **b** is incorrect. Business titles are never abbreviated. It should be *Mr. Richard Thorpe, Senior Editor*, not *Mr. Richard Thorpe, Sr. Ed.* Choice **c** is incorrect. It's permissible to place honorary initials after the name of an addressee; but if you do, omit the beginning title to avoid redundancy. *David X. Liu, Ph.D.* is correct, as opposed to *Dr. David X. Liu, Ph.D.* Choice **d** is the correct answer. In standard formal business letters, the salutation takes one of the following forms: *Dear Mr. Smith:* or *Dear Leslie:* (if you know the person well). But if you have never met and you don't know the person's gender, use the full name instead: *Dear Leslie Smith:* The greeting in a business letter always ends in a colon (*. . . Smith:*).
Section: Writing Conventions
Subsection: Capitalize Title

17. a. Choice **a** is the correct answer. The word *Chinese* is a proper adjective modifying *noodles*. Choice **b** is incorrect. The word *country* does not have to be capitalized. Choice **c** is incorrect. *Italian* is a proper adjective modifying *food*. Choice **d** is incorrect. *Christian* is capitalized as it refers to a religion. It is a proper adjective modifying *music*.
Section: Writing Conventions
Subsection: Proper Adjectives

18. d. Choice **a** is incorrect. Because *Turkish* is the proper adjective for the country of Turkey, it has to be capitalized. Choice **b** is incorrect. *Philadelphia* is capitalized correctly as a proper noun, but *Lawyer* should not be capitalized. Choice **c** is incorrect. *Pleasantville* is a proper noun and should be capitalized. *Libraries* is a common noun and does not need to be capitalized. Choice **d** is the correct answer. *Michigan* is a proper noun and is correctly capitalized.
Section: Writing Conventions
Subsection: Proper Adjectives

19. b. Choice **a** is incorrect. The word *tickets* is a common noun and should not be capitalized. Choice **b** is the correct answer. *European* is a proper adjective modifying *cultures*. It is correctly capitalized. Choice **c** is incorrect. *Chile* is a proper noun, and its adjectival form, *Chilean*, also requires capitalization. Choice **d** is incorrect. *Dutch* is a proper adjective and is capitalized. The names of languages are always capitalized (*Dutch*, *Greek*, *English*, etc.).
Section: Writing Conventions
Subsection: Proper Adjectives

20. d. Choice **a** is incorrect. *British* should be capitalized because it's a proper adjective. The term *prime minister* should not be capitalized in this case, because it's a common noun. But in phrases such as *Prime Minister Thatcher*, the words *Prime Minister* should be capitalized because they function as a title. Choice **b** is incorrect. The word *Spanish* should be capitalized as a proper adjective modifying the noun *countess*. Choice **c** is incorrect. *Russian* should be capitalized. It is a proper adjective modifying the noun *king*. Choice **d** is the correct answer. *Mexican* is a proper adjective modifying the noun *border*.
Section: Writing Conventions
Subsection: Proper Adjectives

Vocabulary

1. b. Choice **a** is incorrect. The word *understandable* is an adjective meaning *able to comprehend*. Choice **b** is the correct answer. The word *ridiculous* is an adjective meaning *absurd*. Choice **c** is incorrect. The word *agreeable* is an adjective meaning *accommodating*. Choice **d** is incorrect. The word *debatable* is an adjective meaning *arguable*.
Section: Vocabulary
Subsection: Word Meaning

2. d. Choice **a** is incorrect. The word *popular* is an adjective meaning *liked by many people*. Choice **b** is incorrect. The word *expensive* is an adjective meaning *costly*. Choice **c** is incorrect. The word *tarnished* is an adjective meaning *dull with oxidation*. Choice **d** is the correct answer. The word *shiny* is an adjective meaning *lustrous*.
Section: Vocabulary
Subsection: Word Meaning

3. c. Choice **a** is incorrect. The word *expensive* is an adjective meaning *of high monetary value*. Choice **b** is incorrect. The word *toxic* is an adjective meaning *harmful*. Choice **c** is the correct answer. The word *relaxing* is an adjective meaning *less tense* or *languid*. Choice **d** is incorrect. The word *busy* is an adjective meaning *attentively engaged*.
Section: Vocabulary
Subsection: Word Meaning

4. a. Choice **a** is the correct answer. The word *postponement* is a noun meaning *to put off to a later time*, as is *reprieve*. Choice **b** is incorrect. The term *guilty verdict* means *an official decision of criminality*. Choice **c** is incorrect. The term *opinion of innocence* means *a statement releasing one from guilt*. Choice **d** is incorrect. The term *valid sentence* means *an appropriate order of punishment or pardon*.
Section: Vocabulary
Subsection: Word Meaning

5. d. Choice **a** is incorrect. The word *uncomfortable* is an adjective meaning *causing distress or discomfort*. Choice **b** is incorrect. The word *energized* is an adjective meaning *full of power*. Choice **c** is incorrect. The word *confusing* is an adjective meaning *not free of doubt*. Choice **d** is the correct answer. One of the definitions of *absorbing* is *fully taking someone's attention*. That's the same meaning as *engrossing*.
Section: Vocabulary
Subsection: Word Meaning

6. b. Choice **a** is incorrect. *Succumb to* means *give in to*, but the definition of acknowledge is *accept the truth of*. Choice **b** is the correct answer. *Yield to* and *succumb* to have similar meanings. Choice **c** is incorrect. *Cure* means *make healthy after an illness* or *provide a solution*. Choice **d** is incorrect. *Yield* does not mean *study*.
Section: Vocabulary
Subsection: Word Meaning

7. c. Choice **a** is incorrect. The word *standoffish* is an adjective meaning *unfriendly and cold*. Choice **b** is incorrect. The word *violent* is an adjective meaning *causing great harm*. Choice **c** is the correct answer. The word *easygoing* is an adjective meaning *mild-mannered*, as is *docile*. Choice **d** is incorrect. The word *diseased* is an adjective meaning *afflicted by an illness*.
Section: Vocabulary
Subsection: Word Meaning

8. d. Choice **a** is incorrect. The word *appreciate* is a verb meaning *to understand the value of*. Choice **b** is incorrect. The word *approve* is a verb meaning *to consent*. Choice **c** is incorrect. The word *discover*, a verb meaning *to find out or learn*, is not a synonym of *dispute*. Choice **d** is the correct answer. *Dispute* is a verb that means *to say or show that something may not be true, correct, or legal* or *to fight*.
Section: Vocabulary
Subsection: Word Meaning

9. d. Choice **a** is incorrect. The word *agree* is a verb meaning *to be in support*. Choice **b** is incorrect. The word *decide* is a verb meaning *to come to a conclusion*. Choice **c** is incorrect. The word *garbage* is a noun meaning *trash* or *waste*. While it completes the first sentence correctly, it does not make sense in the second sentence. Choice **d** is the correct answer. The word *refuse* is both a noun meaning *garbage* and a verb meaning *to be unwilling*.
Section: Vocabulary
Subsection: Multimeaning Words

10. a. Choice **a** is the correct answer. The word *tear* has many meanings and can be both a noun and a verb. It works in the first sentence as a noun meaning *the fluid that comes out of people's eyes when they cry*. In the second, it works as a verb meaning *pull down*. Choice **b** is incorrect. The noun *raindrop* doesn't work logically in the first sentence or logically or grammatically in the second. The second sentence calls for a verb. Choice **c** is incorrect. *Destroy* could work in the second sentence, but it doesn't make sense in the first. Choice **d** is incorrect. *Staple* could work in the second sentence, but it doesn't make sense in the first.
Section: Vocabulary
Subsection: Multimeaning Words

11. b. Choice **a** is incorrect. *Air* doesn't make sense in either sentence. Choice **b** is the correct answer. *Wind* works in the first sentence as a verb meaning *to coil*, and in the second sentence it works as a noun meaning *blowing air*. Choice **c** is incorrect. *Fasten* could work in the first sentence, but it doesn't make sense at all in the second. Choice **d** is incorrect. *Fabric* could make sense in the second sentence, to mean the fabric that the kite is made of, but it wouldn't make any sense in the first.
Section: Vocabulary
Subsection: Multimeaning Words

12. b. Choice **a** is incorrect. *Introduce* works in the first sentence, but it doesn't make sense in the second. Choice **b** is the correct answer. *Subject* is a perfect choice for both sentences. In the first, it operates as a verb meaning *force to experience*. In the second, it operates as a noun meaning *topic*. Choice **c** is incorrect. The noun *assumption* doesn't work in either sentence. The first sentence calls for a verb, not a noun, and in the second sentence, it would make the meaning of the sentence slightly strange. In addition, the article before the blank line is *a*, but *assumption* calls for *an*: *an assumption*. Choice **d** is incorrect. *Matter* makes sense in the second sentence, but it doesn't work in the first.
Section: Vocabulary
Subsection: Multimeaning Words

13. d. Choice **a** is incorrect. The word *experiencing* is a verb meaning *personally encountering*. Choice **b** is incorrect. The word *facilitating* is a verb meaning *enabling*. Choice **c** is incorrect. The word *diagnosing* is a verb meaning *making determination based on fact*. Choice **d** is the correct answer. The word *becoming* fits the grammar and meaning of the sentence.
Section: Vocabulary
Subsection: Words in Context

14. a. Choice **a** is the correct answer. The word *teach* fits the grammar and meaning of the sentence. Choice **b** is incorrect. The word *rally* is a verb meaning *to congregate together* and a noun meaning *a group assembled for a common purpose*. Choice **c** is incorrect. The word *inoculate* is a verb meaning *to administer an injection*. Choice **d** is incorrect. The word *propose* is a verb meaning *to suggest or offer*.
Section: Vocabulary
Subsection: Words in Context

15. a. Choice **a** is the correct answer. The word *located* is a verb meaning *to identify a place* or *established at a site*. It fits the grammar and meaning of the sentence. Choice **b** is incorrect. The word *established* is a verb meaning *to found or institute*. Choice **c** is incorrect. The word *justified* is a verb meaning *to show right or just*. Choice **d** is incorrect. The word *tied* is a verb meaning *to bind or fasten*.
Section: Vocabulary
Subsection: Words in Context

16. c. Choice **a** is incorrect. The word *eluding* is a verb meaning *avoiding*. Choice **b** is incorrect. The word *photographing* is a verb meaning *taking a picture*. Choice **c** is the correct answer. The word *dramatizing* is a verb meaning *to bring to life in a play, movie, or television show*. Choice **d** is incorrect. The word *practicing* is a verb meaning *doing over and over*.
Section: Vocabulary
Subsection: Words in Context

17. b. Choice **a** is incorrect. The word *remedied* is a verb meaning *relieved or cured a disease or ailment*. Choice **b** is the correct answer. The word *enjoyed* fits the grammar and meaning of the sentence. Choice **c** is incorrect. The word *promoted* is a verb meaning *advanced to a higher position*. Choice **d** is incorrect. The word *described* is a verb meaning *explained*.
Section: Vocabulary
Subsection: Words in Context

18. d. Choice **a** is incorrect. *Understanding* would not make sense in the sentence. Choice **b** is incorrect. *Annual* is an adjective meaning *every year*. It doesn't fit the logic or grammar of the sentence. Choice **c** is incorrect. *Variable* is an adjective meaning *likely to change*. It doesn't fit the logic or grammar of the sentence. Choice **d** is the correct answer. The sentence calls for a noun, and the noun *variety*, which means *a collection of different things or people*, fits the logic and grammar of the sentence.
Section: Vocabulary
Subsection: Words in Context

19. d. Choice **a** is incorrect. *Farming* could work in this sentence, but there is a better choice, especially if you consider the meaning of the next sentence. Choice **b** is incorrect. *Position* doesn't make sense in this sentence. Choice **c** is incorrect. *Economics* could work well in this sentence, but if you consider the meaning of the next sentence, there is a better choice. Choice **d** is the correct choice. *Taste* makes the most sense, since the next sentence shares a supporting detail about how some Native Americans would enjoy the taste of popcorn as they sat around a campfire.
Section: Vocabulary
Subsection: Words in Context

20. b. Choice **a** is incorrect. A *garland* is a string of decorative objects. You can't make a garland of popcorn if you *shred*—meaning *tear apart into thin pieces*—the popcorn. Choice **b** is the correct answer. *String*, used here in its verb form, makes perfect sense. Choice **c** is incorrect. *Divide* doesn't make sense. When you make a garland, you join things together, not divide—meaning *separate*—them. Choice **d** is incorrect. For the same reason, *cut* doesn't make sense in this sentence.
Section: Vocabulary
Subsection: Words in Context

Spelling

1. b. Choice **a** is incorrect. *Principle* has the same pronunciation as the correct choice (*principal*), but it has a different definition. It is a noun meaning *a basic theory* or *a moral rule*. Choice **b** is the correct answer. *Principal* is an adjective meaning *most important*. It also serves as a noun meaning *the head of a school*.
Section: Vowel
Subsection: Homonym

2. c. Choice **a** is incorrect. It is an incorrect spelling. Choice **b** is incorrect. It is an incorrect spelling. Choice **c** is the correct answer. This is the correct spelling of the word meaning *a political leader who makes false claims or emotional pleas to gain power*. Choice **d** is incorrect. It is an incorrect spelling.
Section: Consonant
Subsection: Silent Letter

3. d. Choice **a** is incorrect. It is an incorrect spelling. Choice **b** is incorrect. It is an incorrect spelling. Choice **c** is incorrect. It is an incorrect spelling. Choice **d** is the correct answer. It is the correct spelling of the word meaning *to consult with others*.
Section: Vowel
Subsection: R-controlled

4. c. Choice **a** is incorrect. It is an incorrect spelling. Choice **b** is incorrect. It is an incorrect spelling. Choice **c** is the correct answer. This is the correct spelling of the word meaning *food*. Choice **d** is incorrect. It is an incorrect spelling.
Section: Structural Unit
Subsection: Inflectional Ending (Plural)

5. b. Choice **a** is incorrect. *Raise* means *lift up*, which wouldn't make sense in the sentence. Choice **b** is the correct answer. This is the correct spelling for the word meaning *to tear down or demolish*. Choice **c** is incorrect. It is an incorrect spelling. Choice **d** is incorrect. It is an incorrect spelling.
Section: Structural Unit
Subsection: Homonym

6. b. Choice **a** is incorrect. It is an incorrect spelling. Choice **b** is the correct answer. This is the correct spelling of the name of the state in the northeastern United States. Choice **c** is incorrect. It is an incorrect spelling. Choice **d** is incorrect. It is an incorrect spelling.
Section: Consonant
Subsection: Silent Letter

7. b. Choice **a** is incorrect. It is an incorrect spelling. Choice **b** is the correct answer. This is the correct spelling of the word meaning *a rebirth*. Choice **c** is incorrect. It is an incorrect spelling. Choice **d** is incorrect. It is an incorrect spelling.
Section: Consonant
Subsection: Double Letter

8. a. Choice **a** is the correct answer. This is the correct spelling of the word that means *not fearful in addressing a situation*. Choice **b** is incorrect. It is an incorrect spelling. Choice **c** is incorrect. It is an incorrect spelling. Choice **d** is incorrect. It is an incorrect spelling.
Section: Consonant
Subsection: Double Letter

9. a. Choice **a** is the correct answer. This is the correct spelling of a word meaning *ready to happen*. Choice **b** is incorrect. It is an incorrect spelling. Choice **c** is incorrect. It is an incorrect spelling. Choice **d** is incorrect. *Eminent* is the correct spelling of an adjective that means *successful, well-known, and respected*, but it doesn't make sense in this sentence.
Section: Vowel
Subsection: Short Vowel

10. d. Choice **a** is incorrect. It is an incorrect spelling. Choice **b** is incorrect. It is an incorrect spelling. Choice **c** is incorrect. It is an incorrect spelling. Choice **d** is the correct answer. This is the correct spelling of the word meaning *sanction or allow*.
Section: Structural Unit
Subsection: Similar Word Part

11. d. Choice **a** is incorrect. The word is spelled correctly. Choice **b** is incorrect. The word is spelled correctly. Choice **c** is incorrect. The word is spelled correctly. Choice **d** is the correct answer. The word should be spelled *magnificent*.
Section: Consonant
Subsection: Silent Letter

12. c. Choice **a** is incorrect. The word is spelled correctly. Choice **b** is incorrect. The word is spelled correctly. Choice **c** is the correct answer. *Vain* is the correct spelling of an adjective meaning *too proud of one's appearance or achievements*, but that doesn't make sense when paired with the word *weather*. The correct spelling is *vane*. A *weather vane* is a rotating metal object that is placed on a roof to show the direction of the wind. Choice **d** is incorrect. The word is spelled correctly.
Section: Structual Unit
Subsection: Homonym

13. a. Choice **a** is the correct answer. The word should be spelled *physical*. Choice **b** is incorrect. The word is spelled correctly. Choice **c** is incorrect. The word is spelled correctly. Choice **d** is incorrect. The word is spelled correctly.
Section: Consonant
Subsection: Variant Spelling

14. d. Choice **a** is incorrect. The word is spelled correctly. Choice **b** is incorrect. The word is spelled correctly. Choice **c** is incorrect. The word is spelled correctly. Choice **d** is the correct answer. The word should be spelled *potentiation*.
Section: Vowel
Subsection: Long Vowel

15. **c.** Choice **a** is incorrect. The word is spelled correctly. Choice **b** is incorrect. The word is spelled correctly. Choice **c** is the correct answer. *Reseat* is the correct spelling of a verb meaning *to seat again*. But that doesn't make sense when paired with the word *store*. The correct spelling is *receipt*, which means *a slip of paper that details a purchase*. Although the meaning and spelling are different, *receipt* is pronounced the same way as *reseat*. Choice **d** is incorrect. The word is spelled correctly.
Section: Consonant
Subsection: Homonym

16. **a.** Choice **a** is the correct answer. The word should be spelled *parish*. Choice **b** is incorrect. The word is spelled correctly. Choice **c** is incorrect. The word is spelled correctly. Choice **d** is incorrect. The word is spelled correctly.
Section: Consonant
Subsection: Variant Spelling

17. **b.** Choice **a** is incorrect. The word is spelled correctly. Choice **b** is the correct answer. The word should be spelled *oppositional*. Choice **c** is incorrect. The word is spelled correctly. Choice **d** is incorrect. The word is spelled correctly.
Section: Consonant
Subsection: Variant Spelling

18. **d.** Choice **a** is incorrect. The word is spelled correctly. Choice **b** is incorrect. The word is spelled correctly. Choice **c** is incorrect. The word is spelled correctly. Choice **d** is the correct answer. The word should be spelled *immaculate*.
Section: Vowel
Subsection: Short Vowel

19. **d.** Choice **a** is incorrect. The word is spelled correctly. Choice **b** is incorrect. The word is spelled correctly. Choice **c** is incorrect. The word is spelled correctly. Choice **d** is the correct answer. The word should be spelled *conscientious*.
Section: Structural Unit
Subsection: Suffix

20. **b.** Choice **a** is incorrect. The word is spelled correctly. Choice **b** is the correct answer. The word should be spelled *intermediary*. Choice **c** is incorrect. The word is spelled correctly. Choice **d** is incorrect. The word is spelled correctly.
Section: Vowel
Subsection: Short Vowel

Mathematics Computation

1. **b.** Choice **a** is incorrect. $2,653 + 1,007 + (-588) \neq 2,065$. Choice **b** is the correct answer. Working from left to right, add the first two terms: $2,653 + 1,007 = 3,660$. Because the last term is a negative number, subtract it from the previous result: $3,660 - 588 = 3,072$. Choice **c** is incorrect. $2,653 + 1,007 + (-588) \neq 3,660$. Choice **d** is incorrect. $2,653 + 1,007 + (-588) \neq 4,248$.
Section: Integers
Subsection: Addition

2. a. Choice **a** is the correct answer. First, a double negative is present. This converts the sign of 371 to positive and the operator to addition: $-492 + 371$. Because the signs of the terms are now opposites, subtract the smaller absolute value from the larger absolute value. The sign of the final answer is the sign of the larger absolute value: $-492 + 371 = -121$. Choice **b** is incorrect. $-492 - (-371) \neq 121$. Choice **c** is incorrect. $-492 - (-371) \neq -863$. Choice **d** is incorrect. $-492 - (-371) \neq 863$.
Section: Integers
Subsection: Subtraction

3. c. Choice **a** is incorrect. $(10)(17)(-2) \neq -150$. Choice **b** is incorrect. $(10)(17)(-2) \neq 150$. Choice **c** is the correct answer. To multiply signed integers, count the number of negatives. If the count is an even number, the sign of the final answer will be positive. If the count is an odd number, the sign of the final answer will be negative. In this case, there is one negative. One is odd; therefore, the sign of the final answer is negative: $(10)(17)(-2) = -340$. Choice **d** is incorrect. $(10)(17)(-2) \neq 340$. This choice is missing the negative sign.
Section: Integers
Subsection: Multiplication

4. c. Choice **a** is incorrect. $-12,560 \div 8 \neq -157$ Choice **b** is incorrect. $-12,560 \div 8 \neq 157$. Choice **c** is the correct answer. Dividing two integers with different signs results in a negative answer. Divide the integers as usual, and assign a negative sign to the final answer: $-12,560 \div 8 = -1,570$. Choice **d** is incorrect. $-12,560 \div 8 \neq 1,570$. This choice is missing the negative sign.
Section: Integers
Subsection: Division

5. d. Choice **a** is incorrect. $14,255 - (-110) = 14,365$ feet. Choice **b** is incorrect. $14,255 - (-110) = 14,365$ feet. Choice **c** is incorrect. $14,255 - (-110) = 14,365$ feet. Choice **d** is the correct answer. Distance is always found through subtraction of the smaller value from the larger value. The diver is 110 feet below the surface or, put another way, 110 feet below sea level. This measurement can be represented as a -110. The result is $14,255 - (-110) = 14,365$ feet.
Section: Integers
Subsection: Subtraction

6. b. Choice **a** is incorrect. $\$25 \times 13 = \$325$. Choice **b** is the correct answer. Multiplication is a quick way to add the same number several times. Instead of adding $25 by itself 13 times, multiply: $\$25 \times 13 = \$325$. Choice **c** is incorrect. $\$25 \times 13 = \$325$. Choice **d** is incorrect. $\$25 \times 13 = \$325$.
Section: Integers
Subsection: Multiplication

7. a. Choice **a** is the correct answer. Because the total enrollment increase is spread out over seven years, division is required to find the increase for each year: $245 \div 7 = 35$. Choice **b** is incorrect. $245 \div 7 = 35$. Choice **c** is incorrect. $245 \div 7 = 35$. Choice **d** is incorrect. $245 \div 7 = 35$.
Section: Integers
Subsection: Division

8. c. Choice **a** is incorrect. $\frac{7}{15} + \frac{7}{9} = \frac{21}{45} + \frac{35}{45} = \frac{56}{45}$ $= 1\frac{11}{45}$. Choice **b** is incorrect. $\frac{7}{15} + \frac{7}{9} = \frac{21}{45} +$ $\frac{35}{45} = \frac{56}{45} = 1\frac{11}{45}$. Choice **c** is the correct answer. Before adding the fractions, find the least common denominator, or LCD. In this case, the LCD is 45. Convert each fraction to an equivalent fraction with LCD 45: $\frac{7}{15} + \frac{7}{9}$ $= \frac{21}{45} + \frac{35}{45}$. Then, add the numerators and keep the denominator: $\frac{21}{45} + \frac{35}{45} = \frac{56}{45}$. Finally, convert the improper fraction to a mixed number: $\frac{56}{45} = 1\frac{11}{45}$. Choice **d** is incorrect. $\frac{7}{15}$ $+ \frac{7}{9} = \frac{21}{45} + \frac{35}{45} = \frac{56}{45} = 1\frac{11}{45}$.

Section: Fractions

Subsection: Addition

9. d. Choice **a** is incorrect. $\frac{1}{12} - \frac{5}{8} = \frac{2}{24} - \frac{15}{24} = -\frac{13}{24}$. Choice **b** is incorrect. $\frac{1}{12} - \frac{5}{8} = \frac{2}{24} - \frac{15}{24} = -\frac{13}{24}$. Choice **c** is incorrect. $\frac{1}{12} - \frac{5}{8} = \frac{2}{24} - \frac{15}{24} = -\frac{13}{24}$. The original choice is missing a negative sign. Choice **d** is the correct answer. Before subtracting the fractions, find the least common denominator, or LCD. In this case, the LCD is 24. Convert each fraction to an equivalent fraction with LCD 24: $\frac{1}{12} - \frac{5}{8} =$ $\frac{2}{24} - \frac{15}{24}$. Then subtract the numerators and keep the denominator: $\frac{2}{24} - \frac{15}{24} = -\frac{13}{24}$.

Section: Fractions

Subsection: Subtraction

10. a. Choice **a** is the correct answer. To multiply mixed numbers, first convert them to improper fractions: $2\frac{4}{7} \times 5\frac{1}{9} = \frac{18}{7} \times \frac{46}{9}$. Reduce before multiplying: $\frac{18}{7} \times \frac{46}{9} = \frac{2}{7} \times \frac{46}{1}$. Multiply the numerators and denominators: $\frac{2}{7} \times \frac{46}{1} = \frac{92}{7}$. Convert the result to a mixed number: $\frac{92}{7} = 13\frac{1}{7}$. Choice **b** is incorrect. $2\frac{4}{7} \times 5\frac{1}{9} = \frac{18}{7} \times \frac{46}{9} = \frac{2}{7} \times \frac{46}{1} = \frac{92}{7} = 13\frac{1}{7}$. Choice **c** is incorrect. $2\frac{4}{7} \times 5\frac{1}{9} = \frac{18}{7} \times \frac{46}{9} =$ $\frac{2}{7} \times \frac{46}{1} = \frac{92}{7} = 13\frac{1}{7}$. Choice **d** is incorrect. $2\frac{4}{7} \times 5\frac{1}{9} = \frac{18}{7} \times \frac{46}{9} = \frac{2}{7} \times \frac{46}{1} = \frac{92}{7} = 13\frac{1}{7}$.

Section: Fractions

Subsection: Multiplication

11. c. Choice **a** is incorrect. $-\frac{35}{45} \div \frac{10}{15} = -\frac{35}{45} \times \frac{15}{10} =$ $-\frac{7}{3} \times \frac{35}{45} = -\frac{7}{6}$. Choice **b** is incorrect. $-\frac{35}{45} \div$ $\frac{10}{15} = -\frac{35}{45} \times \frac{1}{2} = -\frac{7}{3} \times \frac{1}{2} = -\frac{7}{6}$. Choice **c** is the correct answer. To divide fractions, rewrite the expression as multiplication by keeping the first term and multiplying by the reciprocal of the second term: $-\frac{35}{45} \div \frac{10}{15}$ $= -\frac{35}{45} \times \frac{15}{10}$. Reduce before multiplying: $-\frac{35}{45} \times \frac{15}{10} = -\frac{7}{3} \times \frac{1}{2}$. Multiply the numerators and multiply the denominators: $-\frac{7}{3} \times \frac{1}{2} = -\frac{7}{6}$. Choice **d** is incorrect. $-\frac{35}{45} \div \frac{10}{15} = -\frac{35}{45} \times \frac{15}{10} = -\frac{7}{3} \times \frac{1}{2} = -\frac{7}{6}$. This choice is missing the negative sign.

Section: Fractions

Subsection: Division

12. d. Choice **a** is incorrect. $1\frac{3}{4} + 2\frac{1}{8} + 3\frac{1}{2} = \frac{14}{8} +$ $\frac{17}{8} + \frac{28}{8} = \frac{59}{8} = 7\frac{3}{8}$. Choice **b** is incorrect. $1\frac{3}{4} + 2\frac{1}{8} + 3\frac{1}{2} = \frac{14}{8} + \frac{17}{8} + \frac{28}{8} = \frac{59}{8} = 7\frac{3}{8}$. Choice **c** is incorrect. $1\frac{3}{4} + 2\frac{1}{8} + 3\frac{1}{2} = \frac{14}{8} +$ $\frac{17}{8} + \frac{28}{8} = \frac{59}{8} = 7\frac{3}{8}$. Choice **d** is the correct answer. To find the total, add the three weights. Convert each mixed number to an improper fraction: $1\frac{3}{4} + 2\frac{1}{8} + 3\frac{1}{2} = \frac{7}{4} +$ $\frac{17}{8} + \frac{7}{2}$. Find the LCD and convert each fraction to an equivalent fraction: $\frac{7}{4} + \frac{17}{8} +$ $\frac{7}{2} = \frac{14}{8} + \frac{17}{8} + \frac{28}{8}$. Add the numerators and keep the denominator: $\frac{14}{8} + \frac{17}{8} + \frac{28}{8} = \frac{59}{8}$. Convert the result back into a mixed number: $\frac{59}{8} = 7\frac{3}{8}$.

Section: Fractions

Subsection: Addition

13. a. Choice **a** is the correct answer. Divide the total amount of jelly by the amount each jar holds. Convert the mixed numbers to improper fractions and then change the operation to multiplication. Keep the first term, and multiply by the reciprocal of the second term: $143\frac{1}{2} \div 1\frac{3}{4} = \frac{287}{2} \div \frac{7}{4} = \frac{287}{2} \times \frac{4}{7}$. Reduce before multiplying: $\frac{287}{2} \times \frac{4}{7} = 41 \times 2$. Choice **b** is incorrect. $143\frac{1}{2} \div 1\frac{3}{4} = \frac{287}{2} \div \frac{7}{4} = \frac{287}{2} \times \frac{4}{7} = 41 \times 2 = 82$. Choice **c** is incorrect. $143\frac{1}{2} \div 1\frac{3}{4} = \frac{287}{2} \div \frac{7}{4} = \frac{287}{2} \times \frac{4}{7} = 41 \times 2 = 82$. Choice **d** is incorrect. $143\frac{1}{2} \div 1\frac{3}{4} = \frac{287}{2} \div \frac{7}{4} = \frac{287}{2} \times \frac{4}{7} = 41 \times 2 = 82$.

Section: Fractions
Subsection: Division

14. c. Choice **a** is incorrect. $108\frac{1}{3} \times 90\frac{3}{5} = \frac{325}{3} \times \frac{453}{5} = 65 \times 151 = 9,815$ sq. ft. Choice **b** is incorrect. $108\frac{1}{3} \times 90\frac{3}{5} = \frac{325}{3} \times \frac{453}{5} = 65 \times 151 = 9,815$ sq. ft. Choice **c** is the correct answer. To find area, multiply the playground's length and width: $108\frac{1}{3} \times 90\frac{3}{5}$. Convert the mixed numbers to improper fractions, reduce, then multiply: $108\frac{1}{3} \times 90\frac{3}{5} = \frac{325}{3} \times \frac{453}{5} = 65 \times 151 = 9,815$ sq. ft. Choice **d** is incorrect. $108\frac{1}{3} \times 90\frac{3}{5} = \frac{325}{3} \times \frac{453}{5} = 65 \times 151 = 9,815$ sq. ft.

Section: Fractions
Subsection: Multiplication

15. b. Choice **a** is incorrect. $142.07 + 0.023 + 5.8 = 147.893$. Choice **b** is the correct answer. To add decimals, write the numbers vertically with the decimal points lined up. Zeros may be added at the end as placeholders in order to have the same number of decimal places in all the terms. Add as you would whole numbers, keeping the decimal point in your answer lined up with the decimal points in the problem: $142.070 + 0.023 + 5.800 = 147.893$. Choice **c** is incorrect. $142.07 + 0.023 + 5.8 = 147.893$. Choice **d** is incorrect. $142.07 + 0.023 + 5.8 = 147.893$.

Section: Decimals
Subsection: Addition

16. d. Choice **a** is incorrect. $50.0090 - 1.0762 = 48.9328$. Choice **b** is incorrect. $50.0090 - 1.0762 = 48.9328$. Choice **c** is incorrect. $50.0090 - 1.0762 = 48.9328$. Choice **d** is the correct answer. To subtract decimals, write the numbers vertically with the decimal points lined up. In this case, it is important to add a zero to the end of 50.009 as a placeholder in order to match the number of decimal places in second term. Subtract as you would whole numbers, keeping the decimal point in your answer lined up with the decimal points in the problem: $50.0090 - 1.0762 = 48.9328$.

Section: Decimals
Subsection: Subtraction

17. a. Choice **a** is the correct answer. To multiply decimals, multiply as you would whole numbers: $812 \times 37504 = 30{,}453{,}248$. Count the number of decimal places from both terms. In this case, there are five decimal places. Starting from the rightmost digit in your answer, count five places left. Place the decimal point in front of that digit: $81.2 \times 3.7504 = 304.53248$. Choice **b** is incorrect. $81.2 \times 3.7504 = 304.53248$. Choice **c** is incorrect. $81.2 \times 3.7504 = 304.53248$. Choice **d** is incorrect. $81.2 \times 3.7504 = 304.53248$.
Section: Decimals
Subsection: Multiplication

18. d. Choice **a** is incorrect. $6.254 \div 0.02 = 312.7$. Choice **b** is incorrect. $6.254 \div 0.02 = 312.7$. Choice **c** is incorrect. $6.254 \div 0.02 = 312.7$. Choice **d** is the correct answer. To divide decimals, the divisor must be changed to a whole number. Do so by moving the decimal point in the divisor behind its rightmost nonzero digit. Next, move the decimal point in the dividend the same number of places as in the divisor. Place a decimal point on the answer line so that it lines up with the new dividend. Divide as you would whole numbers, keeping the decimal point in place:

$$\frac{312.7}{2)\overline{625.4}}.$$

Section: Decimals
Subsection: Division

19. a. Choice **a** is the correct answer. To find the change, subtract the total sales, \$247.39, from the amount given to the cashier, \$250. In subtraction, it is important that both terms have the same number of decimal places. Thus, add two zeros after the decimal in \$250 and subtract: $\$250.00 - \$247.39 = \$2.61$. Choice **b** is incorrect. $\$250.00 - \$247.39 = \$2.61$. Choice **c** is incorrect. $\$250.00 - \$247.39 = \$2.61$. Choice **d** is incorrect. $\$250.00 - \$247.39 = \$2.61$.
Section: Decimals
Subsection: Subtraction

20. c. Choice **a** is incorrect. $(1.25)(3.5)(5) = 21.875$ miles. Choice **b** is incorrect. $(1.25)(3.5)(5) = 21.875$ miles. Choice **c** is the correct answer. First, calculate the number of miles Derek jogs each day: $1.25 \times 3.5 = 4.375$. Then, multiply that result by five: $4.375 \times 5 = 21.875$ miles. Choice **d** is incorrect. $(1.25)(3.5)(5) = 21.875$ miles.
Section: Decimals
Subsection: Multiplication

21. b. Choice **a** is incorrect. $7.375 \div 1.125 = 6.\overline{5}$, which yields only six blocks of the desired length. Choice **b** is the correct answer. To find the number of blocks measuring the desired length, divide the total length of the stud by the length of one block: $7.375 \div 1.125 = 6.\overline{5}$. In this result, the decimal represents the leftover wood and cannot be included in the count. Only six blocks measuring 1.125 feet can be cut from the stud. Choice **c** is incorrect. $7.375 \div 1.125 = 6.\overline{5}$, which yields only six blocks of the desired length. Choice **d** is incorrect. $7.375 \div 1.125 = 6.\overline{5}$, which yields only six blocks of the desired length.
Section: Decimals
Subsection: Division

22. b. Choice **a** is incorrect. $2 + 40 \div (-5) + 3 = -3$. The choice is missing the negative sign. Choice **b** is the correct answer. Following order of operations (PEMDAS) division is done before addition: $2 + (-8) + 3$. Then, perform addition left to right: $2 + (-8) + 3 = -6 + 3 = -3$. Choice **c** is incorrect. $2 + 40 \div (-5) + 3 = -3$. Choice **d** is incorrect. $2 + 40 \div (-5) + 3 = -3$.
Section: Order of Operations
Subsection: Order of Operations

23. d. Choice **a** is incorrect. $\frac{12}{5} - \frac{1}{6}(3 - \frac{3}{5}) = \frac{12}{5} - \frac{1}{6}(\frac{12}{5}) = \frac{12}{5} - \frac{2}{5} = \frac{10}{5} = 2$. Choice **b** is incorrect. $\frac{12}{5} - \frac{1}{6}(3 - \frac{3}{5}) = \frac{12}{5} - \frac{1}{6}(\frac{12}{5}) = \frac{12}{5} - \frac{2}{5} = \frac{10}{5} = 2$. Choice **c** is incorrect. $\frac{12}{5} - \frac{1}{6}(3 - \frac{3}{5}) = \frac{12}{5} - \frac{1}{6}(\frac{12}{5}) = 1\frac{12}{5} - \frac{2}{5} = \frac{10}{5} = 2$. Choice **d** is the correct answer. Following order of operations (PEMDAS) any operation inside of parentheses is worked first: $\frac{12}{5} - \frac{1}{6}(\frac{15}{5} - \frac{3}{5}) = \frac{12}{5} - \frac{1}{6}(\frac{12}{5})$. Next, multiplication is done: $\frac{12}{5} - \frac{1}{6}(\frac{12}{5}) = \frac{12}{5} - \frac{2}{5}$. Finally, subtraction is done: $\frac{12}{5} - \frac{2}{5} = \frac{10}{5} = 2$.
Section: Order of Operations
Subsection: Order of Operations

24. c. Choice **a** is incorrect. $\frac{6 - 2(4 + 7^2)}{16 \div 2(8)} = \frac{-25}{16}$. Choice **b** is incorrect. $\frac{6 - 2(4 + 7^2)}{16 \div 2(8)} = \frac{-25}{16}$. Choice **c** is the correct answer. In a fraction such as the one presented, order of operations may be performed on the numerator and denominator simultaneously. Consider the numerator. Following PEMDAS, any operation inside parentheses is worked first. Consider the denominator. In PEMDAS, multiplication and division have the same priority and thus are performed from left to right: $\frac{6 - 2(4 + 7^2)}{16 \div 2(8)} = \frac{6 - 2(4 + 49)}{8(8)} = \frac{6 - 2(53)}{64}$. Consider the numerator. Multiplication is done before subtraction: $\frac{6 - 2(53)}{64} = \frac{6 - 106}{64} = \frac{-100}{64}$. Finally, the fraction is reduced: $\frac{-100}{64} = \frac{-25}{16}$. Choice **d** is incorrect. $\frac{6 - 2(4 + 7^2)}{16 \div 2(8)} = \frac{-25}{16}$.
Section: Order of Operations
Subsection: Order of Operations

25. c. Choice **a** does not contain the error. Multiplication within the parentheses is worked first. Choice **b** does not contain the error. Subtraction is worked next. Choice **c** is the correct answer; it *does* contain the error. The work shows addition of 7 and 3. PEMDAS requires that the multiplication of 3 and −10 be done first. Choice **d** does not contain the error. Based on the previous line's work, the multiplication was done correctly.
Section: Order of Operations
Subsection: Order of Operations

26. a. Choice **a** is the correct answer. Simplify both the numerator and denominator at the same time and use PEMDAS: $\frac{-9 + 18 \div 3(6)}{31 - 4(12) \div 3(2)} = \frac{-9 + 6(6)}{32 - 48 \div 3(2)} = \frac{-9 + 36}{32 - 16(2)} = \frac{27}{32 - 32} = \frac{27}{0}$. Division by zero is undefined. Choice **b** is incorrect. $\frac{-9 + 18 \div 3(6)}{31 - 4(12) \div 3(2)} = \frac{-9 + 36}{32 - 32} = \frac{27}{0}$ is undefined. Choice **c** is incorrect. $\frac{-9 + 18 \div 3(6)}{31 - 4(12) \div 3(2)} = \frac{-9 + 36}{32 - 32} = \frac{27}{0}$ is undefined. Choice **d** is incorrect. $\frac{-9 + 18 \div 3(6)}{31 - 4(12) \div 3(2)} = \frac{-9 + 36}{32 - 32} = \frac{27}{0}$ is undefined.
Section: Order of Operations
Subsection: Order of Operations

27. b. Choice **a** is incorrect. $53 \times 1.2 = 63.6$. Choice **b** is the correct answer. Translate the sentence to an equation of the form: *whole × percent = part*. Convert the percent to its decimal form and solve:

$53 \times 1.2 = part$

$part = 53 \times 1.2 = 63.6$.

Choice **c** is incorrect. $53 \times 1.2 = 63.6$.
Choice **d** is incorrect. $53 \times 1.2 = 63.6$.
Section: Percents
Subsection: Percents

28. **d.** Choice **a** is incorrect. $44.38 \div 0.14 = 317$. Choice **b** is incorrect. $44.38 \div 0.14 = 317$. Choice **c** is incorrect. $44.38 \div 0.14 = 317$. Choice **d** is the correct answer. Translate the sentence to an equation of the form: *whole × percent = part*. Convert the percent to its decimal form and solve:

$$whole \times 0.14 = 44.38$$
$$whole = 44.38 \div 0.14 = 317.$$

Section: Percents
Subsection: Percents

29. **c.** Choice **a** is incorrect. $126 \div 140 = 0.9 = 90\%$. Choice **b** is incorrect. $126 \div 140 = 0.9 = 90\%$. Choice **c** is the correct answer. Translate the sentence to an equation of the form: *whole × percent = part*. Convert the result to its percent form:

$$140 \times percent = 126$$
$$percent = 126 \div 140 = 0.9 = 90\%.$$

Choice **d** is incorrect. $126 \div 140 = 0.9 = 90\%$.

Section: Percents
Subsection: Percents

30. **b.** Choice **a** is incorrect. $30 \times 0.7 = 21$ part-time employees. Choice **b** is the correct answer. Translate the given information to an equation of the form: *whole × percent = part*. Convert the percent to its decimal form and solve:

total number of employees × percent = number of part-time employees
$$30 \times 0.7 = \text{number of part-time employees}$$
number of part-time employees $= 30 \times 0.7 = 21$.

Choice **c** is incorrect. $30 \times 0.7 = 21$ part-time employees. Choice **d** is incorrect. $30 \times 0.7 = 21$ part-time employees.

Section: Percents
Subsection: Percents

31. **c.** Choice **a** is incorrect. $\$1.08 \div \$15 = 0.072 = 7.2\%$. Choice **b** is incorrect. $\$1.08 \div \$15 = 0.072 = 7.2\%$. Choice **c** is the correct answer. Translate the given information to an equation of the form: *whole × percent = part*. Convert the result to its percent form:

price of sweater × sales tax rate = tax
$$\$15 \times \text{sales tax rate} = \$1.08$$
sales tax rate $= \$1.08 \div \$15 = 0.072 = 7.2\%$.

Choice **d** is incorrect. $\$1.08 \div \$15 = 0.072 = 7.2\%$.

Section: Percents
Subsection: Percents

32. **a.** Choice **a** is the correct answer. Translate the given information to an equation of the form: *whole × percent = part*. Convert the percent to its decimal form then solve:

original depth of the pond × percent = increase in depth of pond
original depth of the pond $\times 0.3 = 1.5$
original depth of the pond $= 1.5 \div 0.3 = 5$ feet.

Choice **b** is incorrect. $1.5 \div 0.3 = 5$ feet. Choice **c** is incorrect. $1.5 \div 0.3 = 5$ feet. Choice **d** is incorrect. $1.5 \div 0.3 = 5$ feet.

Section: Percents
Subsection: Percents

33. **d.** Choice **a** is incorrect. $2^3 \times 3^2 = 8 \times 9 = 72$. Choice **b** is incorrect. $2^3 \times 3^2 = 8 \times 9 = 72$. Choice **c** is incorrect. $2^3 \times 3^2 = 8 \times 9 = 72$. Choice **d** is the correct answer. Exponential notation is shorthand for repeated multiplication: $2^3 \times 3^2 = (2)(2)(2) \times (3)(3) = 8 \times 9 = 72$.

Section: Algebraic Operations
Subsection: Computation with Exponents

34. b. Choice **a** is incorrect. $5^3 - (-4)^2 = 125 - 16 = 109$. Choice **b** is the correct answer. Exponential notation is shorthand for repeated multiplication: $5^3 - (-4)^2 = (5)(5)(5) - (-4)(-4) = (125) - (16) = 109$. Choice **c** is incorrect. $5^3 - (-4)^2 = 125 - 16 = 109$. Choice **d** is incorrect. $5^3 - (-4)^2 = 125 - 16 = 109$.

Section: Algebraic Operations
Subsection: Computation with Exponents

35. d. Choice **a** is incorrect. $\sqrt{16 + 9} = \sqrt{25} = 5$. Choice **b** is incorrect. $\sqrt{16 + 9} = \sqrt{25} = 5$. Choice **c** is incorrect. $\sqrt{16 + 9} = \sqrt{25} = 5$. Choice **d** is the correct answer. In this problem, there is an operation inside the square root and as per order of operations, it must be done first. The square root of the result is then calculated: $\sqrt{16 + 9} = \sqrt{25} = 5$.

Section: Algebraic Operations
Subsection: Computation with Roots

36. b. Choice **a** is incorrect. $\frac{\sqrt{100}}{\sqrt{36}} = \frac{10}{6} = \frac{5}{3}$. Choice **b** is the correct answer. Find the square root of the numerator and denominator and reduce the resulting fraction: $\frac{\sqrt{100}}{\sqrt{36}} = \frac{10}{6} = \frac{5}{3}$. Choice **c** is incorrect. $\frac{\sqrt{100}}{\sqrt{36}} = \frac{10}{6} = \frac{5}{3}$. Choice **d** is incorrect. $\frac{\sqrt{100}}{\sqrt{36}} = \frac{10}{6} = \frac{5}{3}$.

Section: Algebraic Operations
Subsection: Computation with Roots

37. a. Choice **a** is the correct answer. To simplify an expression, combine like terms. Like terms match both in variable and exponent. To combine like terms, add the coefficients and keep the variable: $5x^3 + x^3y^2 + x^3 + x^2y^3 = (5x^3 + x^3) + x^3y^2 + x^2y^3 = 6x^3 + x^3y^2 + x^2y^3$. Choice **b** is incorrect. $5x^3 + x^3y^2 + x^3 + x^2y^3 = 6x^3 + x^3y^2 + x^2y^3$. Choice **c** is incorrect. $5x^3 + x^3y^2 + x^3 + x^2y^3 = 6x^3 + x^3y^2 + x^2y^3$. Choice **d** is incorrect. $5x^3 + x^3y^2 + x^3 + x^2y^3 = 6x^3 + x^3y^2 + x^2y^3$.

Section: Algebraic Operations
Subsection: Simplify Expression

38. b. Choice **a** is incorrect. $5(6x + 2) - 7x = 23x + 10$. Choice **b** is the correct answer. To simplify the expression, distribute the five through both terms in the parentheses: $5(6x + 2) - 7x = 30x + 10 - 7x$. Then, combine like terms: $(30x - 7x) + 10 = 23x + 10$. Choice **c** is incorrect. $5(6x + 2) - 7x = 23x + 10$. Choice **d** is incorrect. $5(6x + 2) - 7x = 23x + 10$.

Section: Algebraic Operations
Subsection: Simplify Expression

39. d. Choice **a** is incorrect. $k = 0$ solves $3(k + 17) = 51$. Choice **b** is incorrect. $k = 0$ solves $3(k + 17) = 51$. Choice **c** is incorrect. $k = 0$ solves $3(k + 17) = 51$. Choice **d** is the correct answer. To solve the equation, first remove the parentheses through distribution. Then, isolate the variable by moving 51 to the opposite side of the equals sign through subtraction. Finally, divide both sides by the coefficient on the variable:

$$3(k + 17) = 51$$
$$3k + 51 = 51$$
$$3k + 51 - 51 = 51 - 51$$
$$3k = 0$$
$$k = 0$$

Section: Algebraic Operations
Subsection: Solve Equations

40. c. Choice **a** is incorrect. $n = -5$ solves $9 + 5(n + 3) = 4 + n$. Choice **b** is incorrect. $n = -5$ solves $9 + 5(n + 3) = 4 + n$. Choice **c** is the correct answer. To solve the equation, first remove the parentheses through distribution. Next, combine like terms on the same side of the equals sign. Now, bring all n-variables to one side of the equals sign and all constants to the other. Combine terms. Finally, divide both sides by the coefficient of the variable n.

$$9 + 5n + 15 = 4 + n$$
$$5n + (9 + 15) = 4 + n$$
$$5n + 24 = 4 + n$$
$$5n - n + 24 = 4 + n - n$$
$$4n + 24 - 24 = 4 - 24$$
$$4n = -20$$
$$n = -5$$

Choice **d** is incorrect. $n = -5$ solves $9 + 5(n + 3) = 4 + n$.
Section: Algebraic Operations
Subsection: Solve Equations

Applied Mathematics

1. a. Choice **a** is the correct answer. In front-end rounding, the first digit is rounded, and all other digits go to zero. Consider 3,081. To round 3, look to the digit directly to the right of it. Because 0 is less than 5, 3 remains 3. Therefore, 3,081 rounds down to 3,000. Consider 6,826. To round 6, look to 8. Because 8 is greater than 5, 6 rounds up to 7. Therefore, 6,826 rounds up to 7,000. Therefore, $3,000 + 7,000 = 10,000$. Choice **b** is incorrect. $3,000 + 7,000 \neq 9,000$. Choice **c** is incorrect. $3,000 + 7,000 \neq 7,000$. Choice **d** is incorrect. $3,000 + 7,000 \neq 11,000$.
Section: Estimation
Subsection: Estimation

2. c. Choice **a** is incorrect. $\$2,000 - \$200 \neq \$2,000$. Choice **b** is incorrect. $\$2,000 - \$200 \neq \$1,900$. Choice **c** is the correct answer. In front-end rounding, the first digit is rounded and all other digits go to zero. Consider $1,957. To round 1, look to the digit directly right of it. Because 9 is greater than 5, 1 rounds up to 2. Therefore, $1,957 rounds up to $2,000. Consider $238. To round 2, look to 3. Because 3 is less than five, 2 remains 2. Therefore, $238 rounds down to $200. So, $\$2,000 - \$200 = \$1,800$. Choice **d** is incorrect. $\$2,000 - \$200 \neq \$1,700$.
Section: Estimation
Subsection: Estimation

3. b. Choice **a** is incorrect. 906,854,250 rounds to 906,900,000. Choice **b** is the correct answer. For 906,854,250, the digit in the hundred-thousands place is 8. To round to the nearest hundred-thousand, look to the digit in the ten-thousand place. Because that digit is 5, 8 is rounded up to 9, and all digits behind it go to zero. Therefore, 906,854,250 rounds to 906,900,000. Choice **c** is incorrect. 906,854,250 rounds to 906,900,000. Choice **d** is incorrect. 906,854,250 rounds to 906,900,000.
Section: Estimation
Subsection: Rounding

4. d. Choice **a** is incorrect. 18.2739 is rounded to 18.3, the nearest tenth. Choice **b** is incorrect. 18.2739 is rounded to 18.3, the nearest tenth. Choice **c** is incorrect. 18.2739 is rounded to 18.3, the nearest tenth. Choice **d** is the correct answer. For 18.2739, the digit in the tenths place is 2. To round to the nearest tenth, look to the digit in the hundredths place. Because 7 is greater than 5, 2 is rounded up to 3, and all digits after it go to zero. Therefore, 18.2739 is rounded to 18.3, the nearest tenth.
Section: Estimation
Subsection: Rounding

5. c. Choice **a** is incorrect. 0.004221 converts to 4.211×10^{-3}. Choice **b** is incorrect. 0.004221 converts to 4.211×10^{-3}. Choice **c** is the correct answer. To convert a number into scientific notation, move the decimal after the leftmost non-zero digit, in this case, behind 4. Multiply this number by a power of 10. The exponent on the power of 10 is the number of moves, in this case, 3. If the original number was greater than 1, the exponent on 10 is positive. If the original number is a decimal less than 1, the exponent on 10 is negative. Thus, 0.004221 converts to 4.211×10^{-3}. Choice **d** is incorrect. 0.004221 converts to 4.211×10^{-3}.
Section: Number and Number Operations
Subsection: Exponents, Scientific Notation

6. b. Choice **a** is incorrect. $(6.41 \times 10^5)(3.7 \times 10^{-3})$ $= 2.3717 \times 10^3$. Choice **b** is the correct answer. To solve, multiply the decimals and multiply the powers of ten: (6.41×3.7) $(10^5 \times 10^{-3})$. To multiply the powers of ten, keep the base and add the exponents: $23.717 \times 10^{5+(-3)} = 23.717 \times 10^2$. Convert the result to scientific notation: 2.3717×10^3. Choice **c** is incorrect. (6.41×10^5) $(3.7 \times 10^{-3}) = 2.3717 \times 10^3$. Choice **d** is incorrect. $(6.41 \times 10^5)(3.7 \times 10^{-3}) =$ 2.3717×10^3.
Section: Number and Number Operations
Subsection: Exponents, Scientific Notation

7. d. Choice **a** is incorrect. The ratio form of 2.75 is 11:4. Choice **b** is incorrect. The mixed number form of 2.75 is $2\frac{3}{4}$. Choice **c** is incorrect. The percent form of 2.75 is 275%. Choice **d** is the correct answer. Convert the decimal to a reduced fraction: $0.75 = \frac{3}{4}$. Then, convert the mixed number to an improper fraction: $2.75 = 2\frac{3}{4} = \frac{11}{4}$.
Section: Number and Number Operations
Subsection: Equivalent Forms

8. c. Choice **a** is incorrect. $64 \times 0.08 = 5.12$. Choice **b** is incorrect. $64 \times 0.08 = 5.12$. Choice **c** is the correct answer. To find the percent of a given number, convert the percent to its decimal form, then multiply it by the number: $64 \times 0.08 = 5.12$. Choice **d** is incorrect. $64 \times 0.08 = 5.12$.
Section: Number and Number Operations
Subsection: Percent

9. b. Choice **a** is incorrect. $629 \div 0.85 = 740$. Choice **b** is the correct answer. Translate the sentence to an equation of the form: *whole* $\times$ *percent* = *part*. Convert the percent to its decimal form then solve:

$$whole \times 0.85 = 629$$
$$whole = 629 \div 0.85 = 740$$

Choice **c** is incorrect. $629 \div 0.85 = 740$. Choice **d** is incorrect. $629 \div 0.85 = 740$.
Section: Number and Number Operations
Subsection: Percent

10. d. Choice **a** is incorrect. Three is a factor of each number, but not the greatest common factor. Choice **b** is incorrect. Five is a factor of each number, but not the greatest common factor. Choice **c** is incorrect. Nine is not a factor of 165. Choice **d** is the correct answer. To find the greatest common factor, or GCF, calculate the prime factorization of each value: $165 = 3 \times 5 \times 11$; $315 = 3^2 \times 5 \times 7$; $585 = 3^2 \times 5 \times 13$. Identify the factors that all the numbers share and multiply them: $3 \times 5 = 15$.
Section: Number and Number Operations
Subsection: Factors, Multiples, Divisibility

11. b. Choice **a** is incorrect. 1,050 is not a multiple of 63. Choice **b** is the correct answer. To find the least common multiple, or LCM, for a set of values, first find the prime factorization of each value: $42 = 2 \times 3 \times 7$; $63 = 3^2 \times 7$; $75 = 3 \times 5^2$. Identify the prime numbers that appear in each factorization, note the count of each prime, and choose the highest count. In this case, 2 has a count of 1; 3 has a count of two; 5 has a count of two; and 7 has a count of 1. Multiply these primes with their counts to find the LCM: $2 \times 3^2 \times 5^2 \times 7 = 3,150$. Choice **c** is incorrect. 28,350 is not a multiple of 42. Choice **d** is incorrect. 198,450 is a multiple of the set, but it is not the least common multiple.
Section: Number and Number Operations
Subsection: Factors, Multiples, Divisibility

12. a. Choice **a** is the correct answer. To create this proportion, first change each half of the statement to a ratio: 3 is to $7 = \frac{3}{7}$, and 18 is to $42 = \frac{18}{42}$. Then set each ratio equal to each other: $\frac{3}{7} = \frac{18}{42}$. Choice **b** is incorrect. $\frac{3}{18}$ and $\frac{7}{42}$ are not the proper ratios. Choice **c** is incorrect. $\frac{18}{7}$ and $\frac{3}{42}$ are not the proper ratios. Choice **d** is incorrect. $\frac{3}{42}$ and $\frac{7}{18}$ are not the proper ratios.
Section: Number and Number Operations
Subsection: Ratio, Proportion

13. c. Choice **a** is incorrect. $21 can buy 28 cans of tomato sauce. Choice **b** is incorrect. $21 can buy 28 cans of tomato sauce. Choice **c** is the correct answer. To solve, set up a proportion. The ratio of cans to cost is 12 cans to $9. The proportion is $\frac{12}{\$9}$ cans $= \frac{x}{\$21}$ cans. To solve the proportion, use cross multiplication: $9x = 12(21)$. Then, solve for x: $x = \frac{252}{9} = 28$. Choice **d** is incorrect. $21 can buy 28 cans of tomato sauce.
Section: Number and Number Operations
Subsection: Ratio, Proportion

14. b. Choice **a** is incorrect. $-10 - 4 = -14$. Choice **b** is the correct answer. This pattern follows an arithmetic sequence. Each subsequent value is found by subtracting the same constant from the previous value. The constant for this sequence is 4: $10 - 4 = 6$; $6 - 4 = 2$; $2 - 4 = -2$; $-2 - 4 = -6$; $-6 - 4 = -10$; $-10 - 4 = -14$. Choice **c** is incorrect. $-10 - 4 = -14$. Choice **d** is incorrect. $-10 - 4 = -14$.

Section: Patterns, Functions, Algebra

Subsection: Number Pattern

15. a. Choice **a** is the correct answer. This pattern is two-fold. The pattern for the shapes is dot, ring, target: •, **O**, ⊙. The mathematical pattern is found by adding one to the previous count. The last entry is three targets, so the next entry will be four dots. Choice **b** is incorrect. Four dots is the next entry. Choice **c** is incorrect. Four dots is the next entry. Choice **d** is incorrect. Four dots is the next entry.

Section: Patterns, Functions, Algebra

Subsection: Geometric Pattern

16. d. Choice **a** is incorrect. $2 - 9(x - 4) = 2 - 9x + 36 = -9x + 38$. Choice **b** is incorrect. $2 - 9(x - 4) = 2 - 9x + 36 = -9x + 38$. Choice **c** is incorrect. $2 - 9(x - 4) = 2 - 9x + 36 = -9x + 38$. Choice **d** is the correct answer. First, clear the parentheses through distribution: $2 + [(-9 \times x) + (-9 \times -4)] = 2 + (-9x) + 36$. Then, combine like terms: $-9x + (2 + 36) = -9x + 38$.

Section: Patterns, Functions, Algebra

Subsection: Variable, Expression, Equation

17. c. Choice **a** is incorrect. The result must be positive. Choice **b** is incorrect. The inequality symbol is facing the wrong direction. Choice **c** is the correct answer. To solve the inequality, isolate the variable. Combine the constants by first bringing eight over to seven through subtraction. Then, divide by the coefficient on x. Because the coefficient is negative, the inequality sign must flip:

$$-3x + 8 - 8 > -7 - 8$$
$$-3x > -15$$
$$x < -15 \div -3$$
$$x < 5$$

Choice **d** is incorrect. The inequality symbol must be strictly "less than."

Section: Patterns, Functions, Algebra

Subsection: Inequality

18. b. Choice **a** is incorrect. $x \geq 26$ solves $\$85x - \$310 \geq \$1,900$. Choice **b** is the correct answer. To find the number of apartments Alexis must clean, first create an inequality that models the situation of sales − expenses ≥ profit: $\$85x - \$310 \geq \$1,900$. To solve, isolate the variable:

$$\$85x - \$310 \geq \$1,900$$
$$\$85x - \$310 + \$310 \geq \$1,900 + \$310$$
$$\$85x \geq \$2,210$$
$$\$85x \div \$85 \geq \$2,210 \div \$85$$
$$x \geq 26$$

Choice **c** is incorrect. $x \geq 26$ solves $\$85x - \$310 \geq \$1,900$. Choice **d** is incorrect. $x \geq 26$ solves $\$85x - \$310 \geq \$1,900$.

Section: Patterns, Functions, Algebra

Subsection: Inequality

19. c. Choice **a** is incorrect. From $y = \frac{-3}{2}x + \frac{5}{2}$, the slope is $-\frac{3}{2}$. Choice **b** is incorrect. From $y = \frac{-3}{2}x + \frac{5}{2}$, the slope is $-\frac{3}{2}$. Choice **c** is the correct answer. To find the slope, first convert the equation to slope-intercept form by solving for y: $y = \frac{-3}{2}x + \frac{5}{2}$. Once solved, the slope is the coefficient of x: $-\frac{3}{2}$. Choice **d** is incorrect. From $y = \frac{-3}{2}x + \frac{5}{2}$, the slope is $-\frac{3}{2}$.
Section: Patterns, Functions, Algebra
Subsection: Linear Equation

20. b. Choice **a** is incorrect. Perimeter = $2L + 3W$ = $2(80) + 3(40) = 280$ ft. Choice **b** is the correct answer. The fence will have four sides plus a fifth side inside the corral. The sides include two lengths and three widths: $2L + 3W = 2(80) + 3(40) = 280$ ft. Choice **c** is incorrect. Perimeter = $2L + 3W = 2(80) + 3(40) = 280$ ft. Choice **d** is incorrect. Perimeter = $2L + 3W = 2(80) + 3(40) = 280$ ft.
Section: Measurement
Subsection: Perimeter

21. d. Choice **a** is incorrect. (6 ft. × 8 ft.) + (7 ft. × 9 ft.) + (8 ft. × 10 ft.) = 191 sq. ft. Choice **b** is incorrect. (6 ft. × 8 ft.) + (7 ft. × 9 ft.) + (8 ft. × 10 ft.) = 191 sq. ft. Choice **c** is incorrect. (6 ft. × 8 ft.) + (7 ft. × 9 ft.) + (8 ft. × 10 ft.) = 191 sq. ft. Choice **d** is the correct answer. To calculate the total area of carpet needed, find the area of each room and add the results: (6 ft. × 8 ft.) + (7 ft. × 9 ft.) + (8 ft. × 10 ft.) = 48 sq. ft. + 63 sq. ft. + 80 sq. ft. = 191 sq. ft.
Section: Measurement
Subsection: Area

22. b. Choice **a** is incorrect. $(3.14)(7^2) - (3.14)(4^2)$ = 103.62 cm². Choice **b** is the correct answer. To calculate the area of the shaded region, find the area of the outside circle and the area of the inside circle; then, subtract the results. The area of the outside circle is $\pi r^2 = (3.14)(7^2) = 153.86$ cm². The area of the inside circle is $\pi r^2 = (3.14)(4^2) = 50.24$ cm². The difference is $153.86 - 50.24 = 103.62$ cm². Choice **c** is incorrect. $(3.14)(7^2) - (3.14)(4^2) = 103.62$ cm². Choice **d** is incorrect. $(3.14)(7^2) - (3.14)(4^2) = 103.62$ cm².
Section: Measurement
Subsection: Area

23. b. Choice **a** is incorrect. The circumference of the circle = $\pi d = (3.14)(1.5) = 4.71$ meters. Choice **b** is the correct answer. Because the diameter is given, the circumference can be found by $c = \pi d$. Therefore, $\pi d = (3.14)(1.5) = 4.71$ meters. Choice **c** is incorrect. The circumference of the circle = $\pi d = (3.14)(1.5) = 4.71$ meters. Choice **d** is incorrect. The circumference of the circle = $\pi d = (3.14)(1.5) = 4.71$ meters.
Section: Measurement
Subsection: Circumference

24. c. Choice **a** is incorrect. $6.1 - 1.7 - 2.4 = 2$ miles. Choice **b** is incorrect. $6.1 - 1.7 - 2.4 = 2$ miles. Choice **c** is the correct answer. To find the distance Charles ran on the third day, subtract the distances from the first and second days from the total distance he ran: $6.1 - 1.7 - 2.4 = 2.0$ miles. Choice **d** is incorrect. $6.1 - 1.7 - 2.4 = 2$ miles.
Section: Measurement
Subsection: Length, Distance

25. a. Choice **a** is the correct answer. To find the rate per day, divide the total number of widgets produced by the total number of days: 27,630 widgets ÷ 90 days = 307 widgets/day. Choice **b** is incorrect. The rate is 27,630 widgets ÷ 90 days = 307 widgets/day. Choice **c** is incorrect. The rate is 27,630 widgets ÷ 90 days = 307 widgets/day. Choice **d** is incorrect. The rate is 27,630 widgets ÷ 90 days = 307 widgets/day.
Section: Measurement
Subsection: Rate

26. b. Choice **a** is incorrect. $(3.14)(2.52)(4) =$ 78.5 cu. in. Choice **b** is the correct answer. The volume of a cylinder is found by multiplying the area of the base by the height. Cylinders have circular bases, so the area of the base is found by πr^2. Therefore, the volume is $(3.14)(2.5^2)(4) = 78.5$ cu. in. Choice **c** is incorrect. $(3.14)(2.5^2)(4) =$ 78.5 cu. in. Choice **d** is incorrect. $(3.14)(2.5^2)(4) = 78.5$ cu. in.
Section: Measurement
Subsection: Volume

27. b. Choice **a** is incorrect. $(-3)^2 + (-3) + 2 =$ $9 - 3 + 2 = 8$. Choice **b** is the correct answer. To evaluate the expression, substitute the value $x = -3$ for all the x-variables: $(-3)^2 +$ $(-3) + 2 = 9 - 3 + 2 = 8$. Choice **c** is incorrect. $(-3)^2 + (-3) + 2 = 9 - 3 + 2 = 8$. Choice **d** is incorrect. $(-3)^2 + (-3) + 2 = 9 -$ $3 + 2 = 8$.
Section: Problem Solving and Reason
Subsection: Evaluate Solution

28. c. Choice **a** is incorrect. $5[x + (x + 2)] = 170$ best models this situation. Choice **b** is incorrect. $5[x + (x + 2)] = 170$ best models this situation. Choice **c** is the correct answer. Let $x =$ the first even number. Consecutive even integers are separated by two units, so the next even integer is defined as $x + 2$. The sum of the integers is multiplied by five, and the result is 170: $5[x + (x + 2)] = 170$. Choice **d** is incorrect. $5[x + (x + 2)] = 170$ best models this situation.
Section: Problem Solving and Reason
Subsection: Model Problem Situation

29. a. Choice **a** is the correct answer. Let $w =$ the width of the rectangle. The length is seven more than twice its width, so length = $2w + 7$. We are given that the rectangle's perimeter is 122 inches. Thus:

$$2(\text{length}) + 2(\text{width}) = \text{perimeter}$$
$$2(2w + 7) + 2w = 122$$
$$4w + 14 + 2w = 122$$
$$6w + 14 = 122$$

Choice **b** is incorrect. $2(2w + 7) + 2w = 122$ simplifies to $6w + 14 = 122$. Choice **c** is incorrect. $2(2w + 7) + 2w = 122$ simplifies to $6w + 14 = 122$. Choice **d** is incorrect. $2(2w + 7) + 2w = 122$ simplifies to $6w + 14 = 122$.
Section: Problem Solving and Reason
Subsection: Model Problem Situation

30. b. Choice **a** is incorrect. $x = 15$ solves $4[x + (x + 1) + (x + 2)] = 192$. Choice **b** is the correct answer. Consecutive integers are separated by one unit. Let $x =$ the first integer. Then, $x + 1$ is the second integer, and $(x + 1) + 1 = x + 2$ is the third integer. To solve the problem, create an equation that models the situation: $4[x + (x + 1) + (x + 2)] = 192$. Then isolate the variable, x:

$$4[x + (x + 1) + (x + 2)] = 192$$
$$4(3x + 3) = 192$$
$$12x + 12 = 192$$
$$12x + 12 - 12 = 192 - 12$$
$$12x \div 12 = 180 \div 12$$
$$x = 15; x + 1 = 16; x + 2 = 17$$

Choice **c** is incorrect. $x = 15$ solves $4[x + (x + 1) + (x + 2)] = 192$. Choice **d** is incorrect. $x = 15$ solves $4[x + (x + 1) + (x + 2)] = 192$.
Section: Problem Solving and Reason
Subsection: Solve Problem

31. d. Choice **a** is incorrect. $x = 22$ solves $8x + 4 = 180$. Choice **b** is incorrect. $x = 22$ solves $8x + 4 = 180$. Choice **c** is incorrect. $x = 22$ solves $8x + 4 = 180$. Choice **d** is the correct answer. To solve the problem, first create an equation that models the situation. Let $x =$ the measure of the first angle, then isolate the variable, x:

first angle measure + second angle measure + third angle measure = 180°
$$x + (6x - 5) + (x + 9) = 180$$
$$8x + 4 = 180$$
$$8x + 4 - 4 = 180 - 4$$
$$8x = 176$$
$$8x \div 8 = 176 \div 8$$
$$x = 22$$

Section: Problem Solving and Reason
Subsection: Solve Problem

32. b. Choice **a** is incorrect. $46 \div 0.92 = 50$. Choice **b** is the correct answer. Translate the given information to an equation of the form: *whole × percent = part*. Convert the percent to its decimal form, then solve:

Total number of test problems × percent = number of correct problems
Total number of test problems × 0.92 = 46
Total number of test problems = $46 \div 0.92$
Total number of test problems = 50

Choice **c** is incorrect because $46 \div 0.92 = 50$. Choice **d** is incorrect because $46 \div 0.92 = 50$.
Section: Computation in Context
Subsection: Percents

33. b. Choice **a** is incorrect. $(\$27,500 - \$5,000)(0.25) = \$5,625$. Choice **b** is the correct answer. Jeff's commission is calculated on sales over $5,000. To find his commission, first subtract $5,000 from his sale of $27,500: $27,500 - \$5,000 = \$22,500$. Then, multiply this amount by the decimal form of the commission rate: $\$22,500 \times 0.25 = \$5,625$. Choice **c** is incorrect. $(\$27,500 - \$5,000)(0.25) = \$5,625$. Choice **d** is incorrect. $(\$27,500 - \$5,000)(0.25) = \$5,625$.
Section: Computation in Context
Subsection: Percents

34. c. Choice **a** is incorrect. Percent tip = $13.28 ÷ $63.72 = 0.208 ≈ 21%. Choice **b** is incorrect. Percent tip = $13.28 ÷ $63.72 = 0.208 ≈ 21%. Choice **c** is the correct answer. Translate the information to an equation of the form: *whole × percent = part*. Convert the result to its percent form:

$63.72 × percent = $13.28
percent = $13.28 ÷ $63.72
percent = 0.208 ≈ 21%.

Choice **d** is incorrect. Percent tip = $13.28 ÷ $63.72 = 0.208 ≈ 21%.
Section: Computation in Context
Subsection: Percents

35. a. Choice **a** is the correct answer. Find the amount Heather saves each month: $3,700 × $\left(\frac{1}{4}\right)$ = $925. Then, multiply the result by five months for the total savings: $925 × 5 = $4,625. Choice **b** is incorrect. $3,700 × $\left(\frac{1}{4}\right)$ × 5 = $4,625. Choice **c** is incorrect. $3,700 × $\left(\frac{1}{4}\right)$ × 5 = $4,625. Choice **d** is incorrect. $3,700 × $\left(\frac{1}{4}\right)$ × 5 = $4,625.
Section: Computation in Context
Subsection: Fractions

36. b. Choice **a** is incorrect. 1,200 × $\left(\frac{1}{5}\right)$ = 240. Choice **b** is the correct answer. If $\frac{4}{5}$ of the occupants own their homes, then $\frac{1}{5}$ of the occupants rent their homes. Thus, 1,200 × $\left(\frac{1}{5}\right)$ = 240. Choice **c** is incorrect. 1,200 × $\left(\frac{1}{5}\right)$ = 240. Choice **d** is incorrect. 1,200 × $\left(\frac{1}{5}\right)$ = 240.
Section: Computation in Context
Subsection: Fractions

37. a. Choice **a** is the correct answer. Of the 56 movies released, $\frac{6}{7}$ of them were comedies: 56 × $\left(\frac{6}{7}\right)$ = 48. Of those 48 comedies, $\frac{1}{3}$ of them were rated PG-13: 48 × $\left(\frac{1}{3}\right)$ = 16. Choice **b** is incorrect. 56 × $\left(\frac{6}{7}\right)$ × $\left(\frac{1}{3}\right)$ = 16. Choice **c** is incorrect. 56 × $\left(\frac{6}{7}\right)$ × $\left(\frac{1}{3}\right)$ = 16. Choice **d** is incorrect. 56 × $\left(\frac{6}{7}\right)$ × $\left(\frac{1}{3}\right)$ = 16.
Section: Computation in Context
Subsection: Fractions

38. a. Choice **a** is the correct answer. Line graphs are best for displaying changes in data over time. Choice **b** is incorrect. Bar graphs are best for displaying results in categories. Choice **c** is incorrect. Circle graphs are best for displaying data as percentages. Choice **d** is incorrect. Stem-and-leaf plots are best for displaying data as ordered lists.
Section: Data Analysis
Subsection: Appropriate Data Display

39. c. Choice **a** is incorrect. Rick collected 10 cans in the third week. Choice **b** is incorrect. Diane collected 17 cans in the second week. Choice **c** is the correct answer. In the bar graph, the third week is presented as the second set of bars from the top. Diane's total is represented by the color red. Thus, Diane collected 21 cans in the third week. Choice **d** is incorrect. Rick collected 30 cans in the second week.
Section: Data Analysis
Subsection: Bar, Line, Circle Graph

40. d. Choice **a** is incorrect. Only Group B and Group C share 4 and 20. Choice **b** is incorrect. Only Group C contains both 10 and 20. Choice **c** is incorrect. Only Group A and Group B share only 4 and 13. Choice **d** is the correct answer. When considering where Group A and Group C overlap, the only values are 4 and 16.
Section: Data Analysis
Subsection: Table, Chart, Diagram

41. d. Choice **a** is incorrect. The Apple Strudel had the third-most sales at 28. Choice **b** is incorrect. The Chocolate Torte had the most sales at 45. Choice **c** is incorrect. The Key Lime Pie had the fourth-most sales at 15. Choice **d** is the correct answer. After adding the sales from both days, the Peanut Butter Pie has the second-most sales at 33.
Section: Data Analysis
Subsection: Table, Chart, Diagram

42. **a.** Choice **a** is the correct answer. According to the circle graph, Rico spends 12% of his monthly income on transportation. Multiply his take-home pay of $5,800 by the decimal form of this percent: $5,800 × 0.12 = $696. Choice **b** is incorrect. $5,800 × 0.12 = $696. Choice **c** is incorrect. $5,800 × 0.12 = $696. Choice **d** is incorrect. $5,800 × 0.12 = $696.

Section: Data Analysis

Subsection: Conclusions from Data

43. **b.** Choice **a** is incorrect. The probability is $\frac{2}{3}$. Choice **b** is the correct answer. To calculate a probability, we find the number of possible outcomes for the desired event and divide it by the number of all possible outcomes. In this case, there are four numbers less than five and six total possible outcomes. Thus, $\frac{4}{6}$ is the resulting fraction. Once the fraction is simplified, $\frac{2}{3}$ is the probability of rolling a number less than five. Choice **c** is incorrect. The probability is $\frac{2}{3}$. Choice **d** is incorrect. The probability is $\frac{2}{3}$.

Section: Statistics and Probability

Subsection: Probability

44. **b.** Choice **a** is incorrect. The probability is $\frac{1}{2}$. Choice **b** is the correct answer. To calculate a probability, we find the number of possible outcomes for the desired event and divide it by the number of all possible outcomes. Consider all the possible outcomes: BBB, BBG, BGB, BGG, GBB, GBG, GGB, GGG. There are four outcomes that have at least two girls: BGG, GBG, GGB, GGG. Thus the probability is $\frac{4}{8} = \frac{1}{2}$. Choice **c** is incorrect. The probability is $\frac{1}{2}$. Choice **d** is incorrect. The probability is $\frac{1}{2}$.

Section: Statistics and Probability

Subsection: Probability

45. **c.** Choice **a** is incorrect. $(4.6 + 5.2 + 6.8 + 7.4 + 4.9 + 6.5) ÷ 6 = 35.4 ÷ 6 = 5.9$. Choice **b** is incorrect. $(4.6 + 5.2 + 6.8 + 7.4 + 4.9 + 6.5) ÷ 6 = 35.4 ÷ 6 = 5.9$. Choice **c** is the correct answer. The mean is found by adding all the given values, then dividing the sum by the number of values: $(4.6 + 5.2 + 6.8 + 7.4 + 4.9 + 6.5) ÷ 6 = 35.4 ÷ 6 = 5.9$. Choice **d** is incorrect. $(4.6 + 5.2 + 6.8 + 7.4 + 4.9 + 6.5) ÷ 6 = 35.4 ÷ 6 = 5.9$.

Section: Statistics and Probability

Subsection: Statistics

46. **b.** Choice **a** is incorrect. $85 - 51 = 34$. Choice **b** is the correct answer. To find the range, subtract the lowest value in the data set from the highest value: $85 - 51 = 34$. Choice **c** is incorrect. $85 - 51 = 34$. Choice **d** is incorrect. $85 - 51 = 34$.

Section: Statistics and Probability

Subsection: Statistics

47. **b.** Choice **a** is incorrect. Lines with the same slopes are parallel. Choice **b** is the correct answer. Two lines with the same slope are called parallel lines. Choice **c** is incorrect. Lines with the same slopes are parallel. Choice **d** is incorrect. Lines with the same slopes are parallel.

Section: Geometry and Spatial Sense

Subsection: Point, Ray, Line, Plane

48. **c.** Choice **a** is incorrect. $(\frac{1+7}{2}, \frac{8+(-6)}{2}) = (\frac{8}{2}, \frac{2}{2}) = (4, 1)$. Choice **b** is incorrect. $(\frac{1+7}{2}, \frac{8+(-6)}{2}) = (\frac{8}{2}, \frac{2}{2}) = (4, 1)$. Choice **c** is the correct answer. The midpoint between two points is found by adding the x-coordinates of the two points and dividing by two. Do the same for the y-coordinates. $(\frac{1+7}{2}, \frac{8+(-6)}{2}) = (\frac{8}{2}, \frac{2}{2}) = (4, 1)$. Choice **d** is incorrect. $(\frac{1+7}{2}, \frac{8+(-6)}{2}) = (\frac{8}{2}, \frac{2}{2}) = (4, 1)$.

Section: Geometry and Spatial Sense

Subsection: Coordinate Geometry

49. **b.** Choice **a** is incorrect. $94.2 \div (2 \times 3.14) = 15.0$ cm. Choice **b** is the correct answer. The circumference of a circle is found by $2\pi r$. Because the circumference is given, let $\pi = 3.14$ and solve for the unknown:

$$94.2 = 2\pi r$$
$$94.2 = 2(3.14)r$$
$$r = 94.2 \div (2 \times 3.14)$$
$$r = 15.0 \text{ cm}$$

Choice **c** is incorrect. $94.2 \div (2 \times 3.14) = 15.0$ cm. Choice **d** is incorrect. $94.2 \div (2 \times 3.14) = 15.0$ cm.
Section: Geometry and Spatial Sense
Subsection: Parts of a Circle

50. **a.** Choice **a** is the correct answer. The translation $T(x, y) = (x + 3, y + 5)$ follows the rule, "move three units to the right and five units up." Therefore, $T(0, 0) = (3, 5)$; $T(3, 5) = (6, 10)$; $T(4, 1) = (7, 6)$. Choice **b** is incorrect. $T(0, 0) = (3, 5)$; $T(3, 5) = (6, 10)$; $T(4, 1) = (7, 6)$. Choice **c** is incorrect. $T(0, 0) = (3, 5)$; $T(3, 5) = (6, 10)$; $T(4, 1) = (7, 6)$. Choice **d** is incorrect. $T(0, 0) = (3, 5)$; $T(3, 5) = (6, 10)$; $T(4, 1) = (7, 6)$.
Section: Geometry and Spatial Sense
Subsection: Transformations